Political and
Institutional Issues
of the New International
Economic Order

Pergamon Titles of Related Interest

Laszlo/Kurtzman/Bhattacharya RCDC (REGIONAL COOPERATION AMONG DEVELOPING COUNTRIES)
Nicol/Echeverria/Peccei REGIONALISM AND THE NEW INTERNATIONAL ECONOMIC ORDER

UNITAR-CEESTEM Library on NIEO

Laszlo & Kurtzman Eastern Europe and the New International Economic Order

Laszlo & Kurtzman Western Europe and the New International Economic Order

Laszlo & Kurtzman Political and Institutional Issues of the New International Economic Order

Laszlo & Kurtzman The Structure of the World Economy and the New International Economic Order

Laszlo & Kurtzman The United States, Canada and the New International Economic Order

Laszlo et al. The Implementation of the New International Economic Order

Laszlo et al. World Leadership and the New International Economic Order

Laszlo et al. The Objectives of the New International Economic Order

Laszlo et al. The Obstacles to the New International Economic Order

Lozoya & Bhattacharya The Financial Issues of the New International Economic Order

Lozoya & Cuadra Africa, Middle East and the New International Economic Order

Lozoya & Bhattacharya Asia and the New International Economic Order

Lozoya & Green International Trade, Industrialization and the New International Economic Order

Lozoya & Estevez Latin America and the New International Economic Order

Lozoya & Birgin Social and Cultural Issues of the New International Economic Order

Lozoya et al. Alternative Views of the New International Economic Order

Miljan, Laszlo & Kurtzman Food and Agriculture in Global Perspective

Related Journals *

CHINA INTERNATIONAL BUSINESS
PROGRESS IN PLANNING
WORLD DEVELOPMENT

*Free specimen copies available upon request

PERGAMON POLICY STUDIES

ON THE NEW INTERNATIONAL ECONOMIC ORDER

Political and Institutional Issues of the New International Economic Order

Edited by
Ervin Laszlo
Joel Kurtzman

A Volume in the New International
Economic Order (NIEO) Library
Published for UNITAR and the
Center for Economic and Social
Studies of the Third World (CEESTEM)

Pergamon Press

NEW YORK • OXFORD • TORONTO • SYDNEY • PARIS • FRANKFURT

Pergamon Press Offices:

U.S.A.   Pergamon Press Inc., Maxwell House, Fairview Park,
Elmsford, New York 10523, U.S.A.

U.K.   Pergamon Press Ltd., Headington Hill Hall,
Oxford OX3 OBW, England

CANADA   Pergamon Press Canada Ltd., Suite 104, 150 Consumers Road,
Willowdale, Ontario M2J 1P9, Canada

AUSTRALIA   Pergamon Press (Aust.) Pty. Ltd., P.O. Box 544,
Potts Point, NSW 2011, Australia

FRANCE   Pergamon Press SARL, 24 rue des Ecoles,
75240 Paris, Cedex 05, France

FEDERAL REPUBLIC   Pergamon Press GmbH, Hammerweg 6, Postfach 1305,
OF GERMANY   6242 Kronberg/Taunus, Federal Republic of Germany

Library of Congress Cataloging in Publication Data
Main entry under title:

Political and institutional issues of the new international economic order.

   (Pergamon policy studies on the new international
economic order)
   "A volume in the new international economic order
library."
   Includes index.
   1. International economic relations--Addresses,
essays, lectures. 2. World politics--1945-
--Addresses, essays, lectures. I. Laszlo, Ervin,
1932-   . II. Kurtzman, Joel. III. Series.
HF1411.P59115 1981   337'.09'048   80-27389
ISBN 0-08-025122-6

Printed in the United States of America

Contents

Preface to the
UNITAR-CEESTEM-NIEO Library

The present volume is one in a series of 17 books which make up
the UNITAR-CEESTEM NIEO Library. While each volume covers a
specific aspect of the issues that comprise the New International Economic Order and can be read independently of the
others, it seems useful to provide a brief introduction to
outline the scope of the entire undertaking and put this volume
in its proper context.

In the winter of 1976-77 UNITAR (the United Nations
Institute for Training and Research) initiated with CEESTEM
(the Centro de Estudios Economicos y Sociales del Tercer Mundo,
Mexico) a series of inquiries into problems and opportunities
associated with the establishment of the New International
Economic Order (NIEO). Both institutions agreed that the NIEO
constituted one of the highest priority items on the international agenda, and that independent, objective, and scholarly
investigation of its objectives, obstacles, opportunities, and
indicated strategies may be of great value both to the decision
makers directly concerned with the negotiation of the issues,
and to the international community at large. The UNITAR-
CEESTEM NIEO Library is a result of the research that was
undertaken by the central professional staffs of the institutes, and by their jointly formed international network of
collaboratores and consultants.

What are some of the reasons behind this assessment of the
importance of the NIEO in contemporary economic and world
affairs? Although most people know that the world economy is
encountering serious difficulties on both national and international levels, few people outside a small circle of
experts realize the seriousness of the problems and the breadth
of their scope. Contrary to some current perceptions, the NIEO
is neither a passing pressure of the poor countries on the
rich, nor merely a demand for more aid and assistance.

It is a process which has deep historical precedents, and an undisputed historical significance.

We need not go back further than the end of World War II to find an entire array of historical events which set the stage for the later emergence of the call for the NIEO. While these events arose from their own historical antecedents, they themselves produced the setting for the breakdown of the post-war economic system, and the widening gap between rich and poor nations.

The first and perhaps most decisive event was the liberation of the oppressed peoples of Africa and Asia, in the great wave of decolonization that swept the world in the years following World War II. The newly independent states were said to be sovereign and equal to all other states, old and new, large and small. Their admittance to the UN underscored this. However, the fresh political and juridical status of the new countries was far from matched by their actual economic conditions. The majority felt that their de jure political colonization ended only to be replaced by a de facto economic colonization.

The historical process which gave the majority of the world's population the status of citizens of sovereign and equal states, but left them at the same time in a situation of economic underdevelopment and dependence, triggered the "revolution of rising expectations." Desires for rapid economic growth led Third World governments into ambitious plans and programs of national development. Most of the plans envisaged a quick repetition of the industrial growth processes of the developed world, following a path already long trodden by the countries of Latin America. When the unintended side-effects of traditional patterns of industrialization became evident - uncontrolled growth of cities, relative neglect of rural areas and agriculture, threats to the environment, and the increasing stratification of people in modern and traditional sectors, often with serious damage to social structure and cohesion - many of the original development strategies underwent modification. However, the goal of rapid economic growth was not surrendered. Quantitative growth targets were formally included in the official development strategies of the First and Second UN Development Decades (for the 1960s and the 1970s, respectively).

However, the mid-term review of the achievement of the Second Development Decade's goals showed mixed results. The greatest disappointment came in the area of agricultural production and official development aid. On the average, the UN official development aid targets have not even been half achieved. At the same time, service charges on past loans began to put enormous pressures on developing countries' balance of payments, and world poverty showed no signs of diminishing. There was insufficient progress in commodity trade, inadequate access to the markets of developed countries, particularly for agricultural products; tariffs had escalated, especially for semi-processed and processed products, and new tariff and nontariff restrictions were introduced by many developed countries on a number of items, including textiles and leather goods.   The plight of the least developed, island and land-locked developing countries, gave rise to additional concern.   While some progress was achieved, for example, through the introduction of a generalized system of preferences by the developed countries, and the proposals of the Tokyo Declaration concerning multilateral trade negotiations, the negative developments weighed more heavily in the balance and created widespread dissatisfaction in the developing world.

Another set of factors come into play as well.   This was the sudden and unexpected rise of Third World economic and political power.   The Middle East oil embargo of 1973-1974, and the subsequent four-fold increase in the price of oil created a world energy crisis.   It affected all oil importing nations, developed as well as developing.   It also exhibited the dependence of the developed countries on the developing world for several major natural resources, and proved the ability of the Third World to wield economic and political power effectively. The consequences included rises in the price of food, due to the increased cost of chemical fertilizers, and further tensions between producers and consumers of raw materials.   But the OPEC-type exercise of Third World economic and political power proved unable to improve the condition of the developing countries as a whole.   Despite significantly higher gross resource flows from the oil-exporting to the oil-importing developing countries, the economic plight of the latter worsened due to the higher cost of energy.   Developed countries found themselves beset by economic problems of their own, including not only higher oil prices but inflation, unemployment, and unused industrial capacity.   Economic rates of growth slowed, while in most countries balance of payment deficits grew.   Even where surpluses could still be generated, concerns focused on the domestic economy, and political will to increase levels of aid and assistance to the Third World faltered.

Compounding the economic difficulties of the developed nations were signs of breakdown in the international monetary system which affected all countries, developed as well as developing.   Amidst growing tensions between the United States, Japan and the European Community over matters of trade, the Bretton Woods system collapsed and gave rise to a system of floating exchange rates.   The value of the U.S. dollar began to erode, creating serious difficulties for those countries which, like most of the Third World, held their reserves in dollars. The creation of Special Drawing Rights provided some access to foreign exchange independently of dollar holdings, but such access favored the countries already developed, and the rest remained seriously dissatisfied with the workings of the international monetary system. It became evident that some of the fundamental tenets of the post-war world economy were being called into question, and indeed that some had already collapsed.

The NIEO made its appearance as an international political issue in the context of this series of events. Encouraged by the success of OPEC but fearful of splintering Third World solidarity through the newly won wealth of a few of its countries, Presidents Boumedienne of Algeria and Echeverria of Mexico, among others, called for structural reforms in the international economic system. Their governments' initiative resulted in the adoption of such major UN resolutions as those of the Sixth and Seventh Special Sessions, and the Charter of Economic Rights and Duties of States. These in turn provided the impetus for a long series of declarations, resolutions, position papers and studies on various NIEO issues by the United Nations system and the international community at large.

The coming together of these historical factors was not purely coincidental. The wave of decolonization was the culmination of a long-term historical process of democratization, and the rise of the concept of universal rights for individuals and societies. It led, in turn, to a mounting desire for rapid industrialization by the newly independent countries. This met with major frustrations. But as economic interdependence intensified, as trade and markets expanded, and access to energy and raw materials became crucial to the developed world's giant economic machinery, the concentration of economic power itself was modified. It was no longer wielded by a few powerful governments but also fell into the hands of oil exporting nations and transnational corporations.

The historical process which gave birth to a host of independent nation-states placed into sharp relief the inequities of the previous economic system, and provided some of the developing countries with fresh degrees of economic leverage. Since they not only control the supply of a number of important fuels and raw materials but also absorb about 25 percent of the developed world's exports, their demands can no longer be ignored. And they insist that a healthy growth in the world economy cannot be brought about within the framework of the existing economic system.

When the General Assembly, in December 1977, called for another Special Session in 1980 to assess progress in the establishment of the NIEO, it took a decisive step in bringing the North-South debate to the Organization, where it belongs. It created an ongoing forum for discussions and negotiation in the interim through the Committee of the Whole, which during 1978 managed to define its role and function despite earlier disagreements. Together with the work of the bodies charged with the preparation of the International Development Strategy

for the Third United Nations Development Decade, the Organization created the fora for substantive progress in the area
of restructuring the economic relations of developed and developing countries. Faced with mounting pressures on national
economics in all parts of the world, the international community new finds itself facing a watershed decision: to make
use of these fora, or to continue to use mainly bilateral and
sectoral corrective measures to mitigate tensions while en-
trusting the resolution of problems to the mechanisms of the
free market.

This decision is intimately linked to an entire array of
basic questions. Among them:

The question of cost and benefit. Who will have to bear
the burden of instituting NIEO and will the results be worth
the sacrifices? Will benefits really accrue to the poor people
to help fulfill their basic needs and will developing countries
be made truly more self-reliant - or will the main beneficiaries be the already rich elites? Will the developed countries also benefit from NIEO (a positive-sum game) or will it
mainly mean the redistribution of the current stock of wealth
from them to the developing countries (a zero-sum game)?

The question of legitimacy. Is the free market the basic
mechanism of world trade and the best vehicle of development,
or is it merely a convenient fiction to cover up the current
unjust manipulations of the major economic groups?

The question of morality. Do the rich countries have a
moral obligation to help the poor, and especially the poorest?
Does this responsibility extend to those countries who had no
historical part in the creation of poverty in the Third World?

The question of political feasibility. How strongly will
different organized groups in society support or oppose governmental policies aimed at the achievement of the NIEO - and
how much solidarity exists in these domains internationally,
among the developing and the developed countries themselves?

It is unrealistic to expect that real progress will be
made on specific NIEO issues (such as official development aid,
technical assistance, debt renegotiation, removal of tariff
barriers, technical cooperation among developing countries, the
link between SDRs and development, voting power in the World
Bank and IMF, transfers of technology, regulation of transnational corporations, a system of consultations on industrialization, and restructuring the economic and social sectors of
the United Nations) so long as the basic issues are not resolved and a consensus does not emerge concerning them. NIEO
can be achieved if, and only if, it is perceived that its
benefits are universal and can reach all segments of the
world's population (especially the neediest); if it is held
that its costs do not exceed its benefits; if its regulatory
mechanisms are seen to be legitimate; if some real sense of
moral responsibility exists among members of the human com-

munity, and if sufficient political support is available
nationally as well as internationally for the indicated measures. If one or more of these preconditions are not met, the
NIEO will not be achieved; Member States will continue to
practice the existing, predominantly piecemeal, ad hoc and
mainly bilateral modes of adjusting the stresses and reaching
compromises.

The basic purposes of the UNITAR-CEESTEM NIEO Library is
to provide an independent and objective assessment of these
issues, and to report its findings in time for the historic
events of 1980: the Special Session of the General Assembly
devoted to the assessment of progress toward the NIEO, and the
immediately following regular session, during which the International Development Strategy for the 1980s and beyond (the
UN's Third Development Decade) is to be debated and adopted.
It would be clearly an enormous waste of time and effort to
enter into these negotiations without forming a clear idea of
the issues that bear on their success. But reporting on them
is not a simple matter of using insight and intuition; it
requires painstaking and organized empirical research. The
requirement is to identify the forces that operate for or
against the NIEO in all parts of the world. Intuitive answers
concerning its costs and benefits, legitimacy, morality, and
political feasibility occur to all persons knowledgeable in
these areas, but such answers tend to vary and are thus not
sufficiently reliable. Expert research on the current obstacles and opportunities associated with the NIEO in the
different regions of the world, and with respect to the diverse
sectors of the world economy, needs to be conducted. The
results of such research may shed some much needed light on the
chances of success in establishing a new international economic
order generally, and on the types of objectives and modes of
negotiations that, in the positive case, could lead to it
specifically. For although it is unlikely that a dominant
consensus already exists in the world concerning the costs and
benefits, legitimacy, morality, and political feasibility of
the NIEO (if it did exist, the international community would
probably not be experiencing the sense of frustration it has
today), the precise estimation of costs versus benefits,
legitimacy versus illegitimacy, morality versus indifference,
and political feasibility versus futility by different societal
groups could reveal highly differentiated potentials for
achieving a dominant consensus in the future. Today's chaotic
welter of opinions and pressures concerning the NIEO need not
remain such, but could crystallize into a decisive mood fa-
voring or opposing it. To those who object to such analysis on
the grounds that economic theory, rather than wide-ranging
socio-political considerations, must serve to decide the fate
of NIEO, we may reply that economic theory, while relevant, is
in itself over generous: it can often prove both sides of con-

flicting positions. Since both sides in a dispute can marshal
some variety of economic theory in their defense, and no common
criteria exist for assessing the relative merits of all theories, economic rationality as conveyed by economic theories
becomes marginal in the negotiating process. We need to go one
step deeper, inquiring into the reasons particular theories are
summoned to defend particular points of view, as well as
measuring the intensity of commitment to these viewpoints and
the negotiating power of the parties subscribing to them.

Thus, the focus of the UNITAR-CEESTEM Library is not a
given economic theory, but the perceptions and opinions underlying the positions taken by the diverse actors. The configuration and strength of these perceptions and opinions will
ultimately determine whether negotiations in the area of the
NIEO can be successful, and if so, which strategies will have
optimum chances of success.

The Library contains volumes arranged in three different
series. First, there is a series of overview studies. These
provide background, context, and basic reference data. They
include a volume defining and classifying the principal objectives of the NIEO as agreed or debated in the United Nations
and other major international fora; a volume giving an overview
and assessment of alternative viewpoints on the NIEO espoused
by various nongovernmental groups and researchers in different
parts of the world; a third defining the most critical obstacles confronting the establishment of the NIEO; a fourth
dealing with the specific problems of food and agriculture as
they are debated in the framework of the United Nations. A
fifth volume suggests the basic strategies which appear indicated and appropriate to accelerate progress toward the NIEO;
and a final volume communicates the results of the associated
UNITAR-CEESTEM International Opinion Survey of Decision Makers
and Experts on the crucial questions of the NIEO.

The second series contains geographic studies. Volumes in
this series review the positions and postures of national
governments and the attitudes of business, labor, the public
media, and the opinion of the population at large in various
nations and regions of the world. Individual volumes focus on
the United States and Canada, on Western Europe, on Eastern
Europe including the Soviet Union, on Asia including Australia,
on Latin America, and on Africa and the Middle East.

The third series of the NIEO Library is devoted to functional studies. Here experts give their views and assessments
of such issues as the possible and the desirable structure of
the world economy; of the patterns and problems of international trade and industrial development; of international
financial matters, and of the associated political and institutional, as well as social and cultural problems and opportunities.

Among them, the seventeen volumes of the Library cover practically all the principal issues encountered in efforts to establish a New International Economic Order, through in-depth discussion by independent investigators, coming from different societies in different parts of the world.

The UNITAR-CEESTEM NIEO Library offers wide-ranging analyses, and sometimes divergent viewpoints, on a broad range of topics. It does not offer simplistic solutions, nor advocate one viewpoint indiscriminately over others. It seeks to illuminate the range and complexity of the issues, provide clarification of individual items, and to lend a sense of the vastness and significance of the NIEO as a whole.

It is the hope of all of us, researchers and consultants of the UNITAR-CEESTEM project on the NIEO, that our results, published as the NIEO Library, may render some service to the decision maker and negotiator who must cope with the problems of the international economic order, as well as to the student of international economic and world affairs, interested in further research on these topics. It is our view that the NIEO is a historically necessary, and humanly and politically appropriate attempt to create a world order that is sustainable for generations, equitable for all, and capable of meeting the most urgent needs and demands of the peoples and nations of the world community.

Ervin Laszlo

Project Director

Introduction

It may be said with good reason that the New International Economic Order is economic in terms of its issues, social in regard to its implications, and political in its implementation. Indeed, little progress beyond the mere enunciation of principles can be expected in the establishment of NIEO in the absence of decisive political action. Such action is called for on all levels of decision making, from the national to the global.

That NIEO is primarily a political concern to be handled by governments and international organizations has been affirmed also by an international survey of decision makers carried out in 21 countries.(1) In the opinion of leadership groups in government, business, labor, the media, and the academic community, governments have the greatest responsibility for carrying out measures concerning the world economy, followed by intergovernmental organizations. The private sector received a relatively low rating in this connection, as did other international bodies.

The fact that governments and intergovernmental organizations have the lion's share of the responsibility for implementing measures that could act on, and possibly transform, the existing international economic system lends the NIEO's seemingly purely economic problems and proposals a distinctively political tint. But not only are NIEO issues political in implementation; some of the issues are actually political in their basic substance. These are the issues which are selected for specific consideration in this volume.

Political and institutional issues are closely interlinked in the framework of efforts to implement NIEO. While the NIEO issues of a political nature are those on which political agreement needs to be reached in view of establishing one or another facet of the new order, the institutional issues of

NIEO may be defined as the issues which refer to arrangements of an institutional and administrative kind that must be made if the agreed principles of NIEO are to be translated into practice. Thus, while the specifically political issues form part of the NIEO debate and negotiation, the institutional-administrative issues form the substance of NIEO practice. This volume discusses them in Part One and Part Two respectively.

From the possibly large number of highly detailed issues which are of a specifically political nature, three are selected here for more detailed analysis: the general issue of the sovereignty of states within NIEO; the particular problems raised by the policies and practices of nationalization; and the complex web of issues which make up the debates on the exploitation of the resources of the seas.

The sovereignty of states in the choice of the model and strategy of development is one of the pillars of NIEO. Such freedom has often been entirely lacking for certain states, or it has been used to exploit whatever advantages the present economic system could offer for national economy in the short term. In neither case could governmental action contribute to the establishment of a new order. Yet, as the first study of Part One points out, concerted and responsible action must be taken by national governments themselves in order to transform the economic, political, and social systems within the borders of their own countries.

This requirement holds first of all for those states most interested in the restructuring of the international order: the oppressed and exploited societies and peoples of the Third World. But this does not lessen in any way the responsibility of the richer and more developed countries for political reform, on both the national and the international levels.

Only through the concerted effort of all governments can a new international order be established. The fact that such action must be the result of the free decision of sovereign states calls for a high level of understanding and agreement on the need to restructure the world economic system and create a new order, rather than to merely patch up the existing economic disorder. Such restructuring must start at home, since a new order on the world level must come into existence as a product of new orders on national – and also regional – levels. Self-reliant development, the creation and strengthening of indigenous capacities, long-term socially-oriented financing, the use of appropriate methods and technologies, and the reduction of domestic inequities form essential elements of the proper exercise of the sovereignty of states. They must create the conditions under which a new and equitable international order can be put into place.

The nationalization of certain enterprises and industries is a fundamental, yet still controversial, issue covered especially by the concept of the sovereignty of states over their natural resources. In practice, transferring to the state the ownership of the means of production from local nationals causes fewer problems than the nationalization of foreign-owned enterprises and resources. Controversy shrouds the issue whether such acts are instances of expropriation, or are adequately covered by the agreed principles concerning the free choice of states and their sovereignty not only over the natural resources on their territory but also over the benefits resulting from them. The second study of Part One argues that nationalization is a modern and autonomous legal institution that all states are free to apply with regard to local or foreign-owned enterprises and goods; and that no established legal institution exists concerning the indemnification of the previous owners with regard to the amount and the means of payment. Indeed, the still controversial aspects of nationalization policies are in urgent need of resolution, since the recovery of the full use of, and benefit from, indigenous resources and productive capacities by developing countries is a pressing economic necessity, and frequently a precondition of their economic and social progress and development.

If controversy surrounds the precise application of already agreed principles concerning the use of, and benefits from, the resources and the means of production located on national territories, even more controversy and disagreement clouds the very principles by which access to the benefits of resources located outside national jurisdiction is to be assured. The principle of "common heritage of mankind" is affirmed for such resources but it is diversely interpreted. For some - notably the advanced industrial countries - it means that all who have the means to exploit resources beyond the confines of national jurisdiction should be licensed to do so if they wish. For others - namely the developing countries without adequate means of exploitation - the principle is interpreted to mean an equal distribution of the benefits resulting from all exploitations.

Although complicated by issues of sovereignty extending over coastal waters and continental shelves, and by the problem of compensating the possessors of competing land-based resources, the new global "Law of the Sea" may stand as a test case for NIEO - a test of the will and the solidarity of states to act in the common interest. Should agreement with respect to resources not actually within a national jurisdiction fail to materialize, the chances of agreement on the equitable sharing of benefits from land-based resources within national territories would be even more remote.

The institutional and administrative issues of NIEO are not, as previously noted, questions of agreement or controversy, but of capacity to translate measures into practice. A new order cannot be put into place with the instrumentalities of the present world economic order (or disorder). Existing institutions need to be changed or strengthened; new ones need to be created. The tendency of bureaucracies to perpetrate themselves and to resist change makes the creation of an administrative and institutional framework capable of bringing about and maintaining the new order especially difficult. This difficulty is compounded by the requirement that the new institutional structures should be expert, and flexible - characteristics not shared by most bodies in present public administration.

The studies in Part Two analyze the shortcoming of present institutional and administrative arrangements, and offer suggestions for their rectification. On the level of national administrations, the tasks include not only those connected with carrying out the internationally agreed measures, but tasks of creating the very possibilities for governments to enter into new international agreements. State administrations must at one and the same time implement change and be the subject of - that is, themselves undergo - change. This applies to the three principal domains of public administration: the economic, the social, and the scientific and cultural.

The alienation of governmental administrators from the people whose affairs they administer is a basic obstacle to effective change. In Third World countries, this is often due to administrative practices inherited from the colonial period. Here, decentralization and the creation of more participatory structures appears to be a fundamental condition.

Regional administration constitutes the currently most critical "missing link" between the national level administered by governments and the global level in the hands of the relevant bodies of the UN. The problem on the regional level is not primarily one of restructuring existing systems to cope with the requirements of the new order, but to create new institutions, and give substance to those already in existence.

The need to specify universal global objectives to correspond to local conditions and perceptions has been of increasing concern in recent years. Also the need to enhance the self-reliance of the smaller, poorer, and less-developed members of the international community has become an acknowledged goal of NIEO. Both these objectives call for enhanced regional institutional and administrative capabilities. However, in their understandable desire to create a global system for collective security and the promotion of human and social well-being, the founders of the UN foresaw the need for regional mechanisms mainly in the context of political negotiations and security. The balance of economic, rather than military-political, power was not given sufficient attention. Yet, as economic issues surged to the forefront of the international agenda, the creation of mechanisms to redress the economic imbalances of the trebled UN membership became imperative. Neither the size nor the natural, human, and financial resources of states can be altered by new institutions, but their existing assets and capacities can and must be harmonized, within a new and more beneficial international division of labor. This calls for a new role for regional institutions as mediating and implementing forums, linking global level negotiations with national economic and social decisions and conditions.(2)

There can be no compromise, however, with the effectiveness of the global-level administration of NIEO. This level is the sine qua non not only of the administration, but of the negotiated creation of NIEO. The role of the UN as the only universal intergovernmental body possessing the necessary mandate to negotiate and help implement the complex and wide-ranging NIEO issues is not in question. While there is no substitute for the UN in this matter, the question arises whether that body is capable of fulfilling the task required of it. Does it have the requisite degree of expert competence in the relevant technical fields? Does it provide a sufficiently balanced political forum for the negotiation of the issues? And, equally important, does it possess sufficient authority to supervise and help in the implementation of the agreed measures?

Clearly, the answer is largely negative if we only consider the present structures and decision-making processes of the organization. The question must be rephrased: can the UN evolve itself to respond to these challenges? The more pertinent question thus concerns the restructuring of the UN. The weight of the problem has been recognized: a primary objective of the organization is now its own restructuring, as numerous resolutions of the General Assembly, studies of its specialized organs and of ad hoc commissions, and statements of the Secretary-General indicate. The creation of the Committee of the Whole as an ongoing forum for global economic negotiations, the decision to launch a prolonged round of global negotiations, and the creation of the office of the Director-General for Development and International Economic Co-operation are visible proof of serious attempts to restructure the organization to face the challenge of NIEO. Likewise, the establishment and strengthening of UNCTAD as a technical body on specific issues of concern to developing countries, and the effort to decentralize UN decision making as well as project and program implementation bear witness to the will to rise to the challenge.

The difficulty remains, however, that these and similar measures fail to convince several major economic powers of the need for NIEO and for the UN's role in bringing it about. There are few if any indications to date that such powers would be willing to give up their vested interests in favor of a collective machinery for the allocation of economic benefits and the creation of a new international division of labor. If this difficulty is to be overcome, the UN's decision-making system would have to shift from a political forum of conflict-resolution - or conflict-postponement - to an economic forum for the negotiation of collective benefits. Current voting structures, even when improved by the use of consensus, are poorly adapted to accomplish this: they pitch a majority of the relatively powerless against a minority of the relatively powerful members.

The resolution of this difficulty lies at least in part beyond the immediate confines of the United Nations. It calls for a better match between majority and power, that is, a better balance between the political sovereignty and the economic power of member states. A purely political common front - as practiced in current bloc negotiations - needs to be supplemented with a better distribution of control over economic processes. But this balance cannot be achieved on the global level without the mediation of regional groupings. The latter must enhance the collective self-reliance and the collective negotiating power of the majority of today's Third World states.

Regional economic groupings would not only balance the negotiating position of the partners, but would also make the negotiations themselves more manageable. The parties around the table would be smaller in number and would be better informed of each other's positions. They would have more confidence that the agreements are not merely politically motivated but have a reliable economic foundation. At the same time, representation would be universal, since each regional group would speak for all its members, much as the EEC and a group of socialist countries already do today. A smaller, yet representative, economic negotiating body must eventually replace the current unmanageably large, although universally representative, political forum at the level of the General Assembly, the global round, and their special committees and organs.

The restructuring of the UN, much as the reforming of national administrative systems, implies concurrent changes on several institutional levels. Neither the UN by itself, nor national governments by themselves, can create the mechanisms for establishing NIEO. But a restructured UN, working hand in hand with member governments and their politically representative and economically coordinated groupings, may be equal to the task.

The implementation of NIEO suggests the need for a much higher level of knowledge and communication than is currently achieved in international circles. The research and reflection of social scientists could be the yeast that leavens this process. Unfortunately, contrary to a naive belief, the work of social scientists is not necessarily objective and value free. They, as other members of society, are immersed in a social reality that is highly fragmented and diverse. The basic conceptual modes of today's social scientists - their "paradigms" - are strongly colored by their society's values and beliefs. In this divisive atmosphere, Third World social scientists are at a disadvantage. Research centers in developing countries are fewer and less well endowed than in the industrialized world, and the development of theories responsive to the situation of developing countries suffers in consequence.

If a single, monolithic body of ideas is unlikely to prevail the world over, at least a better distribution of research and theory-generating capabilities should be striven for. This is of crucial importance to developing countries where there is still a shortage of technical experts, and where social scientists are inevitably drawn into the political process.

Studies of the present and the future world order, as the closing chapter of this volume indicates, could and should become a positive force in the international political and economic arena. However, the results of such studies would have to adequately reflect the conditions and perceptions of all societies and population strata, and not only those of the most privileged among them.

No single volume can adequately discuss, or even enumerate, all the complex political and institutional issues which concern the establishment of a new world order. The present volume brings to attention a few key issues which have a crucial role to play in the implementation of NIEO. The studies that follow intend to raise those issues, and to offer their authors' individual perspectives on them. They are elements in the necessary debate and dialogue which must accompany every attempt at the creation of a new set of relationships, binding people and states in our interdependent global community with equity and justice.

Ervin Laszlo
Joel Kurtzman

NOTES

1. For details, see Ervin Laszlo, Jorge Lozoya, John Alexander, Joel Kurtzman, Harry Triandis, A.K. Bhattacharya, Eds. World Leadership and NIEO, NIEO Library (New York: Pergamon Press, scheduled publication 1981).

2. The range of regional tasks and possibilities – no less
   than the spectrum of obstacles – is vast; a more detailed
   overview is provided in Davidson Nicol, Aurelio Peccei,
   Luis Echeverria. <u>Regionalism and the New International
   Economic Order</u>, (New York, Pergamon Press, 1980).

I

Some Political Issues In The Negotiation of the New International Economic Order

1 The Sovereignty of States

Armando Labra
Javier Caballeros
Byron Cardoso
David Colmenares

The purpose of this chapter is to develop the theory that only respect for the sovereign decision of states to launch new national economic orders will lead to the shaping of a New International Economic Order (NIEO). Unless a determined effort is made within their own borders by the countries most seriously affected by the present international economic disorder, the proposed NIEO will continue to progress no further than the stage of well-intentioned discussion in international forums, without any practical effect on the political and economic life of nations.

We have attempted to submit evidence for this idea under four different headings. The first is designed to establish a broader frame of reference than the one from which it stems, and one that includes the demand of the less-developed countries for NIEO; the second attempts to identify the main financial arrangements reflecting the present international economic disorder; an effort is made in the third to describe certain points so far not included in the proposed structure of NIEO, and the fourth proposes a series of steps to be taken toward establishing a New International Economic Order that is based on prior efforts by developing countries and on strengthening the sovereignty of democratic states in order to guarantee results that will benefit the majority of the population.

EVOLUTION AND MEANING OF THE NEW INTERNATIONAL ECONOMIC ORDER

The uninterrupted series of economic imbalances accompanied by severe economic and political crises in the countries that

3

make up the·contemporary market economies has led to a challenge to today's international economic order and to the proposed restructuring of the current system.

The meaning, mechanisms, and limits of that restructuring cause debate and economic and political struggle among the representatives of opposing viewpoints who must join in establishing the new system of relations that is demanded by a majority of the world's peoples with a view to reducing the injustices and inequalities of present-day coexistence. This can only be done by reversing existing trends that are of benefit for the power, consumption, and well-being of merely a minority of nations and social classes.

The unparalleled growth of the capitalist system since World War II has shaped a prevailing pattern of economic relations that extends innumerable advantages to the industrialized nations at the expense of a wide variety of peripheral countries whose inhabitants suffer poverty, hunger, injustice, and the degradation of human dignity. The spectrum of international relations between what are known today as developed and underdeveloped countries is reaching its ultimate limits. The foundations of the international economic system and its consequent power structure threaten to crumble unless measures are taken to shore them up that will either permit the forcible prolongation of the system or lead to the establishment of a new and more rational order, based on a framework of equality and affording opportunities to all societies and peoples of the world to participate and realize their potential.

The essential and universal question to be resolved is this: will we accept our responsibility, in a spirit of honesty, equanimity, and justice, for solving the economic, social, political, cultural, ecological, and other problems afflicting the world, to the extent that we are responsible for them, and make it possible to move to a new and higher stage of civilization, one that gives real access to the material and immaterial benefits and progress envisioned by the world's masses; or will we ourselves to be drawn irreversibly by the prevailing trends toward the deceptive solution of seeking palliatives, rather than a major readjustment of the system established at the end of World War II, and merely put off and add to the eventual force of the social and political explosions that are succeeding one another at increasingly closer intervals?

Once we realize that the solution of this dilemma depends not only on the knowledge, good will, and rationality of our proposals, but also implies the removal of traditional and far-reaching privileges, the denial of powerful interests, the extinction of systems based on domination and the arrogance of power, an end to the potency of expansionist regimes and the demise of societies based on the exploitation and the subordination of the sovereign rights of weaker nations, it

becomes obvious that shaping NIEO will be a process filled with
crisis conflicts and with recurrent disputes with those who
seek to reaffirm, and if possible to further strengthen, the
basic characteristics of the system we know today.

At the same time, the situation of existing national
orders and the conditions prevailing in today's nations cannot
be ignored or evaded in the establishment of NIEO - as they
have been until now - for the obvious reason that these are the
very factors on which its composition - or decomposition - will
depend.   Therefore, analysis of the strategies to be employed
and the obstacles to be met in the establishment of NIEO calls
for a full understanding of the complicated interplay of these
factors.

The conversion of capitalism into a global system within
the framework of a unified world market (characterized by such
processes as the internationalization of production, the accumulation of capital, and the international division of labor
based on the logic of transnational conglomerates) has led to a
sharpening of the tensions existing between the central and
peripheral sectors of the system.

The center-periphery relationship is ruled by a system
that permits the simultaneous existence of opulence and
unemployment, combines the plundering of resources with
scarcities, and parallels the profits obtained from sophisticated technologies with those derived from the exploitation
of the labor force.   The rationality behind the interests of
capital has degenerated into conflicts and contradictions that
make themselves felt with varying degrees of intensity in every
sphere of the world disorder.

Thus, the crises and conflicts confronting mankind have
different meanings for developed and nondeveloped countries,
just as they do for the different classes of their societies.
Inflation, stagnation, unemployment, fuel scarcities, disarmament, international monetary reform, the population ex-
plosion, food production, protection of the environment, and
all the other problems that must be borne in mind in shaping
NIEO are profoundly interrelated, and must therefore be viewed
as a whole.   Overall consideration of these problems will, at
the very least, allow some progress to be made in defining the
limits of responsibilities, and will permit the sort of participation in the general discussion of a new order that is
representative of the plurality and equality of interests
involved in making joint efforts for structural changes and
transformation.   This project can hardly be left to the free
will of economic forces, or to the spontaneous action of
international forums which, when all is said and done, are
simply a reflection of the present power structure - the very
thing that must be changed.

Therefore, if genuine international restructuring is to be
achieved, concerted and responsible action must first be taken

to transform the economic, political, and social orders within national borders by those most interested in seeing that restructuring comes about – the developing countries of the Third World.

The concentration of economic, financial, and technological power in the hands of a very few countries leads to a political and military supremacy whose very existence suffices to block far-reaching changes. There is little evidence to date of any real interest on the part of the dominant actors in the society of nations in remodeling their own structures, much less doing away with their own dominance. Just as lacking, however, are concrete formulas for overcoming the current international economic disorder that is eroding the world community's chances of peaceful survival.

Furthermore, the instruments approved at the world level by the United Nations General Assembly clearly indicate the deliberate political vagueness employed in drafting them, and the consequent failure to provide any viable means of establishing specific mechanisms for putting them into effect. An irritating note is struck by the adopted paternalistic view and the appeals to good will and humanitarian instincts which have so far been viewed as the basis for NIEO, and which, ultimately, suggest the consolidation of the present international disorder more than its evolution toward a new, more just and equitable world rationality.

Projects aimed at bringing about changes in the international society still seem feeble and impracticable; this is true, at any rate, of those projects whose magnitude and intensity would imply the creation of new social systems as an essential prerequisite for any new approach to relations within a given society. History shows that such changes have usually come about as the result of the rise of formerly dominated classes resulting from the political struggle they have waged against contradictions in their society when these become increasingly severe.

It remains to be seen whether the developed countries, in their short-sighted view of their own interests, will eventually recognize the rapidly increasing severity of such contradictions and their own direct responsibility; whether they will continue to act in such a way as to cause a large portion of the world's population, afflicted by the growing accumulation of innumerable problems, to seek increasingly drastic and violent means of escaping the ills that may lead to a world holocaust, or whether they will, in their own interest, permit the establishment of an international regime that can afford respect for the sovereign rights of all nations in terms of equality, equity, and justice. The process by which this goal is achieved may draw its initial impulse from the action taken by national societies within their own borders, or from action taken by the international community itself; in either case, it will relieve the birth pangs of a new society.

OUTLINE OF THE FINANCIAL ASPECTS OF THE PRESENT
INTERNATIONAL ECONOMIC DISORDER

Where financing is concerned, the present international economic disorder stems from the operation of three basic lending sources: bilateral public sources; multilateral public sources; and private sources. A position of particular importance among the bilateral sources is held by those organizations which represent a specific country, such as the United States' EXIMBANK. The latter's loans are generally both tied and hard, and are provided to finance the purchase of goods imported from the United States, the production of strategic materials outside the United States, or they complement private capital.

Multilateral sources include such organizations as the International Monetary Fund (IMF), the International Bank for Reconstruction and Development (IBRD) and the Inter-American Development Bank (IDB). Since all are controlled by American capital, it is obvious, in view of the transnational character of lending capital, that their credits are aimed at ensuring given lines of political conduct, facilities for foreign investment, a role in drafting economic policies, and a favorable attitude toward increasing the role of private capital in the economies applying for loans.(1)

Private sources are the true owners of lending capital and the public lending facilities; the loans they provide are more expensive and run for shorter periods (grace period and amortization period). They are also tied loans, and are used to pay debt service, and to finance purchases of goods and services from the lending source. Irregularities in the handling of these private international financing sources have reached such a point that, in most countries today, fixed interest is being paid on transnational lending capital, with the result that the flow of funds leaving the country is greater than the net earnings on capital. Such loans are generally granted to branches of transnational enterprises and are financed by funds accumulated in the host country. Obviously, this even further decapitalizes and impoverishes the developing countries.

Where financing is concerned, the proposals of NIEO go no further than exhortations to good behavior, in spite of the fact that lending capital escapes the sovereign control of national governments, subordinating the power of those governments to the interests of the lending sources. It would be naive, therefore, for developing countries to hope that good faith will aid in solving their financial problems, since the principal industrial nations have systematically conditioned both their economic and political aid by channeling it through those lending institutions which are the instruments in further consolidating the existing international economic disorder.

The resolutions of the General Assembly of the United Nations have made no positive impact on financing owing to the very nature of this international economic disorder. In the current situation, IMF policies mainly benefit the transnational enterprises and the large private banks that receive a permanent income from the different countries in the form of debt servicing. (These are increasingly dominated by interest payments.) Contradictorily, those most harmed by the IMF and the corporations are the countries they intend to benefit. These find themselves trapped in the vicious circle of indebtedness, the weakness of the state, damage to their national sovereignty, and the growing poverty of their masses. The voting majority they enjoy in the United Nations is of little use to poor countries in making progress toward NIEO at the financial level, since no mechanisms exist that might compel the fulfillment of the precepts set forth in the Declaration and Plan of Action of the New International Economic Order. This is also true of the IMF, where power and the distribution of the benefits obtained from liquidity are in direct proportion to the size of the quotas, which are set in accordance with a country's reserves and its participation in international trade. The same holds true for credit. Under these conditions, any improvement in the situation of developing countries is miniscule, and is quickly wiped out by the negative effects of the inflation it generates.

In addition to disparities in socioeconomic conditions existing in different developing countries, little consideration has been given to the fact that the IMF and the World Bank are United Nations agencies that are not actually controlled by that organization. Rather, they use its initials to carry out their destabilizing mission at the world financial level, and to aid in implanting their economic policy packages in developing countries with a view to manipulating popular support of national governments. The wealthy nations hold meetings such as the one at Rambouillet to study means of employing the illusions of money created by the handling of liquidity as a restraint on the just demands of developing countries and as a weapon in their "economic warfare." The bill for this is eventually passed to the developing countries in the form of loans granted under conditions that favor transnational capital financing. The proposals of industrialized countries to increase the number of tied loans granted by the World Bank and IMF are diversions that serve to shift the attention of developing countries from the struggle they should be waging on behalf of the financial aspects of NIEO.

The Conference for International Economic Cooperation (CIEC, often referred to as the North-South Dialogue) and UNCTAD have had no real effectiveness as far as the poor nations are concerned, since their principal actions (application of a generalized system of preferences by the industrialized nations with respect to the manufactured exports of the developing countries, transfer of 1 percent of the GNP of developed countries, and linkage of SDRs to development assistance), like so many others, have remained mere expressions of goodwill insofar as the actual guidance of transnational financing is concerned. The United States, the world's principal creditor nation, consistently voted against them. The proposed NIEO includes no mechanisms that would oblige participants to fulfill such agreements. Nevertheless, there is evidence of a growing awareness on the part of some of the poor nations that the battle for NIEO can be waged within the framework of a coherent political and economic unity that transcends the sphere of mere joint entreaty.

The promise of IMF aid through its existing mechanisms (oil-facility, compensatory financing, etc.) and through the Trust Fund, established with funds obtained from the auction of one-sixth of its gold reserves, serve to distract attention from matters of basic importance. Another problem is the continued existence of bilateral negotiations making it possible for IMF to introduce orthodox monetary policy programs, due to the financial and political weakness of the Third World countries belonging to the outworn system conceived at Bretton Woods.

The problem of the world economy is not a lack of liquidity, but the unequal distribution of its benefits. This contributes to the increasing poverty of a large percentage of the world's population. Therefore, to insist on solving the national development problems of developing countries by creating such "counterfeit money" as the SDRs is both ingenuous and ill-intentioned. The same is true of the so-called floatation system,which feeds the sort of financial speculation that is occurring today where the dollar and the U.S. "fight" against gold are concerned.

In Latin America, the financial sphere of NIEO must surpass such objectives as merely to increase the capital of multilateral lending institutions. The developing world has sufficient resources of its own to finance development; its ability to exploit them will depend directly on the kind of domestic policies designed by and for the people in each nation. Once the reordering of national affairs has been accomplished, political determination and planned techniques will make it possible to speak of regional integration that will serve as a platform for the struggle for NIEO. A regional financing structure could be created with funds supplied by progressive petroleum-producing countries to provide the foundation for a true process of economic integration.

Within the context of the struggle to establish NIEO, it would be dangerous to forget the nature of the stabilizing programs promoted by the IMF. The funding needs of developing countries are exploited as a means of imposing these programs with the watchword of battling the "priority problem of inflation" that has been brought about, according to spokesmen of the Fund, by state intervention in the economy and by wage increases.   To battle inflation in societies in which the unemployment and underemployment rate exceeds 50 percent of the working-age population, and in which wealth is concentrated in the hands of a minority, is to deepen the crises arising from the situation and to increase dependence at the expense of the welfare of the majority sectors. And, if inflation is an evil, the IMF should not feed it by the reckless issue of "counterfeit money" (Special Drawing Rights-SDRs) or by such speculatory maneuvers as floating the dollar.

As regards financing, NIEO implies abandoning monetary-based concepts of the economy and taking a global view of all the structural factors, and all sound and effective mechanisms offered by domestic financing, so that multilateral lending institutions can become secondary regulators whose interests are subordinated to those of the low-income population groups in developing countries.   Reforms in the international monetary system have given the IMF greater power to control the economies of member countries faced with economic difficulties. This fact has reinforced its role as an instrument for protecting the interests of large banking groups. The latter, while claiming to exert no pressure on behalf of the adoption of any economy policy, in reality, demand the signing of letters of intent approved by the IMF which violate national sovereignties, since credits are contingent on the Fund's endorsement and on its signal to provide banks to grant tied and hard loans.

If the IMF fails to approve the letters of intent that call for the issue of credits to the countries it supports, if it does not supervise the use made of them.   The private banks, then, suspend their aid to developing countries. These countries, because of their internal structural deficiencies, have no other resort than to accept the IMF formulas in spite of their high social, economic, and political costs.   This strengthens the bonds of dependence and contradicts the spirit of NIEO.

Speaking dialectically, it is the groups and factions that favor dependence and that are allied with transnational financing capital that support NIEO without mentioning the terms on which it is to be established.

The fact that, in spite of all the expressions of goodwill by the wealthy nations and the meetings systematically held by the developing countries, there has been no change in the financial aspect of the present international economic disorder is due to the failure to design an NIEO financing strategy that is congruent with world political and economic reality, and with the desired objectives. Similarly, the lack of congruence between these objectives and the action of some governments that do everything possible to obtain moratoriums on their debt, call for the developed nations to assign 0.7 percent of their GNP to them, or presume the issue of counterfeit money provides a solution to their structural and internal economic problems has limited a critical awareness and ability in developing countries to devise measures to be taken on their own initiative, and within their own countries. There can be no NIEO without a prior restatement and modification of domestic financial relations in developing countries within the context of new national economic orders, supported by unified international financing strategies.

Under present conditions, the only immediate step that can be taken to link international financing to the development of Third World countries is to prevent the granting of loans under conditions that are both onerous and damaging to their national sovereignty. To do so, an end must be put to the pressuring of countries by lending institutions to adopt recessive economic policies that are harmful both to their economies and to the social interests of their peoples.

POINTS TO BE INCORPORATED IN NIEO

As we have seen, a great deal has been said to date about NIEO, but almost nothing has been done. This is basically due to the lack of an overall concept of the international system that would permit a large-scale linking of the economic, political, and social measures that must be taken if any real progress is to be made. The major problems of every developing country can be transferred to the international level: unemployment, stagnation, inflation, insufficient food supplies, foreign debt, marginalization, and concentration of income and wealth. Where politics is concerned, the most prevalent problem is the extent to which there is a conscientious and democratic participation of the people.

Without going into the internal causes and effects of the problems inherent in the prevailing national economic disorder in the less-developed countries, it can be seen from the very fact of their existence that the concept of NIEO is limited, since NIEO can only come into existence as a product of the aggregation of new national economic orders. History has shown that these, in turn, depend on the capacity and determination of states to advance in the requisite direction. The essential and realistic thing, therefore, is to realize that the continued political miniaturization of Latin American countries, which is aided and abetted by the centers of power, is the main obstacle to establishment of NIEO. The dimensions of this obstacle can be inferred from the very minor success of integrationist attempts to form a regional economic bloc in that area.

NIEO does not, so far, include any regulation of transnational corporations, in spite of their pernicious effects on
all countries, both wealthy and poor, which they submit to
economic and political pressures that are beyond the control
not only of democratically elected governments, but even of
those whose power rests on bayonets.

Some of the major specific points omitted either voluntarily or involuntarily from the proposed NIEO are the
following:

1. There is no provision for supervision and evaluation of
    the impact of the IDB and the World Bank on the invest-
    ments in the Third World or on the hierarchies and
    priorities set by NIEO. The reason for this omission is
    that these banks are international organizations which,
    like any capitalist bank, are operated for profit. Their
    business is the development of backward countries; their
    decisions are never at variance with the interests of the
    capitalist system that is at the roots of the present
    international economic disorder and which, therefore, does
    more to prolong it than to change it.

2. The existing gap between the few wealthy nations and the
    many poor nations increases the potential threat to the
    peace, security, and stability of the system. Evidence of
    this fact is found in the agreement to channel resources
    in the form of credits to alleviate economic pressures in
    marginalized areas as an indispensable means of checking
    the instability of the system. NIEO sidesteps this grave,
    real, and potential conflict.

3. The proposed NIEO has taken an abstract view of the fact
    that the crisis of the international system seems no
    longer temporary but, rather, permanent – created and
    fomented by the industrialized nations as a result of the
    international concentration of income and wealth, of
    political power, and systemic hegemonies.

4. Another point to be taken into account in presenting a
    detailed design for NIEO is that the armaments race
    channels reserves from the peripheral countries to the
    centers of power and contributes heavily to foreign debt
    and to dependence by encouraging the purchase of weapons
    that are not only obsolete, but unnecessary for peaceful
    and democratic coexistence. The majority of the govern-
    ments that have come to power as a result of coups d'état
    and repressive regimes are sustained by equipment and
    armaments provided by the great powers, and this bogs down
    every attempt at a worldwide readjustment of interests.
    No method is provided in NIEO to alleviate this problem.

5. Population growth represents both a threat to the stabil-
    ity of the system and a product of colonialism and
    exploitation. Again, NIEO will not solve this problem.

6. There is a growing need for increased food production in the developing countries, where the decapitalization of the agriculture and stockbreeding sectors, the autarky of developed zones, and the deterioration of trade conditions make increases in productivity difficult. At the same time, however, the international division of labor obliges developing countries to export foodstuffs under conditions of increasing dependence, thereby reducing domestic supplies. This situation is overlooked in the NIEO proposal.

NOTE

1. For details on the operation of the international financial system, see Jorge Lozoya and A.K. Bhattacharya, eds. Finanicial issues of the New International Economic Order, NIEO Library, 1980.

2 The Policies of Nationalization
Eduardo Novoa

The topic of nationalization is and has been for several decades one of the most controversial issues in international economic relations.(1) In many international gatherings it has divided the Western capital-exporting countries and the developing countries, and set them at odds with each other.(2) It has been one of the basic differences which has led the capital-exporting countries to oppose the passing of the Charter of Economic Rights and Duties of States,(3) and, thereafter, to seek to discredit it.

This controversy has caused many confusions and ambiguities as to concepts and terminology, as a consequence of the antagonists' needs to find arguments to support their respective positions. Thus, the subject of nationalization can be tackled profitably only if there is a prior clarification of the ideas and nomenclature utilized. Only then is it possible to arrive at precise proposals and attempt conclusions to effectively help dispel the obstacles.

In order to clearly understand the concept of nationalization, it is useful to recall its historical origin. The first occasion where measures which can legally be qualified as instances of nationalization were adopted was in Russia in 1917, after the October Revolution.(4) These nationalizations were the most extensive and radical that have ever been undertaken; they applied to goods owned by nationals as well as by foreigners, and did not pay compensation to the affected parties. They had as their objective large estates, banks, insurance, and all large and medium-sized industry in the country.(5)

In the immediate following years, Romania, Czechoslovakia, and Lithuania nationalized land in order to set up their own agrarian reforms. The revolutionary origin of the practice of nationalization must be taken very much into account, since it has shaped the adverse assessments of many Western capital-exporting countries. (It is necessary to remember that France and Great Britain did not recognize the new Soviet government until 1924, and that their courts rejected until then the legal effectiveness of those nationalizations. The United States did not give such recognition until 1933, by virtue of the special Roosevelt-Litvinov agreement.) However, nationalization did not remain a revolutionary measure in its historical development, since it was also put into practice in capital-exporting countries such as France and Great Britain. Indeed, these countries enacted several nationalization acts before World War II (Great Britain nationalized private broadcasting enterprises in 1926, and later, urban passenger transport and air transport. On the other hand, France nationalized war material factories in 1936 and its railroad industry in 1937.), and nationalized new economic activities also in the postwar period. Great Britain nationalized the Bank of England, the coal industry, telecommunications, and civil aviation in 1946; the central cotton purchasing agency and electricity in 1947; the gas industry in 1948; and the iron and steel industries in 1949. France nationalized the coal industry in 1944; the Renault factories, air transport, the Gnome and Rhône factories, and five large banks in 1945; the insurance companies, the gas industry, and electricity and mineral fuels in 1946. These did not correspond to classic norms of expropriation for reasons of public benefit,(6) and so they mark the beginning of a new international practice.

From then on, nationalization extended all over the world and came to be used by governments of every ideological persuasion, although predominantly by developing countries (including some just emerging from colonial status). The constitutions of some developed countries incorporate the concept of nationalization as a special form of property right deprivation, different from that of classical expropriation.(7) In the last few years, more than 100 nationalization measures have been effected in every continent of the world.

Nationalization is an act of sovereignty whereby a state transforms into the property of the entire nation what until then had been privately owned enterprises for the production or distribution of goods and services, with the purpose of continuing their exploitation in the general interest. This constitutes a high-level political act, to reorganize or restructure the bases of the national economy. The state carries out the exploitation by itself, or through special state enterprises or agencies.(8) The essence of nationalization consists, therefore, in the state taking exclusive charge of the means of production previously exploited by private entrepreneurs.

A nationalization measure can be more easily understood if divided into the three facets that constitute it. One is that the state determines that the private entrepreneurs working in a particular industry will no longer engage in this activity. The second consists in the fact that, through a sovereign decree, the state appropriates those goods which it considers necessary to pursue this activity. The last facet involves the state taking over the exploitation of an industry or enterprise, either by means of one of its official agencies or by setting up an autonomous state body for this purpose to take charge of the matter. Of these three facets, only the second (forced acquisition of private property by the state) shows a similarity to traditional expropriating. However, even this facet differs in that a private individual is not deprived of a particular physical property (generally real estate), to be used in the execution of some public work or service but, instead, he is deprived of a set of property goods fit to serve as means of production.

Nationalization can only be used by states that take a decisive role in directing a country's economic life - a participation which can go as far as leading the state to assume an exclusive role as entrepreneur in certain industrial or commercial enterprises. A state which proclaims its absolute nonparticipation in economic activities, or maintains that these correspond exclusively to private individuals (extreme economic liberalism) is not able to accept the institution of nationalization. But as has already been pointed out, today almost all modern states accept nationalization as an appropriate political, legal, and economic measure to better look after the national economy and the welfare of its inhabitants.(9)

Nationalization does not mean "making national" enterprises or industries under foreign ownership. It is a very wide-ranging institution which can be applied to both foreign-owned enterprises and industries and those owned by nationals. To "nationalize" signifies that the means of production or distribution of great economic importance become the property and are set under the exploitation of, the entire nation, not that their ownership is transferred from foreigners to nationals. This does not change the fact that the nationalizations which frequently cause disturbances in international economic relations are only those which concern foreign entrepreneurs. The most spectacular nationalizations of the Third World have been those of Mexico (1938), Iran (1951), Egypt (1956), Indonesia (1957), Cuba (1960), Iraq (1961), Algeria (1967 and 1971), Peru (1968), Chile (1971), and Venezuela (1975). The opposition that such measures often found on the part of the most powerful countries, and the intensity of the international conflicts that arose from them are demonstrated by the fact that several of those nationalizations gave rise to certain military-type actions or the violent overthrow, by means of foreign intervention, of the governments that decreed them. This has been due to the traditional principles of International Law which stipulate that states respect the private property of foreigners, and give the nation to which the foreigners belong the right to grant diplomatic protection.

Those countries which favor nationalization policies, although they have not reached a total consensus, consider that the measures of the last sixty years constitute a new legal phenomenon which has opened the doors to the emergence in international law of a special institution called "nationalization." The foundation for this institution must be the principle of sovereignty and economic independence of states, a principle not presently the subject of controversy at the international level, and one of which all member states of the United Nations have proclaimed themselves in favor.(10) As long as all states have the right to "determine, with complete freedom, when and as they wish, their internal and external political conditions, without outside interference, and pursue, as they consider necessary, their political, economic, social and cultural development,"(11) in view of their right to free choice, they are empowered to decide which means of production and distribution of goods and services shall remain in private hands, and which shall pass into their own control in order to carry on their exploitation in the collective interest. This faculty is held to be unquestionable as regards all goods found within the territory of each state. This is the international principle of territorial sovereignty correctly expressed.

Nationalization is a legal institution different from expropriation, and need not remain subordinated to the traditional rules of the latter, as shown by international practice. It must be governed by the norms established by the nationalizing state, being an expression of sovereignty and economic independence. For this reason, it is acknowledged that it is the laws and courts of the nationalizing state that decide any controversy that may arise. This point of crucial importance was recognized by the Charter of Economic Rights and Duties of States.(12) Nevertheless, countries which favor nationalization have not reached agreement among themselves on whether or not to indemnify the owners whose enterprises are nationalized, and if so, how. While some hold that nationalization in itself does not produce the obligation to indemnify the owners,(13) most believe there is an obligation to indemnify even if it is not a full indemnification,(14) and there are a few who consider it necessary to pay complete indemnification.(15) These latter countries believe that indemnification can be paid in installments, bearing in mind the economic capabilities of the nationalizing state, and can also be paid in bonds or other securities rather than cash.(16)

Western capital-exporting countries hold very different criteria. They refuse to admit that nationalization is a new legal form, different from traditional expropriation. By collapsing these two, they demand the payment of complete indemnification in the case of nationalization. Their interpretation of the terms "just" and "rightful" is that of classical legislation which holds that an expropriating state must pay. In addition, they hold that the inviolability of private property and the respect of rights acquired by foreigners constitutes an integral part of common International Law.(17) To this they add the institution of diplomatic immunity or protection, which permits a state to lend support to a national who claims it for having had his rights infringed upon by a foreign state, so that the dispute over nationalization becomes a controversy between states. As a consequence, Western capital-exporting countries refuse to speak of "nationalization." They call it, instead "expropriation," claiming for the nationalization measures the same conditions they demand for traditional expropriation.(18)

The United States has coined the phrase "speedy, adequate and effective compensation" to point out the indemnification they seek in the event of nationalizations (which they continue calling "expropriations"). This phrase was employed by the American government as a consequence of the Mexican oil nationalization in 1938, and has often been repeated (among others, as a consequence of the Chilean nationalization of copper). It was also included in the text proposed by the United States with the support of the European Economic Council, in the Group of 40 in charge of preparing the CERDS project. It is still being employed in the Conference for International Economic Cooperation (CIEC) of Paris, in an alternative proposal presented by the developed countries. Their desire to see it introduced in some international document is evident, even if it be done craftily.

When the nationalization is effected without providing for this kind of indemnification (compensation), they consider the procedure a "confiscation." The country which has enacted it has then violated what they hold to be the principles of international law. For this reason, the countries which opposed the approval of the Charter of Economic Rights and Duties of States did so on the grounds that this measure could only be adopted for reasons of public benefit or national interest, and that the amount of indemnification paid should observe the standards of international law. But there is no written, systematized, and complete code of international law. Therefore, standards applicable to the conduct of states in their interrelation normally arise as a product of international habit, or the application of certain legal principles which have achieved general acceptance in all countries.

Thus, to determine the contents of international law in a specific case, it is always of foremost importance to know the way international relations are handled in the great majority

of countries that consciously observe a legal rule. It is also
necessary to keep in mind that international law is not im-
mutable but evolves. Its content must be found in modern
international practice, established through the acceptance of
the majority of nations.

There was a time when international law corresponded to a
legal concept imposed by half a dozen powerful European nations, whose legal systems had a great deal of homogeneity
because they were founded on Roman Law and Christian ideas.
Although this prevailed in the past centuries (especially in
the seventeenth and eighteenth centuries, it cannot continue in
the present world, which consists of over 150 sovereign nations
in which the most varied religious, political, social, economic, legal, and cultural ideologies prevail. The old rule
about the inviolability and sacred respect for the right to
private property, which was predominant in the world until the
beginnings of this century, no longer prevails. Neither can
the obligation of states always to respect the property rights
of foreigners be considered as the rule in the practice of
international law. There are many international acts and
reputable opinions, doctrines, and jurisprudence which are
opposed to this.(19)

On the other hand, different acts and doctrines of
generalized application render it possible to speak of international practice as a basis for inching nationalization into a
new institution of international law. Those countries which
favor nationalization are right when, noting its effectiveness,
declare that an institution with characteristics different from
those of expropriation has emerged, and when they deduce its
individuality and special legal character from its practice.

On the basis of what has just been said, we can present
the following premises:

1. Nationalization exists as an autonomous legal form,
    different from that of classical expropriation.
2. The particular result of nationalization is that the
    nationalizing state acquires the property rights to the
    given enterprise or goods by virtue of its sovereign
    powers.
3. The right of each and every state to nationalize enter-
    prises and goods found within its territory is not open to
    discussion, even if they are the property of foreign-
    ers.(20)
4. There is disagreement among nations on whether or not the
    payment of indemnity to the owners of the nationalized
    enterprises or goods is obligatory under international
    law.
5. There is also a difference of opinion among the countries
    that hold that indemnification is obligatory. Some demand
    that a speedy, adequate, and effective indemnification be

made, but the majority believe that a payment within the economic possibilities of the nationalizing state is sufficient, even if it is not equivalent to the commercial value of the goods or enterprises taken and is not paid immediately in cash.

If on the basis of these premises we prepare a legal balance sheet of the present situation, the following two conclusions are inevitable:

1. Nationalization is a modern and autonomous legal institution which all states may apply with regard to foreign-owned enterprises and goods.
2. No agreement exists at the international level either on whether indemnification is obligatory, or about the sum and the way it is to be paid.

It follows that the first point is a rule presently in force within international law. With regard to the second point, no rule of international law can as yet be foreseen, due to serious differences of opinion among countries.

There is at present, a rule of international law which imposes the payment to foreign proprietors of a specific indemnity, or one with certain characteristics. However, we can establish as absurd the claim of Western capital-exporting countries that international law prescribes "minimum standards" of compensation in the event of the nationalization of foreign-owned property. This claim clashes with the overwhelming majority vote against it in the General Assembly of the United Nations. It was here that, when Resolution 3171 (XXVIII) was approved in 1973, it was resolved that, in the event of the nationalization of natural resources, there is only the "possibility" (and not the obligation) of indemnification. When Resolution 3281 (XXIX) (The Charter of Economic Rights and Duties of States) was approved, it was resolved that the compensation to be paid will be determined by the laws of the nationalizating state and controlled by its courts. In both cases, the majorities (108 votes in favor and one against; and 120 in favor and 6 against respectively) make it rationally impossible to invoke international consensus in support of "minimum standards." Without such consensus, no legal rule of international law can arise. This means that no nation can validly hold that a nationalizating state which does not provide a "speedy, adequate, and effective" indemnification is operating contrary to international law.

Despite the legal clarity of the aforementioned situation, Western capital-exporting countries have not, so far, given up their position. This shows that economic interests weigh more heavily in their consideration than reason and logic. However, there are grounds to believe that the present criterion will change in the future. This optimism is based on the marked evolution in the views of the greatest legal experts in these countries. For several years, German, French, Belgian, English, Italian, North American, and Swiss jurists of great prominence have admitted that, regarding authentic nationalization, the state which effects it must recognize the obligation to indemnify the affected proprietor. But they add that, as far as the sum and the way this indemnity is to be paid, there are no fixed rules in present international law. Among others, F. Boulanger, C. Chaumont, L. Delbez, G. Foilloux, P. Guggenheim, E. Lauterpacht, De Nova, L. Oppenheim, A. de la Pradelle, C. de Visscher and G. White, W. Friedmann hold a similar position. For his part, O. Lissitzyn proves the existence of new state actions and practices at the international level, even though this does not lead him to abandon his traditional position. They contradict the thesis of a "minimum standard" or of "speedy, adequate, and effective" payment.

Most promising is the fact that, even among North American internationalists who had stayed loyal to their countries' official positions, strong doubts are beginning to appear about the claims still held by their countries. They are beginning to distinguish between "individual expropriations" (classical expropriations) and "general expropriations" (present-day nationalizations), and admit that the latter must be subject to more flexible, special rules. This advanced position is noticeable in the Project on International Responsibility of States for Damages to Foreigners, prepared, by a special petition of the United Nations, by Harvard University's Law School in 1951, and signed by Professors R. R. Baxter and L. B. Sohn. It continues to influence many North American jurists,(21) who accept granting greater flexibility to the legal rules which apply in the event of nationalization. This is the opinion of Charles N. Brower, as well. It may be that such enlightened opinions will have an effect on the so far intransigent position adopted by the U. S. government. Here, perhaps, lies the best hope of reaching a certain consensus on nationalization policies.

In the head-on conflict between capital-exporting countries (primarily the United States) and the rest of the countries in the world regarding the obligation to indemnify, and the forms and the amounts of indemnification, the existing international legal institutions and agencies are not able to resolve the controversy. Since there is no obligatory jurisdiction that can settle disputes between states that disagree on the legitimacy of nationalization,(22) if the disagreeing countries do not freely decide to go before the International Court of Justice, or before an arbitrational court appointed by common accord, there is no authority that can resolve their differences. Powerful states did not always resign themselves to submit their legal theses on nationalization to a free legal discussion. An example of this is the experience of the Chilean copper nationalization, when Chile suggested applying a procedure of legal arbitration provided for in the Bryan Treaty of 1914. The United States did not accept this suggestion.(23) We must bear in mind the difficulty for a nationalizing state to surrender the decision over the legality or normality of its nationalization to a special tribunal other than its own, maintaining as it does that it has the sovereign faculty to decide on the conditions of nationalization.

Perhaps a binding jurisdiction can be established in the future, to take charge of legal decisions in the event of disagreement between states. It is also possible, although more remotely, that a court can be established to resolve interstate conflicts due to nationalizations. Until then, these controversies will not have a legal solution and will be subjected to de facto circumstances and, primarily, to political, economic, and even military pressures exercised by one state over another. This is certainly not to be wished for in a world in which international principles of rationality, justice, and mutual cooperation should prevail.

On many occasions, foreign companies subjected to nationalization have taken their complaints to local courts in third countries where they also owned property, or where they had markets. In an important number of these cases, however, third-country courts have abstained from receiving their claims.(24) It cannot be considered viable that a sovereign state should be required to accept subordination of the validity of its decisions on domestic public goods to arbitrational bodies or courts of private origin or inspiration, as suggested by representatives of the capital-exporting countries. They have suggested, for example, that disputes over nationalization be submitted to the ICSID (Internacional Centre for Settlement of Investment Disputes), created in 1966 from among the members of the World Bank (IBRD); but it is unlikely that a developing country would submit a decision concerning the legitimacy of its sovereign actions to an organization linked to a Bank which follows the same position of capital-exporting countries with regard to nationalization, and thereby becomes an instrument of economic reprisals against poor nationalizing countries.

It is urgent to find a solution to the conflict over nationalization because: 1) The economic and social problems in many developing countries are sometimes so serious and demand so many and such complete structural reforms, that these countries cannot give up their right to free choice in economic matters, to recover natural resources or nationalize productive or distribution activities of fundamental importance to their development, or to the economic welfare of their inhabitants. 2) If the criterion of the Western capital-exporting countries is imposed, these nationalizations will not be effected at the proper moment (if ever) because of the developing country's financial limitations in producing full indemnification. This would mean, in many cases, that the poorest states would be unable to exercise their most essential sovereign right for lack of economic resources, even if this were indispensable for the good of their country. 3) The absence of a solution to these serious economic and social problems (which might suggest the need for nationalization) could plunge developing countries into serious social turmoil, with unforeseeable consequences.(25) It must be recalled that, as expressed in Resolution 1803 (XVII) of the United Nations General Assembly, general interest prevails over private interest, both national and foreign.

In spite of the above difficulties, some nationalizations have been enacted harmoniously with regard to foreign entrepreneurs and their countries. This has occurred mainly in the case of partial nationalizations, where developing countries have been satisfied with acquiring a part or share of the foreign enterprises; in some cases, the majority share. In this way, mixed enterprises have been formed where the state partly controls the enterprise, and the foreign owners keep some control, in varying proportions. These mixed companies continue functioning under the direction, or at least with the technological contribution, of the foreign entrepreneurs. This procedure has the drawback that it can solve, in a satisfactory and definitive manner, the economic and social problems required for the economic reorganization of the developing country. Certain circumstances, especially technical and technological know-how, can lead to a situation where, legally or de facto, the foreign partner takes complete control of the enterprise. This procedure was employed in Chile with copper by President Frei, in what he called the "Chileanization of copper", first in 1965 and afterwards in 1969, in what was called the "nationalization pact."(26)

Often, these cessions by private foreign entrepreneurs of part of their rights to the local government are actually desired by them. This is because they feel that an association with the state is convenient for the success of their business: it means a better image for the people, the influx of fresh capital or of credit facilities, the removal of the danger of complete nationalization, and the attainment of excellent protection with fewer economic risks, in the operation they previously carried by themselves.(27)

Harmonious nationalizations have also taken place in developing countries with sufficient financial resources to pay the indemnification demanded by foreign entrepreneurs. In such cases, this has been a business transaction freely executed by both sides, state and foreign entrepreneurs, usually to the satisfaction of the latter. This is the case of the Venezuelan oil "nationalization" carried out in 1975. This measure was

adopted after reaching an agreement with the foreign entrepreneurs concerning its conditions, the sums to be paid, and
the advantages the latter would obtain. The criticism is made
in Venezuela that these foreign entrepreneurs have kept great
advantages after the nationalization through certain service
contracts, which would explain their agreement to give up total
control of the enterprise through the payment of a very large
sum which was arrived at without considering some rights
already obtained by Venezuela.(28)

Today, the full and permanent sovereignty of every state
over its natural resources in the interest of national development and the people's welfare constitutes a recognized
principle of international law. This has been recognized, with
no important disagreements, in Resolutions 1803 (XVII), 2692
(XXV), 3171 (XXVIII), 3201 (XXIX) and 3281 (XXIX) of the United
Nations General Assembly. This principle, however, presents a
problem regarding the exact scope of the term "resources."
Does it refer only to tangible substances or goods which can be
extracted from a territory, or does it include also an advantage present in a country due to its territory or its
natural conditions, such as a navigable canal, or conditions
favorable for hydroelectric exploitation? Up until now, the
predominant tendency has been to consider the term in its
widest sense, although there has been no full debate permitting
consideration of all the implications of one or the other
alternative.

Sovereignty over natural resources includes the right to
their possession, use, and disposal in a fashion most appropriate for each country.(29) In order to properly make use of
this faculty, every state is authorized to exercise effective
control over its resources and their proper exploitation in a
way appropriate to its circumstances; that is why a state can
establish rules for the exploration, development, and des-
tination of such resources, and even limit or prohibit these
activities.(30) The sovereignty of a state over its natural
resources can never be restricted, under any circumstances. It
follows that no coercion may be exercised which would limit or
reduce its full and free activity. For this reason, any attack
launched by another country through the adoption of discrimi-
natory or hostile measures against a state exercising its
sovereignty is prohibited by the Lima Declaration of 1975.

According to the Lima Declaration, natural resources
include the terrestrial as well as the maritime resources
corresponding to a nation, and extend to their exploitation,
conservation, processing, and trade. In order to facilitate
the better exploitation of each country's natural resources,
Resolution 3201 provides that the relevant United Nations
agencies will respond to petitions for assistance and advice by
developing nations.

Sovereignty over natural resources authorizes each state to nationalize its own.(31) This does not mean, however, that nationalization should, in general, affect only natural resources, despite some narrow wording - deceptive for that very reason - in Resolutions 1803 (XVII) and 3171 (XXVIII) of the General Assembly and Resolution 88 (XII) of UNCTAD. The Charter of the Economic Rights and Duties of States is sufficiently clear on this point. On the other hand, the correct solution can be obtained from international practice, the opinions of the jurists, and important national legislation. In short, nationalization can affect natural resources as well as any other means of production and distribution of goods and services. Problems that may arise concerning the method and requirements in the nationalization of natural resources are to be solved in the same manner as has been established in considering nationalizations in general.

When dealing with natural resources which are developed, exploited, processed, or marketed through foreign investment, the sovereignty of a country requires that such investment must conform to the rules and conditions freely established by the host country. This is acknowledged in the prevailing and recognized principles. It could be, however, that the treatment of foreign investment by a host country in using the powers to authorize, limit, and prohibit activities related to its natural resources might create difficulties with foreign investors. On this subject, there have been some disagreements between Western capital-exporting and developing countries, based on opposing points of view similar to those examined above. Capital-exporting countries demand that full and permanent sovereignty be exercised "according to international law," a limitation considered nonexistent by developing countries. To clear up this point we can refer to the reasons applicable to nationalization in general.

When economically powerful countries invoke the rules of international law, they do so to attribute current validity to principles which have already been surpassed, especially those concerning the inviolability of private property and the absolute respect for the acquired rights of foreigners. But, as we have seen, it is precisely these principles that have lost force today, and cannot be measured against the needs of a state to protect, first and foremost, the collective interests of its people. This is why point 4 of Resolution 1803 (XVII) states that general national interest is, above all, private interest - be it of nationals or foreigners. If developing countries were not able to exercise sovereignty over natural resources in their territory due to conflict with the private property rights or the acquired rights of foreign investors, this sovereignty would be lacking the "full and permanent" character recognized by general consensus. In addition, this would make the general rights of an entire people subordinate to the private interests of a few foreigners. It follows that this problem can be solved, _mutatis mutandis_, with the same reasoning we explained earlier.

One last point remains to be examined: the responsibility of states that occupy or dominate foreign territory (through colonialism, racial discrimination, apartheid, etc.) to compensate the affected countries and peoples for the exploitation or exhaustion of their natural resources, and for all damage to them.(32) This principle has been confirmed in several international agreements, among which we can mention Resolution 3175 (XXVII) of the United Nations General Assembly. Some of these resolutions deal with the burning Arab-Israeli conflict. In the final analysis, this principle includes the assertion that a territory's natural resources belong fully and permanently to its native inhabitants. It should be applied especially in cases where a newly independent state emerges from foreign domination.

NOTES

1. Report of the General Secretary prepared by the Center for Transnational Corporations, July 20, 1976, about "Issues Involved in the Formulation of a Code of Conduct" (U.N. Doc. E/C 10.17).

2. See the U.N. General Assembly debates which preceded the passing of Resolution 1803 (XVII), 3171 (XXVIII), and 3281 (XXIX).

3. The six votes opposing Resolution 3281 (XXIX) concerning the approval of the Charter came from Belgium, Denmark, the United States, Luxembourg, the United Kingdom, and the Federal Republic of Germany. The ten abstentions were by Australia, Canada, Spain, France, Holland, Ireland, Israel, Japan, and Norway.

4. Some scholars look for cases of nationalization in ancient times. Some attribute this character to certain economic activities undertaken by some states in ancient Egypt, in the Middle Ages, or in other bygone centuries. We think that the nationalizations, without prejudice against the historical interest of such facts and according to the criteria by which they are nowadays considered in the international debate, actually began in Russia in 1917. See, René David and J.N. Hazard, Le Droit Sovietique (Paris: 1954), pp. 9 and 187 ff.

5. The corresponding decrees were enacted beginning November 10, 1917. One, of November 29, 1920, extends nationalization to every enterprise which has more than ten workers or which uses machines and has more than five workers. So, only handicraft activities and small-scale domestic industries are excluded.

6. R. Bindschedler, F. Boulanger, and G. Ripert demonstrate that in those cases the indemnification paid to the old owners was generally lower than the actual value of the nationalized properties. B. Chenot and S. Bastide point out that nationalizing processes in such cases was very different from those demanded by traditional expropriation.

7. Art. 43 of the 1947 Italian Republic Constitution, and paragraph 15 of the Constitution (Fundamental Law) of the Federal Republic of Germany.

8. On the concept and definition of nationalization see Eduardo Novoa, Nacionalización y Recuperación de Recursos Naturales ante la Ley Internacional (México, D.F.: Fondo de Cultura Económica, 1974); "La Nacionalización en su Aspecto Jurídico," in the collective work Derecho Económico Internacional (México, D.F.: Fondo de Cultura Económica, 1976); and Defensa de las Nacionalizaciones ante Tribunales Extranjeros, publication of the National Autonomous University of Mexico, México D.F., 1977.

9. There are authors who believe that even in the United States, state economic enterprises have been formed, and they give as an example the Law of May 28, 1933, referring to the Tennessee Valley Authority. See K. Katzarov, Teoría de la Nacionalización, translation and notes by H. Cuadra (Instituto de Derecho Comparado of the National Autonomous University of Mexico, 1963), p. 66.

10. See Art. 55 of the Charter of the United Nations.

11. Final Document of the Security and Cooperation in Europe Conference in Helsinki, approved in August 1975, 1-a-VIII.

12. Art. 2,2.b of the Charter of the Economic Rights and Duties of States (CERDS).

13. Position held by the USSR and other socialist countries during the discussion preceding the approval of Resolution 1803 (XVII) by the UN General Assembly. This criterion has in its favor some prestigious Western opinions, among which can be mentioned those of Fisher-Williams, Rolin, and Brystricky.

It is very important to point out that this thesis would seem to have won the day in Resolution 3171 (XXVIII) of the General Assembly, since it speaks of the "possible" payment of indemnification, an expression which excludes the idea of an obligatory indemnification. Notice that, faced with such an advanced text, the large capital-exporting countries abstained from voting, rather than vote against. Only the United Kingdom voted negatively.

14. This idea is implicit in the text of CERDS, since it speaks of "appropriate compensation" the amount of which will be determined by disposition of the laws and regulations of the nationalizing state, and any discussion resolved by its courts. We shall see that this position has the support of the most important modern jurists.

15. At least this is the pragmatic attitude adopted by Venezuela in 1975 when it nationalized its petroleum, since it paid the leasing companies a sum which left them entirely satisfied. This does not go against the corresponding law which established that only the book value of the property would be paid.

16. Art. 101 of the Venezuelan Constitution explicitly permits indemnification to the private owner to be paid in installments or, in part, through the emission of bonds which must be acquired by the entrepreneurs. This occurs, in those cases, where there exist "serious reasons of national interest" to do so.

17. Sentence No. 7 pronounced by the Permanent Court of International Justice in 1976, on the expropriation case of German property in Upper Silesia. See: Recueil des Arretes, A series, pp. 30 ff.

18. S. Petren assures us that "Western states whose citizens have been subject to nationalization have wanted to apply the issue of indemnification to customary rules applied to classical-type expropriation, which order the payment of adequate, rapid and effective indemnifications." See "La confiscation des biens étrangéres et les reclamations internationales auxquelles elle peut donner lieu," in Recueil de Cours de l'Académie de Droit International 2 (1963): 495. It should be noted that point 4 of Resolution 1803 (XVII) already quoted and Art. 2, 2.b of CERDS incorrectly identifies nationalization and expropriation. This must be considered a concession of the editors, attempting to obtain the approval of the rich countries. In the Questions and Answers Manual prepared by the World Bank, the North American criterion is followed in speaking of "expropriation" without mentioning the nationalization to which undoubtedly it refers. On the other hand, the document mentioned in our first note correctly speaks of "nationalization."

19. On this subject important opinions by the most reputable modern jurists can be mentioned, among them B. Chenot, E. Jiménez de Aréchaga, F. Münch, G. Fouilloux, S. Petren, C. de Visscher and L. Focsanueanu. Similar jurisprudence coming from West German (FRG), Belgian, French, Dutch, English, Italian, Japanese and North American courts can be found in Novoa, Defensa de las Nacionalizaciones ante Tribunales Extranjeros. Present international practice, for its part, accepts the existence of new rules which enable states, in full use of their economic sovereignty and right to free choice, to adopt the measures considered appropriate for the economic improvement of its peoples, even if this means sacrificing the property rights of private foreign individuals. On this point, consult the works by Novoa cited above.

20. On the occasion of the Suez Canal nationalization by Egypt in 1956, France, Great Britain, and the United States

explicitly recognized the right of states to nationalize. (See AFDI, 1956, p. 844). In 1938, the United States had recognized the right of all states to seize foreign property as a power emanating from sovereignty itself (during the Mexican oil nationalization). Even in the World Bank Manual, mentioned previously, it is established that every state has this right.

21. This can be seen in the recent publications directed by Prof. Richard B. Lillich, from the University of Virginia, with the title of The Valuation Books, in which appear the opinions of the jurists Jessup, Murphy, Sweeney and Wesley which tend to moderate the rigour of the official North American position. Lillich himself seems much more understanding than in his previous position.

22. There is an "optional clause of obligatory juridiction" in art. 36 of the International Court of Justice Statutes, but it is only binding for those few states which have signed an additional protocol.

23. See Eduardo Novoa, La Batalla por el Cobre (Santiago de Chile: 1972), p. 360.

24. See Novoa, Defensa de las Nacionalizaciones ante Tribunales Extranjeros.

25. These are the same concepts developed by Prof. L.B. Sohn in American Journal of International Law, p. 112, when he stated that the inflexible official North American thesis implicitly contributes to revolution in poor countries, since they cannot meet the demands and would be prevented from making necessary social reforms.

26. Concerning the damage this represented to Chilean interests, see Novoa, Chaps. V and VII.

27. From what is expressed by C.D. Michaelson, President of the Metal and Mining Division of Kennecott Corp., in Mining Engineering magazine, April 1969, pp. 73-78, it follows that the "Chileanization" of the said company in Chile in 1965, through the creation of a joint enterprise with majority state participation was contrived by Kennecott Corp. itself, as a solution to its economic problems.

28. On this subject see Novoa, La nacionalización venezolana del petróleo, to be published by the Publications Department of the National Autonomous University of Mexico.

29. Art. 2.1 of the Charter of the Economic Rights and Duties of States.

30. Resolutions 1803 and 3201 already mentioned.

31. Resolutions 1803, 3171, and 3281 already mentioned.

32. Art. 16 of the Charter of the Economic Rights and Duties of States.

3 The Resources of the Seabed
Jorge Castañeda

THE EXPLOITATION OF SEABED RESOURCES AS A
UNIQUE CONTRIBUTION TO NIEO

The exploitation of seabed resources represents a challenge to
a whole generation of internationalists and men of science. In
fact, this is the first experiment in which the international
community is exploiting, managing, and distributing substantial
resources which concern the whole humanity. The exploitation
of the sea bed would contribute to NIEO for the following
reasons.

Better Distribution of Natural Resources

To put a great number of important natural resources at the
disposal of the international community, rather than a limited
number of states, would help in the industrial advancement of
developing countries, insofar as such development depends on
easy access to raw materials. To the extent that these
resources are being exploited under international control,
logically, the needs and interests of developing countries will
be taken into account, which would not be the case if such
exploitation were undertaken by the economically and technologically advanced countries alone.

To Avoid Concentration of Valuable Metals in Few Countries

Equitable exploitation of seabed resources would prevent
valuable metals extracted from the international seabed from
being concentrated in the hands of the very few states with the

necessary financial and technological means. In this way, developing countries will have access to resources which they could not obtain by their own means. It can be supposed that an increase in the supply of these resources will cause a drop in the price of the same raw materials extracted from the ground. Consequently, a number of countries will be affected by this new type of exploitation. Despite the intention to introduce certain corrective measures in order to compensate such countries for any losses they may suffer, the primary objective is for the communal interests of the majority of countries.

To Prevent Exploitation of Hydrocarbons in the International Zone

Mineral resources are not the only ones to be found on the international seabed. Although manganese nodules are the most important, there are also biological and geological resources in the sea. It is known that hydrocarbons are generally found closer to the coast, that is to say, on the continental and insular shelves. Little is known of the existence of hydro-carbons in the oceanic subsoil, although technology allows one to suppose the existence of such deposits in some semi-closed seas, as may be the case in the Sigsbee Fossa in the Gulf of Mexico, the Caribbean Sea, the Mediterranean, the Indonesian Archipelago, the Japan Sea, and others. Again, since there is no reliable data, and it has not yet been possible to develop a specific technology for the purpose, we have to guess about the future exploitation of these resources in the international forum. Up until now, negotiations on the establishment of a system for the exploitation of the zone have related primarily to manganese nodules.

THE LEGAL SYSTEM FOR RESOURCES IN ACCORDANCE WITH INTERNATIONAL LAW

Res Communes and Res Nullius

In the past, the legal system pertaining to the seabed and its resources had not been thoroughly examined. There was little interest in doing so, as such resources could not be exploited. However, different authors had examined whether such resources should be classified in one or another of the categories of property which come to us from Roman Law. Some authors, among them Gidel and others, highly eminent jurists specializing in marine law, maintained that such resources should fall into the category of res communes, i.e., belonging to all and therefore

not susceptible to appropriation by individuals, but only for
the benefit of all, as the air and the sea. On the other hand,
others maintained that res nullius was applicable, i.e., these
resources should belong to no one yet be susceptible to individual appropriation by those who extract or occupy them, as
soon as this is done, as in the case of wild animals and fish.
No argument put forward on either thesis has been really
decisive, and there is no common opinion on the subject.

This writer leans in favor of res communes. This question
has acquired a new dimension since the General Assembly, the
most representative organ of the international community,
adopted the famous Resolution 2749 (XXV) in which it established that these resources are "the common heritage of
mankind" and in particular of developing countries. It can be
said, therefore, that as the Declaration of Principles of the
United Nations concerning such resources adopted the thesis
that they are resources which belong to the whole of humanity,
they, therefore, fit in the category of res communes.

However, these are new problems and such categories, with
their classical concepts, are not appropriate to the presentday
legal classification of such resources.

Limits of Jurisdiction

We are dealing with resources found in what is known as the
zone of sea and oceanic beds and subsoil outside the limits of
national jurisdiction. The first question concerns the actual
limits of national jurisdiction. For this, it is necessary to
take into account some institutions of marine law relevant to
the international zone of the seabed.

According to traditional marine law, national jurisdiction
extends to the outer limits of territorial waters. Since 1940,
the doctrine of the continental shelf has gained weight as a
result of Truman's famous declaration. According to his
doctrine, which has been gaining favor since that time, coastal
states hold sovereign right over all resources found in the
natural prolongation of their territories, i.e., up to 200
meters in depth or any depth where exploitation is possible.
This formula was accepted by the 1958 Geneva Convention on the
Continental Shelf. Due to the vague character of the formula,
it was difficult to give a precise definition of the outer
limit of the shelf, particularly now that technology makes it
possible not only to exceed the 200 meter depth, but also to
exploit up to 200 miles from the coast. Moreover, from the
late 1940s until the 1960s, an international movement sprang
up, particularly in Latin America, which demanded the extension
of juridical limits to 200 miles. It was precisely through
work undertaken since 1974 on marine law by the Third
United Nations Conference on the Law of the Sea that the Latin

American proposals concerning the 200 mile limit were ratified. These concern the exclusive economic zone of 200 miles in which a coastal country can exercise sovereign rights over all animate or inanimate, renewable or nonrenewable resources in the waters, soil, and subsoil.

Some countries, which for reasons of geographical peculiarities - generally of a disadvantageous nature, such as the absence of a continental shelf, or having an enclosed coast - have maintained that the outer limit of the continental shelf should determine the outer limit of the economically exclusive zone. In this way, the limit of sovereign rights for coastal states over their resources in the soil and subsoil would be 200 miles, leaving aside both the criteria of depth and the exploitation of resources.

A number of countries, called wide platform countries, have continental shelves in the geographical sense which extend beyond 200 miles, in many cases considerably so. These include Australia, Argentina, Canada, the Soviet Union, the United States, New Zealand, and others. These countries believe that, according to the 1958 Convention (which is still in force), they have time-honored and acquired rights over this part of the seabed, and they reject the claims made by the Mediterranean countries and others with geographical disadvantages. Their view is that sovereign rights of coastal states should extend up to the limits of the continental shelf and, as we have seen, this can extend well beyond 200 miles. There is little likelihood of change for now. The United Nations Conference on the Law of the Sea has upheld both the doctrine of the continental shelf and the concept of the exclusive economic zone. Logically, these two systems can be applied simultaneously to the same area: the submaritime zone up to 200 miles is covered by one system, while the continental shelf by the other. The two systems are substantially the same and no practical difficulties are expected in this respect. However, it must be made clear that they are not identical. Under the system of the exclusive economic zone, a coastal state has sole sovereign right over the resources but not over the area in which they are found. On the other hand, under the system of the continental shelf, which conforms to the 1958 Convention and is more favorable to coastal states, sovereign rights are held over the continental shelf itself, and not solely over the resources found within it, even if it be used only for the exploitation of such resources. This system gives more power to the coastal states.

Some countries, based on the system of the continental shelf, have considered that they exercise sovereign right over the shelf itself, and some have even incorporated it into their national territory, as in the case of Mexico. But this problem is still to be resolved. In order to satisfy countries without the advantage of a continental shelf, and in the hope of

getting their agreement on the issue of sovereign rights, a
scheme has been devised allowing these countries to benefit
from resources on the continental shelf beyond the 200 mile
limit. It is anticipated that coastal states will be obliged
to share a percentage of the uses obtained from the exploitation of the resources on the continental shelf, above all
petroleum and gas, in that part of the shelf which is beyond
200 miles and up to the geographical limit of the shelf itself,
i.e., the outer limit of the continental border (which is also
the limit of the natural prolongation of the continent). In
the proposals which have been examined by the Conference, some
require that at least 5 percent of the value of products
extracted from the area beyond 200 miles should be kept for
distribution, particularly among developing countries.

THE CONCEPT OF THE COMMON HERITAGE OF MANKIND

Its Origins

The Malta Proposal of 1967. On March 7, 1967, the Social and
Economic Council of the United Nations called for a Resolution
to ask the Secretary-General for a study of the present knowledge about mineral and nutritional resources, excluding fish,
beyond the continental shelf as well as a study of the techniques available for exploiting them. On December 8, 1966, it
asked the Secretary-General to commission a study, in conjunc-
tion with specialist organizations, of scientific activities
and marine technology relating to the expansion of mineral
resources. Finally, on August 17, 1967, Malta's representative
to the United Nations, Ambassador Arvid Pardo, gave a memorable
speech in the presence of the First Committee of the General
Assembly, to which he added an explanatory memorandum.

Pardo suggested that the General Assembly should include
in their agenda the theme of a "Declaration and Treaty on the
Exclusive Reserve for Pacific Aims of the Sea Bed and the
Oceanic Depths, the Marine Depths not included in the Present
Limits of National Jurisdiction, and the Use of Resources for
the Benefit of Mankind." In his memorandum, Pardo explained
that the seabed is the only remaining area of our planet which
has not yet been appropriated for national use, because its
resources are still inaccessible and to use it for defense
purposes or economic exploitation is still a technical im-
possibility. In view of the rapid progress of technology,
Pardo affirms that there is a danger that the situation will
change. The seabed may become the object of national appropriation, which, in turn, could result in its militarization
and the overexploitation and exhaustion of its resources, thus
serving the exclusive advantage of developed countries. Pardo

believed that the moment had come for a declaration on the common heritage of mankind. He requested that a treaty be drawn up immediately, including the following principles: exploration of the seabed should be carried out only under the principles and proposals laid down by the United Nations Charter; economic utilization of these resources be carried out with the object of safeguarding the interests of mankind, and principally in order to promote development in poor countries; and these areas be reserved exclusively for pacific activities.

The Special Committee on the Seabed.   At the end of the 1967 session, as a result of such an interesting initiative, the General Assembly took the first step in what was to lead to the eventual convening of the Third United Nations Conference on the Law of the Sea.   This step involved the setting up of a special committee in charge of studying possible pacific uses of the sea and ocean bed outside the limits of national juris- diction.   This committee met without reaching agreement on a recommendation to the General Assembly.   In 1968, the Assembly reformed the committee, giving it a more permanent character and an increased membership.   On this occasion, the newly formed Commission's work came to fruition.   On December 15, 1969, the General Assembly adopted important resolutions, among them the so-called "Moratorium" Resolution which stands out in its stipulation that, until the establishment of an interna- tional system, countries, physicists, and lawyers would have to abstain from exploitation activities in the area, and no claims for any part of the zone or its resources are to be recognized. However, this recommendation did not establish a legal prece- dent since, among other things, it was passed by 62 in favor, 28 against, and 28 abstentions.

The General Assembly's Declaration of Principles.   The com- mittee continued its work during 1970 in an attempt to formulate a Declaration of Principles on marine depths.   As a result, on December 17, 1970, the General Assembly adopted a most important instrument, which became known as the "new law of the sea."   It was to influence the Resolutions on the New International Economic Order.   We are speaking here of the Declaration of Principles which regulates the sea and ocean bed and subsoil outside the limits of national jurisdiction.

   The Declaration can be summarized as follows: Having established that the actual limits had still to be determined, it was recognized that the existing legal system for the high seas does not supply any real pattern for the regulation of exploration in the zone or for the exploitation of its re- sources.   In addition, the Declaration states that the sea and ocean bed is the common heritage of mankind; no state will be able to claim or exercise sovereign rights over any part of it; all activities relating to the exploration and exploitation of

resources will be controlled by the international regime when
it is established; the area is to serve solely pacific activities; exploration and exploitation of resources will be
carried out exclusively for the benefit of all of mankind
regardless of the geographical location of the States; special
consideration will be given to the interests and needs of
developing countries; by setting up of an international treaty,
universal in character, an international regime will be established, applicable to the zone and its resources, including
an appropriate international mechanism for ensuring the
effectiveness of such provisions.

This Declaration was passed by 108 votes in favor, none
against, and 14 abstentions (among the latter, the group of
socialist states). Many internationalists, particularly those
from developing countries, interpreted this Declaration as an
expression of a certain willingness on behalf of the international community, and thus of international law. Despite
arguments against this interpretation, there is no doubt that,
since the United Nations Conference on the Law of the Sea in
1978, the international community has been united by the
Declaration of Principles as a premise and legal guide for the
international mechanism to be established for the exploration
of the zone and the exploitation of its resources.

Taking this last Declaration and the work done by the
Committee on the Sea Bed from that year until 1973 as a basis,
the General Assembly called for a Third United Nations Conference on the Law of the Sea which, at the time of this
writing, has still not concluded its work.

Historical Significance

The setting up of an international system for the seabed on the
above mentioned principles and implementation in the form put
forward by the United Nations Conference on the Law of the Sea
would make a significant contribution to the New International
Economic Order. Not only would the international system
facilitate a better distribution of valuable resources, it
would also give developing countries a greater opportunity to
obtain metals which are indispensable to their industrialization.

The application of the anticipated international system
would mean that, for the first time in history, the international community would be jointly exploiting goods which
belong to everyone. This represents a new dimension in
international cooperation which has no precedent and which
calls for a much closer understanding and organization of
international solidarity. There has already been a certain
amount of cooperation, with states coordinating their individual and sovereign activities in order to set up scientific

research and international services in aviation, post, and telecommunications, sometimes on a large scale. But so far, there has been no collectively administered communal enterprise, except perhaps, in satellite communications. But mankind has never yet exploited common property collectively.

Such exploitation holds enormous potential, and could open up new roads to international cooperation. From the outset, and most important, an organization will be needed for the administration of these common goods, not merely as a coordinating body for the actions taken by national administrations. This organization will have to comprise all states, acting in everyone's name and for the benefit of all. This will mean that mankind and the community of nations in the political and legal sense will no longer be merely a figment of the imagination. The United Nations would be not just an intergovernmental organization made up of sovereign states with different and often conflicting interests, and would not have to limit individual action in order to maintain peace. Mankind, as such, has not been represented on a political and juridical plane. Thus far, the concept of an international community has only meant a sum of individual states. A body designed to represent and defend the common goals of people does not exist. Mankind possesses neither a juridical nor a representative body responsible for taking care of its interests. If the system we hope for is established, it will mean that, for the first time, titular rights on goods will be ascribed to mankind in a juridical form, at least in the limited area of exploiting and maintaining such goods equitably. Mankind will have its own heritage, different from the heritage of its component parts. The organization charged with the exploitation of these riches will represent mankind and defend its interests. It will take on a new international juridical form first, perhaps; but, in the end, it will become a recognized entity with its own identifiable goals and resources. It will establish organs to act in its name and look after its interests. This new and revolutionary concept has great significance and enormous potential.

In reality, the revolutionary principle of the common heritage of mankind will allow people to transcend the artificial borders which separate them, and enable them to see that their interests often lie beyond such borders.

The concept of common heritage can also be applied in other fields, mainly in the biosphere, the Antarctic, and the high seas and outer space, including the moon and other planets. Due to the particular characteristics of these areas, it will be necessary to considerably reinforce international cooperation. These are regions which, as the seabed, are outside the national jurisdiction of states. Therefore, if their resources are to be usable and accessible, they will have to be subject to an international regime. In the Third United

Nations Conference on the Law of the Sea, certain delegates suggested extending the concept of common heritage beyond the mineral resources on the seabed to the living organisms in the high seas outside national jurisdiction. Therefore, fish would also be subject to an international regime.

There is a case where the international community has already taken the first steps toward extending the concept of common heritage to other areas. This is the case of outer space. On December 16, 1966, through Resolution 2222 (XXI) of the General Assembly, a declaration was adopted regulating activity by individual states in their exploration and util- ization of outer space, including the moon and other planets. Two months later, this declaration became an international treaty. It is precisely in this field that, even before the 1970 declaration on the seabed, a concept was originated in which any activity in the exploration and utilization of outer space would be carried out exclusively for the benefit of all mankind. The difference lies in the fact that, in this particular case, it is not a question of the exploitation of a natural resource: present day technology does not yet allow any economic use from resources found in outer space. This does show, however, that international technology and cooperation can be applied to areas outside the national jurisdiction of states.

THE COMMON HERITAGE CONCEPT CONCERNING
THE INTERNATIONAL SEABED

Meaning and Scope of the Concept of
"Common Heritage"

Since the 1970 Declaration of Principles was adopted, an enormous force has been released to establish an international regime designed to implement the concept of the common heritage of mankind. Possibly one of the greatest obstacles has been overcoming the different understandings of the meaning and scope of the concept of common heritage by the various coun- tries. In countries under the Anglo-Saxon juridical system, the concept of "common heritage" is different from the under- standing of "common heritage" by countries with a civil or continental juridical system. In the latter case, the concept is of common property, which must be exploited on a communal basis and for the benefit of all members of the community; therefore, individual exploitation is impossible. In the former case, however, the concept suggests that such goods are common property, at the disposal of each member of the com- munity, according to his possibilities. As we will see, these differences in perception have influenced the different types of international proposals put forward by groups of countries.

Exploitation for the Benefit of All Mankind, in Particular for the Benefit of Developing Countries

The exploitation of resources on the seabed for the benefit of all mankind and not only for the benefit of those with the means of exploiting such resources would be reinforced if the concept of a "common heritage" were prevalent, and even more so if it were for the benefit of developing countries. A strict application of the concept of "common heritage" would practically exclude developing countries from obtaining any benefit derived from the exploitation of these resources, as these countries would not be able to exploit such common resources, not having the means to do so.

The Need for an International System and an International Authority Concerning the Exploitation of the "Common Heritage"

For developing countries, the existence of an international regime and authority is essential, since only through this can they be sure that the benefits will be equally distributed among all countries. The developed countries are not concerned with the establishment of an international regime and authority, as it is enough for them to participate individually in the benefits of these common goods. While these countries are not objecting to the negotiations for an international regime and authority, they give them a meaning that would merely grant a seal of legitimacy to activities which they are themselves undertaking in the exploitation of these resources.

Prohibition of the Use of Sovereignty and Appropriation in the "Common Heritage" of Mankind

As an inevitable corollary to the concept of "common heritage," the Declaration of Principles had to establish a norm to prohibit any member of the international community, or any physical or legal entity, from carrying out any action which would imply the exercise of sovereignty or appropriation over any part or portion of the common goods belonging to mankind. This is implicit in the recognition that any exploitation of the resources of the seabed can only be carried out under the standard of an internationally agreed regime, and under the supervision and participation of an international authority, which would become the representative of mankind. In this way, any individual act affecting or breaking up the common good would be illegal under law.

Exploitation Exclusively for Pacific Uses

In dealing with a zone outside national jurisdiction in which the special rights of the community of nations have been recognized, it is considered necessary to limit all activity undertaken in the area to exclusively pacific uses. In the same year the Declaration was adopted, a convention was held in which it was decided that the placing of weapons of mass destruction on the sea and ocean bed outside the limits of national jurisdiction was to be prohibited. Unfortunately, such prohibition was applicable only to the type of weapons mentioned, so it has been possible to interpret the meaning of the convention in such a way as to allow the placing of certain types of installations, arms, and devices, other than arms of mass destruction. This is, of course, contrary to the interests of mankind in the area, and efforts will have to be directed toward a total disarmament of the international seabed.

THE INSTRUMENTATION OF THE PRINCIPLE IN PRACTICE: THE ESTABLISHMENT OF A REGIME FOR THE INTERNATIONAL SEABED

The Committee on the Sea Bed (1967-69) and the Preparatory Committee of the Conference (1971-73)

As has already been outlined, the General Assembly, having considered Ambassador Arvid Pardo's proposal, established a special committee which, in 1968, took on a more permanent character and increased in size. In 1970, the Committee changed in preparation for what was to be the Third United Nations Conference on the Law of the Sea. This preparatory Committee worked until 1973 with its newly increased membership.

The Commission also started to outline certain proposals on the way to implement the concept of common heritage of mankind. However, no basic agreement on the content of a system was reached, so it was still far from being worked out when the Commission finished its work. The only proposal approved by the majority, and that only within the Group of 77, was the proposal put forward by 13 Latin American countries. They suggested a system of joint service contracts and joint companies, with an international authority. As will be seen later, this proposal had a decisive influence on the future work of the Conference. On the other hand, the United States presented a project (worked out by the Nixon administration), which put forward a very different conception.

The Third United Nations Conference on the
Law of the Sea (UNCLOS)(1974-)

The Third UNCLOS began its work in Caracas in the summer of
1974, after a series of sessions on matters of procedure, which
took place in New York in December 1973. The Conference has
since held seven sessions, in New York and Geneva. It carries
out its work in three plenary committees, although a great part
of the negotiations is carried out by smaller groups. The
First Committee, under the presidency of Paul Bamel Engo of the
Cameroons, is concerned with the regime for the international
seabed.
      In the Second and Third Committees, enormous advances have
been made and work is practically completed. The Second
Committee is concerned with general questions of marine law:
territorial waters, interior waters, channels, adjacent zones,
continental and insular shelves, exclusive economic zones and
the high seas, the conservation of living resources in the high
seas, and the question of archipelagos and inland countries
and others in disadvantageous geographical positions. The main
theme of the new law of the seas is undoubtedly the exclusive
economic zone of 200 miles. The Third Committee, which deals
with the protection of the marine environment, including
questions of pollution, scientific research, and the spread of
marine technology, also made substantial advances, so that it
can be said that practically complete consensus has been
reached by these two organs.
      Only in the First Committee is there still much work to be
done. The obstacles have been enormous, as discussed above.
Nevertheless, appreciable advances have been made, such as the
agreement on the adoption of an international system and the
establishment of an international authority. But negotiations
are still in progress on certain fundamental issues.

OBSTACLES TO THE IMPLEMENTATION OF THE NEW
INTERNATIONAL ECONOMIC ORDER WITH REGARD TO A
REGIME FOR THE INTERNATIONAL SEABED

As already mentioned, during the work of the Committee on
marine depths, 13 Latin American countries presented a document
dealing with the problem of giving the concept of the common
heritage of mankind a realistic content. These countries
realized that it would be impossible to implement such a
concept without the financial and technological participation
of the great powers. The Latin American proposal attempted to
reconcile the inevitable need for financial and technological
help by developed countries with the establishment of an
authority, strong enough to ensure that any exploitation would

be done for the benefit of all mankind. A price would have to be paid in allowing the great powers a certain amount of access, so that they would share their technology and finance. It was felt best not to insist on the establishment of an international authority with virtual monopoly on activities in the area. It would be necessary to establish a system of participation, and this was the idea behind the proposal for service contracts and joint companies. This would break up as little as possible the common heritage in favor of the members of the authority. The Latin American proposal was enthusiastically received by the Group of 77 in the Caracas session. Moreover, in order to give correct weight to the matter, the proposal was introduced by the African group in the Plenary Session of the Group of 77. When adopted by the Group it was presented by it to the First Committee.

The developed countries took as the basis for their response the document originally presented by the United States. They would not accept an interpretation of common heritage which would in any way restrict direct access to the resources of the seabed. Disregarding the original interpretation, which had been accepted in the Declaration of Principles in 1970, the United States began to argue that, despite the Declaration, the freedom of the high seas should include the exploitation of marine depths. In other words, they implied that each nation had a right to exploit unilaterally and to its own advantage the common goods found on the seabed. They would not agree to any sharing through the authority of benefits of exploitation with other countries. They proposed, however, the establishment of an authority which would limit itself to issuing automatic licenses to nations that asked for them in order to legitimize their access. Obviously, this system would only benefit those with the financial and technological means to make use of such licenses. In this way, the authority would be nothing but a permit office, granting automatic licenses to the handful of countries able to satisfy the conditions. The authority would merely look on, as the powerful countries exploited the seabed, while possibly paying a monetary contribution which would be of no great benefit to mankind.

Polarization of the Positions and the Acceptance of a Virtual "Draw"

This situation prevailed during the Caracas session as well as the session which took place in Geneva in the spring of 1975. Positions became increasingly radical and eventually crystallized. The Conference reached a deadlock on the negotiations. Different intermediate positions were tried, but all were rejected by one or the other, and sometimes by both sides. By the end of the Geneva session, it was accepted, although tacitly, that a kind of draw had been reached, and that neither side had the slightest intention of encouraging agreement.

However, during this session, the seed was planted which was to become the essence of the agreement which exists today, although in a more general form, on a regime for the exploitation of the seabed. This consisted of the idea, interpreted differently by both sides, of creating a system in which the authority could reserve certain areas and portions of the international seabed area for its own exploitation in the future, in return for giving over other areas to exploitation individual states and companies under its control and jurisdiction. This idea, originally called the "banking system" by the United States, gave rise in later negotiations to a version which, although different from the original concept, was based on a division of the international seabed.

In Search of an Agreement

A proposal was then made by the developing countries for a so-called "parallel" system; through this any contractor who is to take part in the exploitation of the zone would offer the international authority an exploitation area divided into two parts of similar commercial value: the first of these, the contractual area, would be exploited by the state or contractor concerned; while the second, the reserve area, would be for exploitation by the international authority. The authority would have the right to choose its reserve area from the two areas of equal value.

The developing countries saw visible disadvantages in that it virtually divided the seabed into two parts. The authority could obviously not exploit its reserve area without its own financial and technological means. Moreover, the supporters of this type of system were demanding the automatic granting of contracts in the contractual area. Obviously, a country with financial and technological means would prefer to have access to the contractual areas, in order to avoid sharing with the authority in the reserved area and being subject to its vigilance. In this way, the reserved areas would become "dead hands" until all contractual areas of greater value had been exploited, which could take centuries. The developing countries would be mere witnesses of the exploitation by the few of the common heritage of mankind. The parallel system was not accepted as a base for negotiation and was rejected by the Group of 77.

However, the developed countries tried all they could to impose the system on the Group of 77. For this reason, the fourth session, which took place in New York in the spring of 1976, ended, as did the First Committee, in a deadlock. This pressure of the developed countries proved unfruitful and, if

anything, provoked frustration among the delegations which made
negotiation impossible. One was beginning to think that the
Conference would inevitably end in a breakdown in negotiations.

During the fifth session, which took place in New York in
the same year, another attempt was made to get out of this
"impasse." The Secretary of State of the United States at that
time, Henry Kissinger, made a speech in which he offered a
voluntary contribution from the United States to the authority
so that it could begin exploitation in the reserved area.
However, the Group of 77 did not regard these voluntary contributions as reliable, since no similar offers in the past had
ever materialized. Moreover, relying for the future of the
international authority and on the goodwill of individual
states to give their contributions would be unthinkable. On
the contrary, the aim was for the authority to have enough
autonomous resources to enable it to exploit the reserved area
without having to depend on the goodwill of states.

At the reunion of a group called Evensen, the Group of 77
made an enormous effort to try and open up possibilities for an
agreement before the sixth session in New York. On this occasion, the Mexican delegation proposed that the authority
should be given autonomous technological and financial resources through a system in which a contractor would be subject
to the payment for initial rights in order to obtain contracts
as well as taxes to be paid on the exploitation, and payments
for the privilege of exploitation. The Mexican proposals led
to a reopening of the dialogue and, once the sixth session had
started, they were used as a base for negotiation and were
adopted by the Group of 77. These proposals were very different from the original parallel system.

The "modified" parallel system, conforming to the proposals of India, Mexico, and other countries, consisted mainly
in the intention to establish certain ties and links between
the reserved and contractual areas. According to this system,
the reserved area would be exploited by the authority with its
own resources while access to contractual areas would not be
automatic; it would be subject, not only to those payments
mentioned earlier, but also to a series of requisites which
would have to be satisfied by the contractors. The problems
encountered in the final negotiations of the modified parallel
system will be analyzed later.

Main Differences Between the Industrialized
Countries and the Third World

The differences between the two extremes are best seen in their
negotiation for a New International Economic Order. The theme
of the seabed has, to a certain extent, turned into an important experiment in the establishment of a New International

Economic Order.   For this reason, the developing countries have
fought to establish a precedent for future negotiations.   Let
us   look   at   the   main   differences   between   these   two groups.

The principle of free access.   Undoubtedly, the first obstacle
to negotiations has been the difference in attitude toward the
degree of access to the international seabed enjoyed by contractors.   In developed countries, the prevailing concept has
been that of immediate freedom of access for those who demand
it from the authority.   In this way, the authority would be
reduced to merely administrative tasks, with the only limitation of deciding whether or not to grant contracts.   On the
other hand, the developing countries, as we have already mentioned, have fought hard to retain a greater discretionary
power for the authority, so that it may grant contracts only
when they are in the interest of all states.

An example of this is the situation that would arise if
two competitive applications were made to the authority for the
same portion of the international seabed.   According to the
Group of 77, the authority would have to use its discretion in
choosing and approving the application which it felt would
offer the best advantages in terms of the transfer of funds and
technology, the duration of the contract, and other factors
which could benefit the authority.   On the other hand, the
developed countries' view was that the authority should choose
applications on a "first come first served" principle, regardless of whether the first application offered better or
worse conditions to the authority.   In reality, the developed
countries see no problem of competition.   According to the
industrialized countries, all applications would be dealt with
in chronological order to protect the producers on the ground.
This will be dealt with later.

The transfer of technology to the authority and developing
countries.   Apart from the controversial themes, there has also
been the question of the transfer of technology to the authority.   From the very first sessions of the Conference, it became
obvious that, despite the availability of sufficient funds to
the authority for exploitation activities, they would be useless without simultaneous access to the sophisticated and
expensive technology needed to undertake these activities.   The
developed countries did not want the transfer of technology to
be a requisite for the granting of contracts.   They argued
that, as technology is not in the hands of states but rather in
those of private companies, it would not be possible to come to
an international agreement on the transfer of technology to the
authority.   It would not be legally possible for a government
to oblige a company with this technology to transfer it to the
authority.   On the other hand, from the point of view of developing countries, it was not a question of the legal obli-

gations of governments, but an indispensible condition for the granting of a contract. The authority would have to have, at least, the discretion to choose those contracts which guaranteed a transfer of technology. In this way, an incentive would be created to encourage contractors to offer the greatest transfer possible.

One of the questions that came up from the beginning was that developing countries should obtain a certain amount of technology. According to the Brazilian delegation, this could take the form of a clause in which a contractor would be obliged to transfer technology to developing countries through the authority. Developing countries would then be able to exploit the international seabed in association with others. This clause, which would only be of use to developing countries with relatively developed economies, was rejected by the Group of 77. This Group was in favor of transferring directly to the authority. In any case, this clause was unacceptable to the developed countries. After hard negotiations, some great advances were made. In the texts which came out of the later periods from the negotiation groups established for this purpose, stipulations were made for the transferring of technology from companies to the authority. This in itself was a great advance for the developing countries. Moreover, it represented an important occasion in the debates for the establishment of a New International Economic order, in that the developing countries achieved an advantageous compromise.

Agreements on "joint ventures" with the authority as conditions and incentives to obtain contracts. Other advances attained in the negotiations have been the establishment of certain links between the reserved and contractual areas. However, these have not been very optimistic. Faced with obstacles which the great powers had created in order to dilute the concept of the modified parallel system, some countries, India in particular, suggested another requisite for the granting of a contract in the specified area; this was proposed to allow participation in "joint ventures" with the authority, thus making it possible to exploit the reserved area.

In other words, an unbreakable link between the exploitation of both areas was formed. Negotiations took place on the basis of how such a link should be structured and whether it should be a compulsory condition imposed on the contractors, or whether, as was virtually agreed in the end, it should serve as an incentive for the authority to give preference to those willing to participate in a joint venture. On this last point, the proposals of Mexico and India had an enormous influence.

The policies of resources. Obstacles to production. Another point of great importance has been the so-called "policies of production". As was mentioned earlier, the increase in supply of minerals extracted from the seabed inevitably will lead to a fall in the price of those same minerals extracted from mines in the ground. Among those affected by such price drops are both the developed and developing countries, although in the case of the latter, the negative affects will be more detrimental, particularly in those countries which depend primarily on the production of minerals for the development of their economies. This problem was recognized from the beginning by the Committee on Marine Depths and was, therefore, included in its agenda. The Group of 77 made efforts to protect those countries producing minerals from the ground which are also found in the marine depths.

Yet again, on this point, the Group of 77 and the industrial powers took different stands. Therefore, it was suggested that only half the annual increase in demand should be covered by the exploitation of the seabed, i.e., a formula of 50 percent for an increase in production from the ground, and 50 percent for the seas. These positions became clear when it became necessary to study the different possibilities for compromise. For example, Minister Jens Evensen of Norway, in one of the great efforts of conciliation, proposed a formula of 75 percent for the marine depths and 25 percent for production from the ground. However, this was rejected by the Group of 77.

A study of this situation showed that an increase in the annual demand for nickel could serve as an index to the increase in demand for metals extracted from the zone. This is because nickel, which is the most valuable of metals obtained from the zone, has registered a stable increase in annual production demand from the ground. This increase has also been reflected in price, which has been more stable for nickel than for other metals. To a certain extent, it can be said that this situation favored the Group of 77 because the major nickel producer, Canada, while directly involved in negotiations, on this occasion, was in opposition to the other developed powers. No common conclusions were accepted on the way in which copper would be affected by marine production. It was agreed, in various forums, however, that the production of copper from the ground would not be greatly affected. The case of cobalt is different since the only major producer of this mineral is Zaire. In this particular case, no one doubted that Zaire would have to be compensated for any losses suffered through the extraction of cobalt from the seabed. Since no agreement could be reached to cover all metals, it was decided to use the increase in demand for nickel as criterion.

In the Integrated Text to the Aims of Negotiation which was presented by the president of the First Committee to the Conference, in the sixth, president Engo suggested a formula divided into two parts. This was the outcome of several attempts at a compromise. This formula consisted, in the first place, of dividing the policies of production control into two phases. In the first phase, which would last for a provisional period of seven years, there would be no control on production; this would allow the increase in demand to be covered from the sea, and the first activities in the zone would be encouraged. At the end of this period, however, a policy of production would be implemented, attributing only 60 percent of annual increase in the demand for nickel to marine production. The 60/40 percent formula was one of transition which was finally consolidated when it was accepted by Canada and the United States. Evidently, the Group of 77 agreed to this compromise. Unfortunately, although it was thought that the United States was the spokesman for all developed countries, the European Economic Community was not in agreement with the adopted formula, and in the seventh session, voiced objections. It can be estimated, however, that the formula which will finally be accepted will most likely be similar to the one just described.

Article 150 of the Integrated Text to the Aims of Negotiation contains, among other things, two principles which are essential to this study. In the first place, in clause b) of paragraph 1, it is established that the activities in the Zone will take place in such a way as to ensure "fair, stable and remunerative prices for raw materials from the zone, which are produced also outside the area and an ever increasing availability of these minerals in order to promote an equilibrium of demand and supply." Moreover, in clause g) of the same paragraph, it is stipulated that one will have to assure "the protection of developing countries faced with adverse effects on their economies and income as a result of falls in the price of the minerals concerned and in the volume of exports of such minerals, to the extent that such reductions are a result of activities in the zone. . . . "

The reason one can estimate that the EEC will eventually accept a limitation formula, similar to the one described earlier, is that the principles in article 150 represent a basic agreement between the participants of the Conference, which are reflected, in a more or less fair position, in the 60/40 percent system.

Composition and powers of the organs of the authority. On top of the problems which have hindered the success of the work of the First Committee was the problem of the composition of the organs of the International Sea Bed Authority. Also, there was a question of the powers and means of such organs. The problem can be summarized in the dilemma of whether the composition and power of the organs of the authority will consist of international, formal, and pure democracy, or whether a political realism will emerge allowing these organs to function in practice. From this, the Group of 77 foresaw the need to establish a supreme parliamentary organ for the authority (the Assembly) in which international democracy would prevail through the representation of all the members of the organization with each member having a vote of equal value. This would give the Group of 77, which is made up of about 120 states, a majority. Moreover, it would encourage the establishment of an Assembly with wide powers, in such a way that policies would be adopted to guide all activities in the zone. It was considered essential for the Assembly to be powerful in order to confront the groups which dominate the financial and technological means needed to undertake activities in the zone.

As expected, the great powers opposed these ideas and tried to prevent the Assembly from using such power to become, as was said, a forum for the "tyranny of the majority." They, therefore, pushed for the establishment of an executive organ, the Council, which would concentrate all powers. The problem with the composition of this Council has been one of the most tricky in the negotiations on the marine depths, in that its composition would reflect the strength of different power groups in the weight of decisions concerning the exploitation of the common heritage of mankind. The negotiations dealt with the powers of the respective organs. During the fifth session in 1976, the first glimpse of a possible compromise was seen when many of the participants recognized that the Council should include certain "special interests" for those groups affected by activities in the zone or those groups most actively involved in such activities. The need to define these special interests was seen and this proved to be an immensely difficult task. The recognition of these special interests implied that the decisions of the Council would be made on the basis of a need to harmonize the conflicting interests of the various groups of countries participating in the zone: those with financial and technological means, and developing countries whose economies would be affected by the activities undertaken in the zone. Inevitably, the drawing up of a list of special interests turned into a competition for inclusion in the list. Special circumstances were put forward, such as size of territory, the production of certain minerals, total population and population increase, the disadvantageous geographical location of some countries, etc. An agreement on certain criteria for the definition of special interests was finally reached, although it has remained open. Moreover, the question of how many seats in the Council should be assigned to each category of special interests is still pending.

Article 159 of the Integrated Text offers a possible compromise. It stipulates the establishment of a Council with 36 members, four of which would be chosen from among those countries which have made the greatest contribution to the exploration and exploitation of resources in the zone, shown by

substantial investment or the use of high technology in relation to resources in the zone. This group would have to
include at least one country from Eastern Europe. With this
criterion, the special interests of those with the financial
and technological means to undertake activities in the zone
would be well recognized. Another group of four members would
be chosen from those who, on the basis of production in areas
under their own jurisdiction, were large exporters of those
metals found in the zone. This group would have to include at
least two developing countries. Six other members would be
developing countries who represent various special interests
such as large populations, inland countries or countries at a
geographical disadvantage, countries being great exporters of
the categories of minerals obtained in the zone, and the less
advanced developing countries. Finally, the other 18 members
would be chosen according to the principle of an equitable
geographical distribution, with the condition that each geographical region would have a least one elected member. Article 159 insists on making sure that inland countries and
those at a geographical disadvantage be represented in the
Council in a similar proportion to their representation in the
Assembly.

Although the formula for the composition of the Council
has not yet been finalized, there appears to be a line for
negotiation around which a final compromise will be reached.
There have been attempts to increase the membership of the
Council in order to make room for more special interests.
However, it was considered that this would lead to a never
ending situation in the sense that no one could monopolize all
special interests, which would result in the Council becoming
like a supreme organ.

The formula for the composition in article 159 is based
on a recognition that the Council will really be a powerful
organ of the authority, which will mean that the Assembly is
partially lacking in its true quality as the supreme organ of
the Authority. A compromise has, therefore, been reached on
the basis of international reality.

Financial agreements. One of the signs of the advance in
negotiations has been that it has already been possible to
discuss financial arrangements between the authority and the
contractors. Once advances have been made on certain fundamental questions, particularly in production policies and the
basic principles of the modified parallel system for the exploitation of the deep seabed, the time has come to begin
negotiations on the cost of this system; which includes the way
in which those having the financial and technological means
should pay for access to the zone, so that the authority may
eventually depend on its own resources to undertake activities
in its reserved zone. These negotiations proved extremely

difficult due to a lack of experience necessary to reach conclusions on the amounts and form these payments should take.

The main element taken into consideration in the negotiations has been that the charge to contractors should not be
a discouragement but, rather, an incentive to the exploitation
of resources in the zone, without prejudicing the rights and
interests of mankind, or the owners of these minerals. At the
same time, one has foreseen certain initial payments to be made
at the beginning of operations, "front-end payment" and also,
payments that are to be made by the contractors during the
different phases. Such payments or taxes would be charged
depending on the various activities of the contractors, but so
far no agreement has been reached on which of these phases
should be included. The last negotiations were on the subject
of the categorization of these phases, beginning with pros-
pecting in specific areas in the zone, continuing with exploration, exploitation, extraction, transport, processing, and
the marketing of the minerals.

Precisely because of the lack of experience, it has been
difficult to calculate which of these activities should be
subject to payments and taxes and in what way this should be
done. According to the industrialized countries, taxes should
only be paid on those activities undertaken in the zone itself.
They argue that transport and the processing of minerals takes
place outside the zone. The first of these takes place on the
high seas which is covered by the freedom of navigation in the
oceans. The second is done under the territorial sovereignty
of the countries in which processing takes place. Apart from
establishing that each of these phases should be covered, even
the developing countries, who proposed that collection should
take place at every stage, had problems in including the last
phase (processing) in view of the fact that this could be done
in their own territories. Negotiations on financial arrangements will have to take place through a political type of
compromise. No historical experience is available to help
arrive at valid calculations and conclusions.

The Revision Conference. As can be seen by the description of
the conflicts which have arisen out of the negotiations, none
of the agreements which were reached in principle were able to
satisfy in a definite form the interests of all parties concerned. Even the agreement in principle on a system of exploitation was not satisfactory for either the developed or
developing countries. For this reason, a conclusion was
tentatively reached on the necessity to establish a mechanism
which would give flexibility to agreements and to items still
under negotiation. In this matter, the Mexican delegation made
a valuable contribution, in the Evensen Group in Geneva in the
spring of 1977, by suggesting conditions and methods for a
future Revision Conference, to examine the practical gains of

the system which would have been agreed upon in the final treaty. The Revision Conference represents an escape valve for certain groups, in that it would enable one to foresee that the approved system will not become an indefinite straitjacket but rather a system which will be revised once sufficient experience has been gained to make fitting adjustments. The Mexican formula was finally adopted within the Integrated Text to the Aims of Negotiation.

However, in the incorporation of this formula, the president of the First Committee favored the interpretation of a limited number of developing countries, which stated that if the Revision Conference did not reach agreement on a way of continuing the operation of the system, in a modified form or not, it would revert, ipso facto, to a unitary system of exploitation, as the one originally suggested by the developing countries as far back as the time of the Committee on the Marine Depths. This unitary system reserved the monopoly of activities in the zone to the authority, through its operational organ, the "Company." This came from the concept in the proposal of the thirteen Latin American countries, based on the idea of service contracts and joint ventures.

In accordance with the Mexican proposal, twenty years after the Convention came into effect, the Assembly of the authority would automatically call a Revision Conference to the Convention and its annexes, examining pertinent arrangements in depth in the light of acquired experience, in order to ensure that the aims had been fulfilled in all aspects; and, above all, to determine whether the resources of the zone had been fairly distributed, without there being an excessive concentration of resources in the hands of a small number of states. It would also ensure that the principles incorporated in the production policy, already mentioned in reference to Article 159, had been complied with. Moreover, such a Revision Conference would try to find out whether the system of exploitation had benefited developing countries and whether an equilibrium had been maintained between the reserved and contractual areas. The Mexican formula proposed that if the Conference were not able to reach agreement on amendments to the Convention provisions, it should at least maintain the principle of the common heritage of mankind; the international system for the equitable exploitation to the benefit of all countries, particularly those in the process of development; and an authority which will undertake, organize, and control the activities in the zone.

Norway added other principles which should be preserved: relating to no claims being made or sovereign right exercised on any part of the zone, the general behavior of states in the zone, the prevention of the monopolizing of activities by a small number of states, the use of the zone for pacific ends alone, the economic aspects of the activities in the zone, scientific research, the transfer of technology, the protection of the marine environment and human life, the rights of coastal states, the juridical statute of the waters and the air immediately above, and the harmonization of the various forms of activities in the zone and the oceans. That is to say that, regardless of any concrete agreements that may be reached by the Revision Conference or, above all, regardless of the lack of agreements, the principles in the 1970 Declaration should be preserved.

The Mexican proposal pursued the following objective: there would be no juridical vacuum if the Revision Conference became stuck through a lack of majority agreement, either on modifications to the system or continuation of the former system. The president of the First Committee included a formula in the Integrated Text which foresaw a reversion to a unitary system based on service contracts and joint ventures in the case where no agreements had been reached. This is considered totally unacceptable by the developed countries. It is difficult for the formula of the Integrated Text to constitute a basis for a consensus on the subject.

The Major Obstacle to the NIEO: Unilateral Exploitation of the Seabed

So far, we have examined the main differences in attitude between the industrial and developing countries. They oppose each other on a general agreement for the establishment of a universal system which would allow the seabed to be exploited for the benefit of all mankind. From this point of view, these differences present a real threat to the establishment of a New International Economic Order. We will now examine another obstacle, of a distinctive nature, which is much more serious and could demolish not only any hope of establishing an international system for the seabed, but could even be an obstacle to a general treaty on the Law of the Sea which incorporates all questions already agreed and which is of great importance to the establishment of a New International Economic Order.

This fundamental obstacle is the manifest intention of some maritime powers (and to a large extent this has been put into practice) to exploit the seabed unilaterally outside an international system negotiated and agreed under the auspices of the United Nations. In view of the difficulties that were encountered from the beginning of the 1954 Conference in Caracas, the maritime powers began to support the thesis, initially in corridors and later in more or less formal public declarations, that if it were not possible to reach agreement on the collective exploitation of the seabed, within an international system, this should not prevent countries with the means to exploit resources from doing so. Of course, they did not deny the validity of the principle that these resources should be exploited for the benefit of all mankind, nor did they agree that any state should be allowed to exercise sovereignty or appropriate for itself parts of the seabed. But they maintain that the exploitation of resources is not forbidden under general traditional international law which also covers the seabed but, rather, is permitted under this general order. In other words, they maintain that the legal opportunity to exploit these resources is included in the general principle of the freedom of the seas and that no legal obstacle may prevent them from extracting and appropriating the resources of the seabed so long as no reclamation of sovereignty is made.

Of course, the developing countries took the exact opposite view on this principle. These countries supported the thesis that, as there is no precedent in the exploitation of the seabed, the traditional system of the high seas cannot really be applied to this question in any way. Yet, faced with a judicial vacuum, the solemn Declaration, adopted by the General Assembly with no votes against and only a few abstentions, was a clear expression of the willingness of the community of nations to the way in which these resources should be exploited. The Declaration of Principles was clear and categorical in this area: exploitation should be done within an international system, negotiated and accepted by all countries, and within which exploitation would be done through the establishment of an international organ which would look after the interests of the international community and ensure, in particular, benefit for the whole of mankind. It was obvious, moreover, that unilateral exploitation by a few states would neither be to the benefit of all mankind nor to the benefit of the international community, even if the exploiting states, voluntarily (i.e. ex gratia) actually kept to their proposal of reserving what they call a reasonable part of the benefits for distribution among all states.

With time and increasing difficulties in reaching agreement, the intentions, expressed in declarations, became more pressing. In particular, the United States pushed this possibility on many occasions. Its fundamental argument was that there was a great urgency to exploit these resources; that ultimately their exploitation would benefit the whole of mankind; and that, if no agreement could be reached for the communal exploitation of these resources, the United States would find itself obliged to do it itself.

The reasons for such urgency were never well understood. Of course, at the moment, ground deposits more than satisfy the demand for these valuable resources. No one suggests that they are on the point of being exhausted. On the other hand, the United States denied having the intention to create reserves of these metals of a strategic type, and also denied that some of

these metals would be in the hands of states of doubtful re-
liability as steady suppliers to Western industrial countries.
What was argued with more insistence was that the large mineral
companies and others, which have dedicated themselves to pros-
pecting and exploration and have made considerable investment
in trying out methods of extraction, face considerable risks.
Of course it can be argued, and in fact has been argued, that
nobody is forcing these companies to begin such operations
before they have a more or less firm basis on which to do so,
and that they have been investing at this time purely for gain,
and were cognizant of the risks and the existing legal and
political situation, as laid out in the fifteen points of the
Declaration of Principles of the Assembly in 1970. Also, since
the argument that once experimental operations are started they
cannot be stopped does not seem a convincing one, and, in any
case, not reason enough to claim unilateral rights to exploitation since this would violate the clear wishes of the community of nations, then exploitation can only take place under
an international system. One must ask oneself, moreover,
whether, in reality, there are any valid reasons to justify
this urgency, or whether these proposals to exploit the seabed
unilaterally are not, rather, a form of pressure employed by
the industrial powers in order to force the developing countries to come to their point of view and to be willing to make
agreements on the basis of the industrial countries' interests.
    These threats have, in fact, become operative. Initia-
tives have been presented to the United States government to
grant concessions to North American companies in order to
exploit the seabed unilaterally. These initiatives have been
carried through to a fairly high level in the legislative
process, to the extent that one of them has been approved by
the House of Representatives, although it did not win approval
in the Senate. In this legislation, the United States does not
claim any sovereignty, nor does it maintain that other states
should not have rights over the same sites. It deals with
permissive legislation which would only cover North American
companies. However, this is only the first phase.
    In view of the fact that other Western countries might
also have the capacity to exploit the seabed, and because they
would be attempting to exploit the same areas that would have
been explored at high cost by North American companies, a
scheme was finally completed in the form of a "mini-treaty"
between the main Western industrial powers and Japan, in which
any reclamation made on mineral sites would be mutually re-
spected. The possibility was even mentioned that this "mini-
treaty" would be open to developing countries willing to accept
this type of exploitation. Of course, this has not been an
open subject in the Conference. But in private conversations
and also in certain public forums, the representatives of
developing countries have stated that not only is such a scheme

totally unacceptable but, also, that they propose fighting it
through all legal channels. It was also stated that this would
cause a series of confrontations with all developing countries,
not only in relation to the exploitation of the seabed, but
also in relation to all matters in the North-South dialogue.
This would inevitably be a serious obstacle to the establishment of a New International Economic Order. The so-called
"mini-treaty" would be the best way to exacerbate opposition
and conflict between the two groups of nations. This would
mean that the few countries having the necessary financial and
technological means to exploit the seabed would do so for their
own benefit and, in this way, would exclude the greatest number
of states, i.e., the developing world, from participating in
the benefits gained from the exploitation of resources which
belong to the whole of mankind, and to all states.

The developing countries have shown, on many occasions,
that such a scheme would not only be completely incompatible
with the principles acclaimed by the Assembly, but also contrary to international law. It would be an illegal form of
exploitation and an exclusive appropriation by a few states, of
that which is the heritage of all mankind. The last, carefully
prepared pronouncement by the developing countries highlights
not only the political consequences of such threats, but also
the legal reasons why such exploitation by a few states would
be contrary to international law. This pronouncement was read
by the President of the Group of 77 in the name of the whole
group, i.e., the whole membership of about 120 countries,
without exception. It was read in the plenary of the seventh
session of the Conference of the United Nations on the Law of
the Sea. The pertinent sections of the declaration are as
follows:

> The Group of 77 rejects completely the basis of the
> said legislation (unilateral), and in particular the
> premise that the right to extract resources from the
> sea bed outside the limits of national jurisdiction
> is one of the legal rights in the freedom of the high
> seas. There is nothing in practice, and more impor-
> tant, no legal precedent, which could be considered
> authentic rights or deeds for the exploitation of
> these resources. Nor is there a general treaty which
> authorises the exploitation of the sea bed. The
> Declaration of Principles, incorporated in resolution
> 2749 (XXV), expressly excludes the unfounded argument
> according to which the freedom of the high seas could
> be extended to the sea bed, and moreover, it places
> exploration and exploitation of the sea bed under an
> international system which is still to be estab-
> lished. The situation is therefore exactly the
> opposite to that which applies to exploitation of the

resources of the high seas. In this case, three centuries of customs and innumerable treaties provide the necessary precedent to maintain the freedom of the high seas in regard to the exploitation of its resources. But, in the case of the sea bed beyond national jurisdiction, there is a total lack of precedent in international law to allow such exploitation to be done to the benefit of individual states.

The absence of an already existent legal system for the sea bed, means that the Declaration of Principles in Resolution 2749 (XXV) of the General Assembly, which declares that the sea bed and its resources are "the common heritage of mankind," acquire a special significance, content and value. It has the effect of creating the basis of a legal system which this Conference was in charge of formulating. The Declaration of Principles can no longer be ignored by merely saying that the resolutions of the Assembly are not obligatory and only resolutions of recommendation. The Declaration was not merely a recommendation inviting states to behave in any way. It was substantially more than that. It was a solemn proclamation by the most representative organ of the international community, which declared that the resources of the sea bed, outside the limits of national jurisdiction, are the common heritage of mankind as a whole, and that exploitation can only take place under an international system and its resources can not be appropriated unilaterally.

The Declaration of Principles was adopted without opposition. All the groups of countries accepted the principle of common heritage, the international character of the sea bed and its resources outside the limits of national jurisdiction, as well as the inevitable legal consequence of this which is that unilateral exploitation is incompatible with this principle. The Declaration of Principles is, therefore, the authorized expression of international law on the system for the sea bed outside national jurisdiction. One must also remember, that the Declaration of Principles was the outcome of many years of preparatory work and intense negotiations both in the General Assembly and in the Committee on the Sea Bed. In view of all this, it cannot be dismissed or rejected as just one of the resolutions of the United Nations; on the contrary, it establishes a principle in international law in the exact sense of article 38

of the Statute of the International Court of Justice
and represents an authorized expression of the opinion of the international community on the matter.

Therefore, it is clear, that no country can legally
violate the principles established in the Declaration
of Principles. And, what is more, each state, under
the terms of the Declaration, "will be responsible
for ensuring that the activities in the area . . .
will be undertaken in accordance with the international system which is being established." Unilateral exploitation would be a clear violation of the
international law which would result in appropriate
legal liability. The fact that actual claims of
sovereignty are not made is totally irrelevant.
Unilateral exploitation and appropriation of resources is as much as claims of sovereignty. It
is, in fact, equivalent to the exercising of sovereignty. The fact of reserving a small portion of
the benefits, by unilateral decision, for developing
countries is not the same as complying with the
obligation of exploiting resources under an international system still to be established. . . .

The Group of 77 cannot accept that any state, person
or body should acquire rights through such unilateral
means. . . .

The dark clouds that envelop the Conference by these
actions could not only prejudice the conclusions of a
treaty as a whole, but could also precipitate a chaotic situation in the whole of marine law. The consequences could have terrible repercussions. . . .
In reality, the clash in the Conference, the largest
in the history of the United Nations, could have a
disastrous effect on the whole system of multilateral
negotiations which are taking place under the auspices of the United Nations. Repercussions of this
could be felt by future generations.

Such important considerations should be blamed on
those who, with their narrow-mindedness and narrow
interests, tend to ignore the long term interest of
creating pacific and ordered world institutions. It
is these countries that must take full responsibility
for these irreparable consequences.

POSSIBLE STRATEGIES

An examination of possible strategies which could be followed
so that the exploitation of the seabed may greatly contribute
to the establishment of a New International Economic Order
entails examining the best solutions to reach a universal
agreement and, therefore, a global treaty on a system for the
sea and ocean bed.

We have examined the main obstacles to such an agreement.
Despite the threat which weighs on the Conference and the final
agreement, this threat being unilateral exploitation, it is
hoped – and in the opinion of the author, it is to be believed
even today – that the industrial powers will ultimately prefer
the establishment of an international system which will allow
them to participate in the exploitation of the seabed, certainly to their own benefit, but also within a normative
universal order, accepted by the whole community of nations,
giving them greater security, both in the juridical and political fields in order to undertake such exploitation. It is
believed that the threat of unilateral exploitation is, more
than anything, simply a threat, a type of pressure which is
used to influence negotiations.

There is still a great possibility of reaching an agreement. Both sides have powerful instruments of negotiation. In
the end, an agreement would be convenient for everybody.
Therefore, in order to examine possible strategies to consolidate a New International Economic Order, it will be necessary
to reexamine the solutions which could lead to such an agreement.

The Possibility of a Treaty in Which
Points of Rule and Detail are Omitted

Since the end of the second part of the seventh session of the
Conference, more promising perspectives have been opened. We
will examine them first.

From the beginning, the developing countries maintained that
only the treaty itself should contain the features and principles essential and basic to a system on the seabed. We
believe that a great number of statutory questions, that is,
those dealing with the granting of contracts, financial agreements, etc., could be left to decisions taken by the organs of
the authority, once these are established, because the main
principles dealing with these matters should only be included
in the treaty itself. However, this thesis, advanced by the
developing countries, was rejected by the maritime powers.
These powers maintained that, because of the uncertain way in

which these organs would be operated, and because they fear
that, one way or another, their interests would be put aside,
as the majority would be held by the developing countries, it
would be necessary, first, to agree to every last detail in the
treaty itself and to its annexes. In other words, they demanded the establishment of a real mining code, without giving
any aspect of future negotiation or decision to the organs,
once the authority is established.

The difficulties in reaching an agreement are obvious.
This is due to the complexity of the problems themselves, the
intrinsic difficulties of negotiation and the fact that, in
many of the matters concerned, there is no experience to fall
back on, in that there is no precedent of similar exploitation
since everything is new and, to a certain extent, unknown. One
cannot know the real cost of extracting such minerals; one
still does not know the success, from a technical point of
view, of the different systems of extraction which are being
experimented; among other problems, the real cost of processing
to obtain pure metals is unknown. In these conditions, at the
end of the second part of the seventh session of the Conference, in the winter of 1978, the idea was revived of iden-
tifying those questions of normative principles, that is to
say, essential rules which would become the basis of future
agreements on all obligatory questions, and which may lead to
the solution of many pending problems in the future, above all,
in that which deals with financial arrangements and many
problems relating to the system of exploitation itself -
contracts, mining sites, etc.

In any case, negotiation has advanced considerably. In
this way, it may be indispensable to keep the whole question of
production policy in the treaty - the limits that should be
fixed to production, so as not to damage the producers of
minerals from the ground. In the same way, certain main principles concerning financial arrangements should be agreed upon
and basic principles on the system of exploitation should be
stated. But, if it is decided to postpone solutions to those
problems which have caused so much trouble, it will be impossible to reach an agreement now.

One can say that this would not only postpone the problem.
If the most essential principles were agreed upon and a global
agreement were reached, it would be possible to ratify, in the
very near future, all general agreements on marine law. As has
already been said, most parts of this are already well advanced
and have practicaly reached consensus point. For the purpose
of consolidating these, and also consolidating those basic
principles on which agreement has been reached in matters
relating to the exploitation of the seabed, a rapid ratification of the treaty would be desirable. If this led to
signing of the already agreed and consolidated parts, which
would be an enormous advance, it would be the best impediment

to the attempts of unilateral action by the industrial powers. Thus, the essential principles would remain consecrated in the treaty. This would clearly invalidate any attempts to exploit resources outside this sytem.

In due course, this solution would have the great advantage of giving a breathing space, and maybe quite a long one, to solve pending problems. Probably, in time, better knowledge and experience will be gained of the practicalities involved in the exploitation of the seabed and, perhaps, states will be able to resolve pending concrete problems with more knowledge of the facts. In the same way, maybe the fact of having a treaty would become an incentive to the different groups to reach agreement on still unresolved matters.

Future solutions to problems of rules and details could take two forms: One would be through real negotiation in which all parties would take part within a provisional type of system, between the time when the treaty is signed and the time when, in a few years, it comes into effect, once all the necessary ratifications have been made. This would necessitate all parties agreeing to questions still pending. The second way would be that, once unresolved problems had been negotiated, these would become compulsory decisions of the organs of the authority. However, in the case of adopting the second solution, agreements would have. to be reached on problems of the composition, function, powers, and decision making methods of the various organs of the authority. This would be difficult but not impossible, and it would have the effect of assuring the different groups that they would not be overwhelmed by these organs. It has already been stated that there seems to be a general hope that the method of simplifying and abbreviating the treaty could reach agreement. Hopefully, by the beginning of the next Conference in (March 1981), an agreement in principle on preparatory work will have been reached in order to carry on with these new work methods, even it there are still difficulties present. A lot of time and effort has been put into the negotiation of unresolved problems. However, there are some who believe that to change the course of negotiation at this point would be counterproductive.

Possibility of Agreement on Still
Unresolved Important Questions

If one looks at the heart of the problem, rather than at work methods, it is clear that the main obstacle to a system of the seabed contributing to a New International Economic Order is the seven different points already indicated, on which the developing countries and the industrial countries disagree. From the developing countries' point of view, the way to overcome this obstacle would be for the industrial countries to

come over to their way of thinking. However, it is obvious
that this is impossible. In indicating what these differences
are, we stated the position of the developing countries and the
perspectives that could be acceptable. For example, in the
question of the production policy and the production stopper,
it is very probable that the limit suggested by the developing
countries who support the agreement between Canada and the
United States to limit underwater production to 60 percent of
the average annual increase in the demand for nickel, is
acceptable to all. In other cases, it is unlikely that agreements will be reached on the basis of the developing countries'
position. For example, in the case of the 20 year Revision
Conference, should the Conference fail to reach agreement on a
new system, a formula different from that in the Integrated
Text will probably be accepted. In the case of the transfer of
technology, it is unlikely that the developing countries'
position will be accepted as the basis for an agreement. In
other questions, it appears that these differences, although
very great, can be negotiated and that agreement can be reached
through an intermediate or distinct solution.

In conclusion, it can be seen that developing countries
have shown a great capacity to maintain unity and fight together for well-thought-out and well-structured common positions. This encourages one to hope that the final result will
be a just and balanced solution which would take into account
the interests of the whole of mankind and, above all, those of
developing countries, and, at the same time, would be realistic
and viable enough to begin the exploitation of resources with
the indispensable contribution of the industrial powers.

Perspectives

It is difficult to know which will be the correct formulas
needed to reach a general agreement which would result in the
signing of a universal and comprehensive treaty on the law of
the sea. Some countries would have more interest than others
in the signing of such a treaty. Some authors have already
shown the advantages that can be gained from a general treaty
by countries such as the United States, France, and, appar-
ently, for some Latin American countries as well. It can be
affirmed that the parties are already agreed on matters referring to the general laws of the sea, particularly in certain
aspects such as territorial waters, rights of passage through
channels and straits, and above all, the exclusive economic
zone. The implicit agreement, which has already been reached
through successive negotiations culminating in the Integrated
Text, represents a certain proof of the incorporation of all
these rules in the body of international law. In other words,
it can be said that, although there is no treaty, the exclu-

sive economic zone, which is of interest to so many coastal
countries, has already become an accepted institution which,
although arrived at indirectly, is nonetheless efficient. The
point is that a great number of countries, sixty or more since
the beginning of the Conference, have already established
unilaterally exclusive economic zones. This observation is
certain. However, there is a vision defect in this thesis. It
is also certain that the lack of a treaty could never mean a
return to the situation prevailing before the Conference, that
is, the traditional law of the sea. It is also certain that
this absence of a treaty would have a great influence with
regard to the content and scope of very many juridical rules
which are applied daily on the utilization of the seas. This
could easily cause chaos and anarchy in the utilization of the
seas. The absence of a treaty could lead to a series of
unilateral declarations of various kinds, suitable to each
country, which are likely not to remain within the limits of
the Integrated Text. The resulting anarchy could have the
gravest consequences for international relations and could,
more importantly in the long run, become an obstacle rather
than a contribution to the New International Economic Order.

In conclusion, I believe that all countries would gain
something from a treaty, while all countries would lose
something if there were no general agreement. This explains
the importance I have given this matter throughout this whole
chapter. The lack of a treaty with regard to a system for the
sea bed would be really disastrous for the establishment of a
New International Economic Order because, in practice, however
much the developing countries have tried to stop it, it would
result in the exploitation of the valuable seabed resources for
the benefit of a few countries only and not for the benefit of
the whole of mankind.

APPENDIX TO CHAPTER 3

Apart from the numerous biological and organic resources which
are to be found in the seas, on the seabed itself one finds
vast mineral resources. Among them, the polymetallic nolules
stand out for their economic potential. These nodules are
located primarily on the ocean and seabeds and in their subsoil
in areas outside national jurisdiction. They are also found on
the continental and insular shelves of a small number of
countries. Information on their numbers is still quite limited
to date, particularly because research made so far covers
hardly 3 percent of the surface area of the zone.

Formation and Dimensions of Nodules

Polymetallic nodules (also known as manganese nodules because they contain a high concentration of this metal) are formed by a process which can be summarized in the following way: the oceans are saturated with manganese and iron which come from rivers, volcanic eruptions, and underwater springs. As these minerals are compounded by the effects of currents, colloidal (noncrystalline) particles are formed, which again attract a variety of minerals found in the water and in detritus deposits. Falling to the bottom, these particles attach themselves to any protruding object, such as fragments of stones, rocks, or the bones of micrometeoric marine animals. The deepwater currents bring with them more particles which begin to build up around the object, which itself serves as a nucleus. This nucleus, or nodule, increases layer by layer, until it reaches appreciable dimensions. This means that, to a certain extent, we are dealing with a renewable resource. Their size varies greatly, from small or even minute grains to rocks weighing 1,770 pounds, as those found to the east of the Philippines. Most of them measure somewhere between one and twenty centimeters, and the average size is five centimeters. The nodules are of a dark coffee color, smooth, brittle, and porous. The growth rate is 0.01 to 1 millimeter per thousand years, although those found closer to the shore increase in size more rapidly. Speed of growth is also greater around unstable or recent objects. This foregoing description is one of the most accepted explanations of the formation of manganese nodules, although a scientific theory acceptable to all experts has yet to be found.

Composition and Location

Nodules are generally composed of the following minerals: manganese, iron, silicon, lead, aluminum, copper, nickel, and cobalt - the last three being the most important in economic terms. A typical nodule of the Pacific Ocean is generally composed of 25 percent manganese 1 percent copper, and 0.60 percent cobalt.

Nodules are normally found at depths of 4,000 to 5,000 meters, although they can also be found in shallower waters on the continental and insular shelves. Areas rich in copper, nickel, and cobalt, and where the highest concentration of nodules is found, are called primary areas. The largest number of primary areas is found in the Pacific Ocean, especially in the central and east-central zones. It is estimated that there are more than 1,500 billion metric tons of nodules in the Pacific Ocean, and that they are forming at a rate of 10 million metric tons per year. It is calculated that in the southeast Pacific, there are 14 to 15 kilograms of nodules per square meter. The nodules with the highest manganese content are found 500 to 800 kilometers off the coasts of North and South America, particularly off the coast of Northern Mexico. Other deposits, not quite so rich, can be found in the Atlantic and Indian Oceans.

Economic Potential

The most well accepted calculations supply the following data on the wealth and potential of these reserves, in accordance with the rate of consumption for 1970:

- Aluminum: 43 billion tons, equivalent to a 200,000 year reserve, compared to 100 year known reserves of aluminum deposits in the ground.
- Manganese: 358 billion tons, equivalent to reserves of 400,000 years (ground deposits: 100 years).
- Nickel: 14.7 billion tons, equivalent to reserves of 150,000 years (ground deposits 100 years).
- Cobalt: 5.2 billion tons, equivalent to reserves of 200,000 years (ground deposits: 40 years).

Moreover, it is calculated that in the Pacific Ocean there are 207 billion tons of iron, 10 of titanium, 25 of magnesium, 1.3 of lead, and 800 million of vanadium. It is estimated that, by the end of the 1980s, 20 to 30 million tons of polymetallic nodules will be extracted every year.

II

Institutional and
Administrative Issues of
the New International
Economic Order

4 The Administrative Apparatus of States and the Implementation of the NIEO
Gérard Timsit

The connections between the New International Economic Order
and the old administrative order of states are not often
recognized, but they exist and are stronger than one might have
thought. Undoubtedly, the goal of the writers of the Charter
of Economic Rights and Duties of States, as stated in the
Declaration adopted by the United Nations General Assembly in
Resolution 3201 (S-VI) of May 1, 1974, "was to eliminate the
widening gap between the developed and the developing countries." To achieve this, it was necessary to formulate a set
of legal principles and rules to govern international economic
relations based on "equity, sovereign equality, interdependence, common interest and co-operation among all States,
irrespective of their economic and social systems."(1) The
main purpose of the Charter was thus to define and elaborate
the basis and nature of the relationship to be established
among the members of the international community. It has,
however, important implications with regard to the domestic
administration of states.

The government and domestic administrative apparatus of
states may play a key role in the "world solidarity revolution"
required for the establishment of a New International Economic
Order, as illustrated by the different scenarios presented in
Goals for Mankind, a report to the Club of Rome,(2) and by the
task allotted to states of disseminating the ideas and principles of NIEO. The importance of the administrative machinery

---

*The first part of this study owes much to the various reports
presented at the Sousse Colloquium, particularly of Sadok
Chaabane, Guy Caire, Violaine Dallemagne, Pierre-Yves Maurice,
Alain Euzeby, Michèle Voisset, Paule Gentot, and M. André
Gauron.

in this context raises questions about the relationship between the national administration and the NIEO.

The simplest approach is to consider the effects of the New International Economic Order on national administration, that is NIEO——>Administration. The New International Economic Order brings about or should bring about changes: what are they, or what should they be?

The relationship may be reversed, however, as follows: NIEO <——Administration. The administration strives to establish a New International Economic Order. To what extent can it do so? Is it an obstacle or a positive factor in establishing NIEO? This important question is at the heart of the problem of restructuring the United Nations system, since the United Nations General Assembly has entrusted to all organizations, institutions, subsidiary bodies, and conferences within the system the task of implementing the Programme of Action on the Establishment of a New International Economic Order, a task which is also assigned to the internal machinery of States. Both relationships, NIEO ——>Administration and NIEO<——Administration, must be considered. The first requires analytical thinking, while the second calls for empirical, concrete studies, an evaluation of projected administrative structures, and machinery to check their adaptability to the establishment of NIEO. The two approaches, although theoretically separate, intermingle in practice: analysis is difficult without the background of a preliminary evaluation and concrete study which requires analytical thinking.

The structure and functions of today's national administrative machinery make it a serious obstacle to the establishment of NIEO, since NIEO calls for both development and democracy. In the various states of the world, and particularly in the Third World, the national administrative apparatus is responsible for initiating development, which is one of the fundamental changes required by the concept of NIEO. The national administrative apparatus must not, however, be considered solely as an agent of change. It is also a subject of change to the extent that, if its internal machinery is not radically reformed, especially in the direction of greater democracy, the state might, through the very force of its own inertia, obstruct the implementation of NIEO principles.

Consequently, in its relationship with the New International Economic Order, the national administrative apparatus must be seen from two angles: as agent of change, and as a subject of change.

THE NATIONAL STATE ADMINISTRATIVE APPARATUS
AS AGENT OF CHANGE

The administrative structure of numerous developing countries is, and remains to this day, one that was borrowed from their colonizers during certain periods of their histories. The administrative institutions they inherited upon their accession to independence thus have a high "colonial coefficient."(3) Even though these administrative structures seem mere imitations of those of the industrialized countries, they are, in fact, overburdened with characteristics that radically modify their nature and significance and render them incompatible, in their functions as well as their very structures, with the demands of NIEO. Not only are they characterized by rigidity and complexity, but they remain partially conditioned by the priorities of the colonial period: maintenance of law and order, and exploitation of economic resources to supply the metropolitan power with raw materials.

Progress has certainly been made since accession of many developing countries to independence, but their administrative structure still bears the stigma of colonialism. This administrative structure, to be entirely readapted by NIEO, is sluggish and unwieldy, and some of its sectors that are essential for NIEO are underdeveloped. Reform of the state administrative machinery must be carried out to equip it to promote change and development, and to adapt it to its new tasks.

It is clear that NIEO requires the rejection of all initiative forms of administration. Article 1 of the Charter of Economic Rights and Duties of States advances the principle that "each State has the sovereign and inalienable right to choose its economic as well as its political, social and cultural systems in accordance with the will of its people, without outside interference, coercion or threat in any form whatsoever." It thereby affirms the right of each state to create its own form of administration, not a mere replica of a foreign administrative system or, in the case of a country having suffered colonial domination, one left over from the colonizers.

Domination, if understood to mean the adoption by a society of the "behaviour models of a foreign society forced on it by political power or economic necessity and/or because it values foreign standards to the detriment of its own,"(4) produced administrative structures and procedures in some countries that are extraordinarily similar to those of countries in which the political, economic, and social environment is quite different. The idea of NIEO, however, implies endogenous development: "it springs from the heart of each society, which relies first on its own strength and resources and defines in sovereignty the vision of its future."(5)

Administrative development, therefore, calls for a re-organization of existing administrative models which might range from simple modifications of those that had been borrowed from industrialized countries to actual administrative revolutions aimed at "facilitating the creation of conditions in which societies may satisfy their own needs, . . . eliminating the transfer of rural surpluses to benefit the urban 'elite' and introducing self-determination and management of enterprises at all levels, from the local to the national, through decentralization, inter alia."(6)

On the other hand, NIEO requires a general increase in administrative action and, consequently, in administrative structures. At the end of the nineteenth century, a German economist noted the existence of a "law of evolution of State activity." "Experience," he wrote, "permits one to deduce from history . . . a 'law' of the evolution of State activity among civilized peoples: the law of the growing expansion of public or State activity among advancing civilized peoples."(7) Although general, this law could be refined by introducing a law of the acceleration of the growth of state activity in periods of domestic or international crises when the state serves as a vehicle, instrument, or agent of change. It can, however, fully carry out this function only when two requirements are met: if its tasks have been redistributed, and if the structures and procedures of its internal administrative machinery have been reorganized.

REORGANIZATION OF THE NATIONAL
ADMINISTRATIVE APPARATUS

Instruments for such reorganization exist, although at present they are not necessarily used for the purposes of development. For the establishment of NIEO, these instruments must be used primarily to reach the goals set in the Charter of Economic Rights and Duties of States. Each State has the responsibility to "promote the economic, social and cultural development of its people" (Charter, article 7). This means that existing administrative bodies must be reoriented in favor of the sectors to be established as priorities in future under NIEO, and that human resources in particular must be available to them so that the reorientation will be effective.

Reorientation Sectors

NIEO stresses the need to mobilize national resources (Charter, article 7), including the state's own, which it has the right to use in: regulating foreign investment, regulating and supervising the activities of transnational corporations, and nationalizing, expropriating, or transferring ownership of foreign property (article 2, subparagraphs 2 (a), (b) and (c)). It can also mobilize resources shared by two or more countries in the exploitation of which a system of information and prior consultation may be established in order to achieve their optimum use (article 3).

Resources may further be mobilized in two other ways: the first involves exploiting existing resources by promoting international scientific and technological cooperation and the transfer of technology, particularly by facilitating the access of Third World countries to the "achievements of modern science and technology and the creation of indigenous technology for the benefit of developing countries" (article 13, paragraph 2); the second involves utilizing the resources released by effective disarmament measures for the development needs of Third World countries (article 15).

This emphasis on the mobilization of national resources demands greater importance for three forms of administration: economic, social, and scientific-cultural.

Economic administration. There are three sectors of economic administration that appear a priori necessary for the establishment of NIEO.

1. Foreign trade administration is a priority area. In particular, article 6 of the Charter of Economic Rights and Duties of States clearly affirms that "it is the duty of States to contribute to the development of international trade of goods, particularly by means of arrangements and by the conclusion of long-term multilateral commodity agreements, where appropriate, and taking into account the interests of producers and consumers." Export assistance, custom barriers, commercial cooperation and the marketing of raw materials (cotton, wood, etc.) require a sound foreign trade administration and, consequently, the growth of this sector of state activity. By the same token, efforts should be made to establish strong, efficient administrative bodies specially responsible for supervising foreign investment and the activities of transnational corporations. Currently, however, there are virtually no administrative bodies dealing specifically with problems caused by the rise and proliferation of the economic (fiscal, customs, etc.) delinquency of transnational corporations.

2. Energy administration is another field accorded priority under NIEO. The energy crisis linked with the transformation of international economic relations means that, for countries lacking in energy resources, and energy administration equipped to deal with the crisis must be established, with leads to the overloading of the administrative sector through the proliferation of commissions, committees, agencies, delegations, offices, etc. which, in France, for example, are

rapidly increasing. Also "light-weight" administrative bodies must be established, i.e., those with small staffs and a high level of technological competence, which perform the vital functions of instigating and organizing.

3. Planning administration is another sector that might be particularly affected by the establishment of NIEO. The instability of the international environment caused by the ongoing negotiations makes medium-term planning all the more necessary.

Social administration. Social security administration is of special interest by virtue of the vital contribution it can make to development. It is necessary, therefore, to consider the problems presented by the establishment of such administrations in countries that do not have them as yet. The problems include a) the size and position of such a body within the entire administrative structure, b) the status it should be given to avoid its bureaucratization, and c) the problem of training officials for the new tasks.

Similar problems are encountered in other sectors of social administration where the establishment of NIEO would have a strong impact, for instance health and environmental administration, to which the Dag Hammarskjöld report attaches prime importance.(8) Labor administration, however, is in the first ranks of the social administrations that should expand most dramatically in the developed as well as in the developing countries. The crisis in the developing countries forces them to reorganize old administrative bodies or create new ones to enable them to deal with the employment problems they face.

The recent establishment in France of a Labour Delegation, an interministerial and some departmental committees for the promotion of employment, and an interministerial commission under the Secretary of State for Immigrant Workers, bear this out. In developing countries, aside from the employment problems they share, the development of transnational corporations and the privileged position they are accorded demands the formulation of a body of social rules which can only be accomplished by national labor administrations, possibly in close cooperation with international organizations.

Scientific-cultural administrations. Research provides indispensable support for health activities. As stated in the Dag Hammarskjöld Report, "research towards specific problems of each society"(9) is an essential condition for development. Article 13 of the Charter is explicit in that regard: "Every State has the right to benefit from the advances and developments in science and technology for the acceleration of its economic and social development . . . the developed countries should co-operate with the developing countries in the establishment, strengthening and development of their scientific and technological infrastructures and their scientific research and technological activities so as to help to expand and transform the economies of developing countries."

With a view to the establishment of NIEO, therefore, research administration in developing countries calls for "developing domestic capacity to use and create knowledge and acquiring knowledge from abroad."(10) Such capacity is some-times nonexistent or skeletal, inefficient and unable to supervise research in these countries. This creates the serious problem of the nationalization of these administrations and, in the industrialized countries, of the establishment of new structures to facilitate cooperation with developing countries.

The information administration sector should also be radically transformed for the establishment of NIEO. This sector, which is currently characterized by "the absence of a set of regional and Third World exchange and transmission systems to break up the oligopoly of the major news agen-cies,"(11) must adopt a two-pronged approach: on the one hand, for internal purposes, it must establish or develop an in-formation administration equipped, if not to control, at least to organize "the ever-broader dissemination of an ever-increasing range of information;"(12) and, on the other hand, for external purposes, it must adjust the information imbalance between the center and the periphery of the creation of "regional agency pools to replace the dominator-dominated relationship with an equitable relationship,"(13) and to transform the current one-way flow of information to make it a true exchange between developed and developing countries.

Reorientation Resources

Resources, particularly human ones, are required to restructure the domestic administrative apparatus of states and to redirect it toward the mobilization of natural resources. Such efforts would be fruitless if, for example, the sectors toward which it was redirected did not possess staffs of sufficiently high quality and specially trained in the required fields and technologies.

The establishment of NIEO calls for a decreased growth rate or even, in the industrialized countries, a regression in administrative systems. This requirement is due to two series of events: on the one hand, the "rise to stardom" of technical ministries which are anxious to be represented by their own officials in the negotiations. (It would be a paradox, re-marked a participant in a conference organized by the Royal Institute of International Affairs in London,(14) if these administrations were to regress at the very moment when foreign problems were taking on increased importance.) On the other hand, this is due to the quantitative deficit in, and lack of economic training of, officials of foreign affairs who, being too few, uninformed, and undertrained in economic problems, are forced to defer to the officials of other ministries in international economic negotiations. If this were to become the pattern, the administration would be divested of its coordinating function which could result in fragmentation of the economic policies of states.

Restructuring the national administrative machinery thus entails the acquisition of additional resources and the training of new officials, better qualified than today to deal with national and international economic problems. It is easy to see the importance of national or international programs for specialized and advanced training for officials to systematically prepare them for the new tasks they must undertake in the implementation of NIEO.

RESTRUCTURING THE NATIONAL ADMINISTRATIVE APPARATUS

The restructuring of the state's internal administrative apparatus is the second condition which must be fulfilled if that apparatus is to be able to perform its role as an agent of change. It is not enough merely to rearrange the existing administrative bodies. They must also be made more effective through the reorganization of structures and the revision of procedures, in order to permit the optimum use of the administration if it is to be devoted to the establishment of NIEO.

Reorganization of Structures

Although the implementation of the Charter of Economic Rights and Duties of States requires that administrative structures should be better equipped to perform effectively the functions which are henceforth to be assigned to them, the changes they have undergone since the accession of states to independence have not necessarily made them more reliable.

The original institutional nucleus from which the administrative structures of developing countries have evolved — inherited from the colonial period - has certainly undergone changes designed to ensure their adaptation to the new tasks assigned to them. However, the expansion of administrative structures poses problems of coordination among the various administrative segments and consequently requires the proliferation of coordinating bodies which, all situated in the same strategic administrative structures - presidency, prime minister, coordinating bodies par excellence - are concentrated in sectors which are so narrow that they can be decongested only by delegation or dismemberment. What we are witnessing, therefore, is a "bellows" phenomenon: expansion, coordination, overload, dismemberment of the administration; the latter movement both arising from coordination and calling it into question. The structural changes which have so far taken place in connection with NIEO have not, therefore, been sufficient to make the administration better equipped to perform the func tions incumbent on it.

Unburdening the administrative structures seems to be both a condition for and a consequence of NIEO. The need to react quickly to the crises which confront them lead states to multiply the number of agencies, delegations, departments, and other offices, bodies characterized by their lightweight structure, small number of staff, and high degree of technical competence. While the establishment of these bodies has not resulted in the parallel elimination of existing ministerial organs, it has relieved the latter of part of their substance, through the transfers of competencies.

These coordination and study-oriented structures are able to react much more quickly to events and, thus, ensure more effective administrative action. One may wonder about their future, and the significance of their recent proliferation. Certainly, neither their appearance nor even their development is linked exclusively to the establishment or consequences of NIEO. However, the acceleration of this trend does seem to be its direct consequence. Thus, with regard to the administra- tive implications of the NIEO, the problem arises of knowing whether the establishment of a new international economic and social order will give rise to the creation of a new administrative model. This model would combine a central administration reduced to its essential functions with auton- omous administrative bodies which, while fulfilling, the required conditions of effectiveness (through their special- ization, flexibility, and lightweight structure) would also be socially integrated into the community for which they are responsible.

REVISION OF PROCEDURES

If revision is to serve the purpose of NIEO, it seems that it must take the form of the modernization of administrative procedures. The crisis provoked for developed countries by the demand for NIEO and the restructuring which is required in the developing countries calls for a reexamination of the proce- dures and methods used until now - in France, for example, the modernization of the machinery for processing statistical data and the improvement of coordination between the planning

machinery and the governmental authorities. Doubtless, effects
of a similar kind could be found in other countries, particularly developing ones, especially in the field of international
and regional administrative procedures. In this respect, the
proosals made by the Dag Hammarskjöld Foundation seem to offer
some interesting perspectives.

The Foundation's 1975 report states:

> The present level of Third World countries' joint
> negotiating capacity and that of most Third World
> countries taken individually is inadequate. The more
> industrial economies agree to negotiate seriously as
> opposed to passively rejecting broad demands or
> making selective, "take it or leave it" offers, the
> more serious this inadequacy will become. Two evi-
> dent routes to strengthening capacity in this field
> are:
>
> •   Third World global, interrregional, or regional
>   technical and research units linked to existing
>   political forums and conferences
> •   Greater use of a constituency system in negoti-
>   ations, allowing any individual poor country to
>   concentrate expertise and personnel on a limited
>   number of issues. . . .
>
> The Non-Aligned Conference should build up serious
> technical and negotiating secretariats with duties
> far beyond resolution drafting.(15)

THE ADMINISTRATIVE APPARATUS OF STATES AS SUBJECT OF CHANGE

The administrative apparatus of the state can contribute to
change - the promotion of the economic, social, and cultural
development of its people, as provided in article 7 of the
Charter of Economic Rights and Duties of States - only insofar
as: (1) Its technical effectiveness is increased: the essential
means of achieving this are the reorganization and restructuring dealt with above; and (2) it is motivated by political
will. In this respect, it must be said that in many cases the
political will to promote the objectives of NIEO does not exist
or is not successfully brought to bear. This results from a
deliberate decision by the political authorities of a country
or from the influence exerted on the country's political and
administrative authorities by multinational economic powers
which are hostile to the new order.(16) Even where political
will exists, it is not always translated into practice, because
of the inertia or dysfunctions which analyze the administrative
apparatus even though the latter should take priority as an

instrument for the establishment of NIEO. Therefore, it is not enough to consider the administrative apparatus as the vehicle or agent of change and to increase its purely technical efficiency.

It is also vital that the administrative apparatus should not constitute a screen separating the political authorities from the citizens. The state must, therefore, be more firmly rooted in the people. This is in accordance with the formal requirements of NIEO. The concepts of collective endogenous development and self-reliance are fundamental.

The administrative apparatus of the state must become a subject of change. If the state is to be able to implement the necessary changes for the introduction of NIEO, it must begin by changing itself, in accordance with the principles of the new order which it is to establish. To promote the economic, social, and cultural development of the people, the state must itself be socially and culturally rooted in its people.

This is a precondition for administrative action; and unless it is, the administration, whose effectiveness would certainly be assured by the technical measures analyzed above, would lack the foundation it needs to implement the changes implied by NIEO.

THE NEED FOR THE STATE TO BE ROOTED IN THE PEOPLE

Frequently, of the two vital functions which are, in every state, incumbent in the administration – the functions of control and mediation – only one is performed, overshadowing the other and profoundly distorting the administration's action. Therefore, it is necessary to analyze how, and with what consequences, the administration becomes reduced to one or the other of these functions.

Reduction of the Administration to its Function of Control

Control was the administration's sole function during the colonial period, when it was seen as the tool of the colonial power. All too often, this remained so after the country's accession to independence, when the "nationalization" of the public service – which is often effected by the accelerated training of the colonial power's former employees – amounted to nothing more than the substitution of nationals for foreigners in posts of authority in the administrative hierarchy. "The decolonizing operation was mounted under the pretext that the true nature of the colonial administration lay in its own internal organization and not in its coercion of the people of

the villages."(17) This is by no means the case. Often there
is no fundamental change in relations between national officials and the people, and the administration is merely the
successor to the power of domination formerly exercised by
foreigners. "They tell us we're independent; what is independence? Independence is for officials and people in the
towns, not the village people."(18)

Gérard Althabe accurately dissected this sense of false
independence which was deeply resented by rural communities in
one formerly colonized country: When, in 1962, the authorities
in that country decided to replace the traditional national
holiday of the former colonial power by the anniversary of the
proclamation of the country's independence, they met with
strong resistance from the village communities for whom the
latter was only an "officials' holiday: it's nothing to do with
us villagers."(19) And the officials' power is doubly deprived
of legitimacy because it is only the exercise of the function
of control which can no longer be justified by the subordination of the person exercising it to the power of the foreigners
who have now left the country: "The village world seems to be
still trapped in the colonial structure which survives despite
institutional reforms and innovations; these it either diverts
from their declared course or transforms into reflections of
what exists in the nation on which it is patterned."(20) The
administrative machinery which retains or continues to perform
only those functions which are linked to the country's former
subordination to a foreign power forgets its other functions
and itself becomes foreign to the people over which it wields
its power: "Thus, its appearance is that of an administrative
machinery which exhausts its reality in its functionality; and
its true nature is that of a hierarchical network"(21) which is
confined to the sole function of control.

Analysis of administrations in other developing countries
do not contradict this interpretation of an "alien modern-
ity"(22) from which the rural population remains estranged and
finally manages to escape: "Hukoumat, the Government, is . . .
"them," up there. Elsewhere, the new structures . . . have
failed to overthrow the local, particularistic systems."(23)
The same is true in black Africa where, as Georges Balandier
shows "the material strength of the colonizing society . . .,
as well as its superior administrative ability, explains the
importance of what one might call clandestine or indirect
reactions and, made possible by the manner in which the
"duplication processes" operate. Underlying the apparent
fulfillment of administrative orders or exaggerated professions
of co-operation, independent activities are organized and basic
opposition is manifested. . . ."(24) The very modernization of
this administration is likely to render it relatively ineffective. Since it is resented at times as alien to the socio-
cultural traditions of the groups on which it is imposed, it
provokes evasive behavior which undermines its authority.

REDUCTION OF ADMINISTRATION TO ITS FUNCTION
OF MEDIATION

It is the people's "expectations" of the state which lead to
the reduction of the administration to its function of mediation between the individual and authority – between society and
the state. Doubtless, people expect from the state the normal
benefits which every state provides for its citizens. But, in
the developing countries, there also exist specific expectations of the state, which Jean Leca and Jean-Claude Vatin
define as "the demand for administrative services as a
right."(25) They continue:

> the Algerian citizen is above all an aggressive
> consumer who expects from the national State all that
> the colonial State refused him: the urban petty
> bourgeoisie asks occasionally for political power and
> always for the standard of living enjoyed by the
> former colonizers, the urban proletariat demands
> security of employment and higher wages, while the
> rural poor want work . . . and, above all, education,
> which is viewed as the vital or, in any case, the
> only available means of social advancement.(26)

And it is true that the administration in developing countries
performs many roles which go beyond or replace those purely
technical ones which in theory it is to perform: it substitutes
for a political power which is lacking, a social mobility for
the groups which put it in office, it is a source of reward in
the form of patronage and nepotism, for the support and loyalty
given to holders of power; it is a systematic and privileged
source of employment in countries where unemployment is high.
The administrative bureaucracy constitutes a sort of providence
for those few who can gain entry to or make use of it. It has
been said of Latin America:

> while the bureacuracy provides the ruling group with
> patronage and support for the régime, and the middle
> groups with employment, the national community re-
> ceives in turn only a minimum level of essential
> services as compared with its size and cost. . . .
> Socio-economic destruction makes a considerable dif-
> ference in terms of accessibility and quality of
> services being offered and received. Socio-cultural
> differentials tend to widen the gap between bureau-
> cracies and the large group of lower strata com-
> position.(27)

The administration's tendency to "attract (to itself) the various feelings of disinheritance" of the citizens of the formerly colonized country has been carried over from its colonial origins: in their eyes, the administration has been vested with a function of mediation between them and all that they hope to obtain - or all from which they hope to escape - because of their country's accession to independnce. The administration is perceived as an intermediary and it is doubly so because the official is the "provider of all sorts of services" - he holds the papers, the certificates, the rubber-stamps, new symbols of the violence which is inflicted on all through these intermediary élites and through the needs they spread. It is the triumph of the cousins' republic "in a relationship of vulnerability-protection,"(28) and because the official is also the person who provides the links, the passage between the two worlds in which he participates, that of the modern administration of which he is the official representative, and the traditional world from which he originated and with which he retains contact. Truly, "contrary to appearances, there are three systems, not two: the liaison agents are the officials but also the émigres, the city dwellers, the educated, who spread the new ideology."(29) Administrative activity is often reduced to this function of mediation, while its function of control is contested and rejected by the people. As Jean Leca and Jean-Claude Vatin explain, "the [people's] expectations of the State go hand-in-hand with the very opposite of those expectations: by expecting the State to solve all contradictions, society . . . must inevitably be disappointed when the State reveals that it is still only an ineffective entrepreneur and a point of confrontation between conflicting forces."(30) And they go on to state

> despite the classical and frequently accurate distinction between, on the one hand, the beneficiaries and élites of the system who would be better able to master the political process and develop a participant culture and, on the other hand, the masses who are estranged from this process and either withdraw into micro-politics or are infused with millenarianism, it seems to us that what is characteristic of both groups is the coexistence of intense expectations of the State and distrust of its machinery.(31)

The forms are different; the result is the same: the administration - reduced to one or the other of its functions - is emptied of its substance. It is resented as being alien to its socio-cultural environment; it is the object of distrust and therefore ignored, diverted, or contested. This situation can scarcely fail to have a detrimental effect on the administration's action, even when its technical effectiveness has been improved. Under these conditions, the pursuit of the objectives of NIEO might well be completely in vain. It is, therefore, necessary for the state to be more firmly rooted. How might this be achieved?

Reduction of the administration to one or other of its normal roles of control and mediation is a consequence of the maladjustment of administrative institutions to their socio-cultural environment; under-administration is basically a form of adjustment. Solving this problem calls for defining the exact nature of the various kinds of underadministration.

THE SCENARIOS OF UNDERADMINISTRATION: FOUR HYPOTHESES

1. The first hypothesis is the one most frequently encountered, and can be summed up as combining a sharp diff- erentiation in the administrative structure with a low level of social integration. Such a situation can be seen in coun- tries with a modern administrative apparatus which is very specialized in its structure, while the social group over which the administrative apparatus exercises its jurisdiction is still characterized by the juxtaposition of different ethnic, tribal, and religious communities. The low level of social integration then coincides with structural differentiation and reinforces its effects to the point of disintegration or dislocation of the administrative structures. The first example of underadministration corresponds to a socio-cultural phenomenon which might be termed a crisis of national identity; the community does not have a socio-cultural pattern which could be adopted by the great majority of its members.(32) Each ethno-cultural group identifies with one of the admin- istrative structures and uses its protection to consolidate its own position; this gives rise to the phenomenon of feudal administrative domains which threaten the unity of the state.

2. The second hypothesis is the opposite of the first. It refers to a high degree of integration combined with a low level of differentiation. It applies to the situation pre- vailing in the basic community units - village communities, rural groups, etc. - where the degree of social integration is extremely high, since the administrative radius is confined within the dimensions of the ethno-cultural group itself. On the other hand, the administrative apparatus is often greatly under-specialized, if indeed it exists at all. This is a typical case of underadministration in the usual sense of the term. The administrative apparatus, by virtue of its non- existence or inadequacy, is not in a position to satisfy the needs of the community. This second example of underadmin- istration corresponds to another of the crises confronting contemporary states: the crisis in the allocation of resources

among its citizens resulting from inadequate administrative machinery, usually at the level of local communities.

3. The third hypothesis also corresponds to a crisis in the allocation of resources among the citizens of the state, but in this instance it is due, not to inadequate administrative machinery, but to the enormous "expectations" projected upon that machinery, which is seen essentially as mediating between the citizens and the authorities - as dispenser, provider, as providence itself. Obviously, it cannot act as total provider because of the discrepancy between the hopes projected upon the state - which are the greater by virtue of having been held back during the colonial period - and the state's capacity to fulfill those hopes, a capacity which can, at best, scarcely be superior to that of the industrialized countries whose administration operates in optimum conditions.

4. The fourth hypothesis refers to a crisis of legitimacy: it is the existence of an administrative apparatus which is confined to the exercise of its role of control and which is felt as alien and illegitimate by those over whom it exerts authority. It elicits evasive behavior on the part of the citizens subject to it. This makes the apparatus ineffective in that its role of control achieves results which are precisely the opposite of those desired.

Obviously, these four hypotheses of underadministration never exist in a pure form in developing countries. Most often they coexist, and their coexistence corresponds to the crises of identity, legitimacy, and allocation which confront these countries and which make it more difficult to solve the problems of underadministration afflicting them, whereas the industrialized countries were able to confront the various crises successively.(33)

In short, there is a duality of "modern" and rudimentary administrative systems. The former is resented as foreign and, ultimately, because it is both modern and alien, as virtually threatening "ethnocide."(34) On the other hand, the latter, if it is socially and culturally integrated with its environment, runs the risk of being totally inefficient as a result of its rudimentary nature. Thus, the problem is to establish an administrative apparatus which is both effective in practice and rooted in its socio-cultural environment.

No partial solution to this problem seems possible since it is linked to the simultaneous crises affecting the developing countries. The state must be restructued as a whole, since the three kinds of crises affecting it must be tackled simultaneously.

CRISES AFFECTING THE STATE

The Crisis of Identity

The crisis of identity is undoubtedly the most difficult to solve. The remedy for such a crisis runs counter to a seemingly irresistible trend toward abandoning socio-cultural traditions, seen as the precondition for progress in the community. There are "images" of the traditional society(35) to which many researchers are deeply attached and which portray traditional society as rigid, as "repetitive society replicating itself from generation to generation, and without significant structural variation";(36) a "society situated outside history or on its margin, a 'frozen society' which stays at zero degree historical temperature, according to Claude Levi-Strauss."(37) Such images reinforce the idea that these so-called traditional societies are utterly opposed to any progress, and, going beyond even this idea, that their values can only be hostile to, or incompatible with, development. "The society is structured but impervious to economic stimuli; for its ethos it turns to an affrmation of the past; it forms an integral part of an immediately intelligible world. Traditional structures are obstacles to new stimuli."(38) Such a society would have "a retrospective vision of the world . . . The stability of its institutions, the strictness of its morals and its belief in ancestral values make such a society essentially conservative."(39)

Obviously, these images are scarcely conducive to the establishment of a new administrative system, nor can they encourage any expectation that such a system would contribute to change. Yet, perhaps the problems of under-administration in developing countries might be solved were the administration to sink roots in traditional society. It should be noted that the rigid or retrograde aspect of many so-called traditional societies derives more from illusion than from established fact. It is undoubtedly easier to formalize the "simple," the "fixed," whether referring to structures or to behavior, than the complex or the mobile. Yet society cannot be treated in this reductive fashion without, to some extent, being denatured, in a "state of rigor mortis."(40) Indeed, as Georges Balandier observes, "almost all traditional or pre-developed societies are the arenas of profound change,"(41) and it is important to take into account all the factors of change. In this light, one can discern the ambivalence of certain elements which have usually been seen as obstacles to development:(42) it is surely true that the social practice of the extended family, although it is most often seen as a hindrance to development because of the burdens it places on the authorities, ensures, through the bonds between the public-servant

and the members of the family group to which he belongs, a flow
of information which the dislocation of the administrative
structures might have curtailed - information gathered via
means and channels other than those usual in modern government
departments, but information nonetheless.(43) And it has been
shown that the eradication of certain factors linked to socio-
cultural traditions is in no way the precondition of all social
progress; it and can be postponed, or could even be unneces-
sary.(44) Is it not possible that a similar situation might
apply in the administrative field?

     Furthermore, the mere presence of a public service, i.e.,
an official within a community should not be taken as a sign
that the state has taken root in its socio-cultural environment. The official must also be in direct contact with the
people, and must provide them with the necessary impetus for
involvement in the tasks of development. This condition can be
met only when the official is not a stranger to the community
for which he is responsible, i.e., when he originates in it;
otherwise the identity crisis will continue.

> These are at once the traditions of most African
> civilizations and the requirements for real devel-
> opment, requirements which make it imperative to seek
> new forms of decision-making and management in the
> public services and, at the various levels, public
> servants of a new kind. When progress is made in
> this direction and when these processes gain momentum
> it soon emerges that peasants and city-dwellers are
> quite capable of finding from among their own ranks
> people capable of carrying out tasks hitherto (badly)
> performed by officials, and that they are just as
> able to control public servants and to demand from
> them both services and a very different attitude to
> that which can be seen today.(45)

The use of public servants drawn from the communities themselves to provide administration implies not merely that they
originate in the communities, but also that they are chosen by
them. Solutions to the crisis of identity are thus found in
searching to solve the crisis of legitimacy.

                    The Crisis of Legitimacy

The crisis of legitimacy is unlikely to be resolved without
recourse to the establishment of a public service which is no
longer confined to the function of control alone. Popular
participation seems to be the only way to achieve such an
objective, since it would permit the appointment of public
servants who would no longer be considered wielding illegiti-

mate authority over the community. This would eliminate the evasive behavior which is the response to the alien character of the public service in some developing countries: "In short, it is when those concerned in the villages and districts choose their local officials, and when those officials are trained primarily on the spot, rather than at institutes where they reproduce extraneous models, that a public service can be refashioned, which would be capable of communicating with those it is supposed to serve."(46)   In the traditional triad of civil servants, consumers, and citizens, instead of giving free rein to officials appointed by authority, a growing role should be assigned to the consumers of administrative services, and more generally to the citizens of the community for which these services are provided.

The Crisis of Allocation

A solution, or attempted solution, of the twin crises of identity and legitimacy will not ensure that all the opportunities for solving the problems of underadministration are brought together. Such action must be extended through the establishment of an administration capable of meeting the demands for the allocation of resources which confront developing states. The aim must be to remedy the crises confronting the state and to ensure for that purpose both its effectiveness and its environment. The two closely-linked ideas of "endogenous collective development" and "self-reliance," which are fundamental to NIEO, imply a greater use of decentralization.

Endogenous collective development appears to be a type of development which presupposes (a) severance of the links of dependence maintained by the dominant countries within the "international system"; (b) total mobilization of national resources and capabilities; (c) strengthened cooperation between the developing countries, and (d) redirection of development efforts towards meeting the basic needs of the peoples concerned.(47)

The "autonomous definition of development-styles and life-styles" can only be meaningful if it is extended from the international level to the national level. It should be "a means of endowing political independence with economic content," without going so far as to be narrowed to a kind of isolationism. It should take hold at the grass-roots level among the local communities.

In fact, one can imagine, and sometimes observe, the example of a ruling class in a Third World country, whether or not belonging to OPEC, improving its economic relations with

the industrialized world by applying the principle of national
or collective self-reliance while, at the same time, increasing
the burden of its domination over its own people. "Self-
reliance does not work without structural reforms to provide
the poorest with the means to improve their lot."(48)   Each
community must find its own solution to as many of the problems
it faces as possible.

> In other words, each basic community unit, relying on
> its own energies, should be in a position to manage
> its own affairs and to enter into relations with its
> opposite numbers on equal terms in order to resolve
> common problems, while the State looks after the
> regulation of social mechanisms and, in particular,
> sees to it that the rights of the weakest communities
> or individuals are protected and assured.(49)

The decentralization of administrative structures is one of the
characteristic implications of the establishment of NIEO and
this involves participation. Participation seems all the more
necessary in that it often appears to be the only possible
compensation for the ineluctable extension of public-service
bureaucracies, known to all countries, whether developed or
not.

It is foreseeable that "another Sweden"(50) would introduce a more direct supervision of the administration by its
citizens for the sake of avoiding political reforms that reach
those citizens "in the form of peremptory circulars issued by
harrassed bureaucrats."(51)   Radical decentralization,(52) of a
kind which would promote community participation, leaving the
higher echelon to deal only with problems which cannot be
solved at lower levels, is an essential condition for the
establishment of NIEO.   Combined with participation, such
decentralization provides the only possible solution to the
three-fold crisis affecting developing countries: the crisis of
identity (the absence of a socio-cultural model with which the
vast majority of the national community can identify); the
crisis of legitimacy (the existence of an administrative
apparatus restricted solely to the function of exercising
control and resented as alien and illegitimate by the community); and the crisis in the allocation of resources (due to
the inability of the administrative apparatus, through its
inadequacy, to satisfy the community's needs).
    Decentralization should not be confined to territorial
communities: it should also be extended to the management of
central administrative services and should involve the participation of public servants, through their trade-unions, in
the organization of their work.   In this way, it might be
possible to avoid the symptoms of rejection or withdrawal

engendered by a public service which draws too much upon extraneous models. This would also confer on the proliferation of public enterprises, state-owned companies, agencies, and corporations a stringency and logic which they lack at present.

Decentralization in developing countries today takes merely the form of specialized and autonomous administrative services involving enterprises, corporations, and other agencies which have multiplied over a period of one or two decades. Such decentralization can provide a partial solution to only one of the three crises affecting the developing countries; the crisis in the allocation of resources. Under such a system, autonomous governmental agencies generally have an effectiveness and freedom of action unavailable to traditional administrative systems based on ministries. However, the crises of identity and legitimacy remain unsolved. The importance of a trend toward decentralization and participation is clear: without it, central state governments would be liable to remain monstrous machines exercising a pointless control over a community in which they have no roots. If nothing is changed, this phenomenon will only be exacerbated, deepening the gulf already separating the "modern" central administration from the local authorities still operating at the traditional level.(53) The changes called for in NIEO can be brought about only through corresponding changes in the state administrative apparatus.

NOTES

This preliminary draft report on the administrative apparatus of states is based on earlier research conducted by the author and refers in particular to the following publications:

Les administrations publiques des Etats du Tiers-monde et le nouvel ordre économique international. Annuaire du Tiers-Monde 1976. Editions Berger-Levrault 1977. p. 397 et seq; Administration publique et Environnement socio-culturel. Rapport à le réunion d'Experts sur l'adaptation de 1 administration publique et de la gestion aux différents contextes socio-culturels, (UNESCO - Tanger, 26-30 Septembre 1977) Revue Française d'Administration Publique, 1978, No. 7, pp. 21 to 36; Les implications administrative d'un nouvel ordre international économique et social. Rapport introductif au Colloque de l'Institut international des Sciences Administratives (Sousse - Mai 1978) A paraître in: Administration et N.O.E.I. Editions Cujas 1979.

1. Preamble to the Charter of Economic Rights and Duties of States. United Nations General Assembly, Resolution 3281 (XXIX), December 12, 1974.

2. Expression borrowed from E. Laszlo et al., Goals for Mankind: A Report to the Club of Rome on the New Horizons of Global Community (New York: Signet Books, New American Library, 1978), p. 350.

3. Jacques Bugnicourt, "Le Mimétisme administratif en Afrique," Revue française de science politique, 1973, p. 1253.

4. A. Nicolai, "Analyse idéologique du concept de domination," in L'Economique et les sciences humaines, under the direction of G. Palmade, Dunod, 1967, Vol. II, p. 541. "For lack of a better word let us use domination as a generic term that conveys the idea of an asymmetrical relationship, either potential or actual, conscious or unconscious, formal or informal, sought, accepted, suffered, opposed or rejected, between at least two entities: bodies, staffs, forms, groups, societies or cultures" (Ibid., p. 450).

5. 1975 Dag Hammarskjöld Report on Development and International Co-operation prepared on the occasion of the Seventh Special Session of the United Nations General Assembly. Development Dialogue: a journal of international development co-operation published by the Dag Hammarskjöld Foundation, Uppsala. No. 112, 1975, p. 7.

6. Conclusions of a special working group on finding a new cooperation model (xeroxed document). "International colloquium on the implications of a new international economic order," Institut international d'études sociales. Geneva, January 19-23, 1976, p. 2.

7. A. Wagner, Les fondements de l'economie politique, translated by L. Polak (Paris, 1904), Vol. III, p. 363. Quoted in L. Fontvieille, Evolution et croissance de l'Etat (français, 1915-1969. Cahiers de l'I.S.M.E.A., series A-F, No. 13). September-December 1976, Vol. X, p. 1694.

8. Cf. article 30 of the Charter and the Report quoted above, p. 32. While it is accepted that health depends first on food, habitat and preventive measures, all the practical implications of this assertion have not yet been drawn. The satisfaction of health needs calls for, in particular: a reallocation of available resources directed toward prevention; the integration of health services into development services as a whole; the adaptation of health services to specific circumstances; and using local resources, to the maximum, instead of imitating models from countries in which conditions, notably the epidemiology, are different.

9. Dag Hammaersjöld Report, p. 33.

10. Ibid., p. 82.

11. Ibid., p. 83

12. Ibid., p. 83.

13. Mustapha Masmoudi, "Conférence sur le nouvel ordre mondial de l'information et le rôle de la presse dans la promotion du dialogue euro-arabe," La Documentation Française (Paris) June 20, 1977, No.324, p. 16.

14. "Problems of foreign policy making in Britain, France and Germany:" Report of a trilateral conference on the management of interdependence. The Royal Institute of International Affairs, London, March 10-12, 1976, p. 4.

15. Dag Hammarskjöld Report, pp. 75-76.

16. Moïse Ikonicoff, "L'Etat-relais," Tiers Monde, 1978.

17. Gérard Althabe, "Opression et libération dans l'imaginaire, les communautés villageoises de la Côte Orientale de Madagascar," Preface de Georges Balandier, Ed. Maspéro, Coll. textes à l'appui 1976. p. 50.

18. Ibid., p. 39, note 15.

19. Ibid.

20. Ibid., p. 51.

21. Ibid., p. 55.

22. Bruno Etienne, Algérie (Cultures et Révolution, Seuil, Coll. L'Histoire immédiate, 1977), p. 299.

23. Ibid., p. 114.

24. Georges Balandier, "Sociologie de l'Afrique noire," Bibliothèque de sociologie contemporaine, 1971, pp. 494-96.

25. Jean Leca and Jean-Claude Vatin, L'Algérie politique, institutions et régime (Presses de la Fondation nationale des sciences politiques, 1975).

26. Ibid., p. 316.

27. Jorge I. Tapia-Videla, "Understanding Organization and Environments: A Comparative Perspective," Public Administration Review, 36 (6) (November-December 1976): 633.

28. Etienne, Algiers, p. 107.

29. Ibid., p. 108.

30. Leca and Vatin, L'Argérie politique, p. 319.

31. Ibid., p. 313.

32. "In the ethno-cultural sense," a system is pluralist when it is constituted by a variable number of ethno-cultural groups which retain their characteristics (modified to a greater or lesser extent), which has attained only a low level of effective integration, and which does not possess a body of socio-cultural patterns that are accepted by the great majority of members of the society." L. Beltran, "Dualism et pluralisme en Afrique tropicale indépendante," Cahiers Internationaux de sociologie 47 (July-December 1969): 101.

33. With regard to the simultaneity and periodicity of crises in underdeveloped and in industrialized countries, see M. F. Lochie, "Gouvernement représentatif, bureaucratie et développement politique: le cas africain," in: Cahiers africains de'administration publique no. 16 (1976) pp. 151 ff.

34. Etienne, Algiers.

35. Georges Balandier, "Anthropo-logiques, P.U.F.," Sociologie d'aujourd'hui, Chap. 5, p. 215-30.

36. Ibid., p. 216.

37. Ibid.

38. Philippe Hugon, Les blocages Socio-Culturels du Developpement en Afrique Noire Tiers-Monde, 1967, p. 699.

39. Ibid., p. 700.

40. Georges Balandier, Anthropo-Logiques, Précité. p. 217.

41. Ibid.

42. Albert O. Hirschman, "Classification et quasi-démantèlement des obstacles au développement," Tiers-Monde (1966), p. 285.

43. Jacques Bugnicourt, "Communication et Choc des Cultures à Travers L'Action Administrative en Afrique," Recherches pédagogique et culture, Paris (January February 1976), pp. 9-19.

44. "The cultural and institutional conditions for development tend to have many more variables than our limited experience initially led us to believe. . . . Abbeglen has shown in great detail, in a revealing study of industrial enterprises in Japan, that "nationalization and depersonalization are not indispensable to the adoption of a Western-type industrial economy," Hirschman, "Classification," p. 293.

45. Bugnicourt, "Communication et Choc des cultures."

46. Ibid.

47. Enrique Oteiza and Francisco Sercovich. "Développement Collectif Auto-Centré," Revue internationale des sciences sociales 28 (1976): 724.

48. Dag Hammarskjöld Report, p. 35.

49. Ibid., p. 39.

50. Ibid., p. 45 (Document prepared for the Dag Hammarskjöld Project by two members of the future studies office attached to the Prime Minister's Cabinet in Stockholm).

51. Ibid., p. 56.

52. Ibid., p. 33.

53. Cf., with regard to this point, Julio Tresierra, "Fonctions et dysfonctions de la bureaucratie dans les sociétés transitoires," in Sociologie de l'Impérialisme VIIe Congrès mondial de sociologie, Varna 1970, sous la direction de Anouar Abdelmalek, Ed. Anthropos, 1971, p. 621.

5 The Regional Institutional Requirements of the NIEO

Mario Bettati
Gérard Timsit

PROMOTING REGIONAL ADMINISTRATIONS

Collective self-reliance, notwithstanding the many procla-
mations of its necessity, has not developed along lines
concordant with the New International Economic Order on the
institutional and operational levels. Various political,
legal, and technical obstacles slow the regionalization of
development in the Third World. With due respect for the
sovereignty of states and their desire to determine their own
development, some indications may be advanced to provide a
basis for the reinforcement of certain means and capacities on
the regional and sectoral areas.

Regional administration furthering the goals of the NIEO
may take varied forms and may bring institutional machinery
into play on different levels.

Regionalism may first assert itself on an overall level in
a very general way among all the developing countries through
the increased negotiating capacity of the entire Group of 77.
It may next progress on the level of the actual regions, i.e.,
the continental or subregional geographical or geopolitical
areas, and, finally, be stimulated interregionally by mechanisms for liaison among the secretariats of the groupings that
have already been formed.

An Overall Institutional Framework Comprising
Solely Developing Countries

The notion of collective self-reliance, as understood by developing countries, includes a determination to establish an NIEO
as the result of worldwide joint action by them. The confer-

ence of the Third World regional and subregional economic
grouping, which met for the first time on the secretariat level
on April 10, 1978 at Geneva, was doubtless an unprecedented
event.

Like the Ministerial Meetings of the Group of 77, it expressed the need for mutual consultation felt by the countries
concerned which desire effectively to implement an overall
system of South-South economic cooperation. But to be put into
effect, that intention largely depends on the existence of an
overall institutional framework comprising solely developing
countries.

Meetings such as those just mentioned, whose means and
influence are indeed limited by their very nature, are insufficient. They can only be held periodically, and their lack of
permanence prevents them from dealing with the everyday
problems which face their participants both as regards their
cooperation and the negotiations they have to conduct with the
industrialized countries.

The aims and objectives of an institutional mechanism
would be to provide an overall framework for formulating,
studying, and presenting the general economic cooperation
policies and programs of the developing countries. It would
also give them the essential technical support for negotiations, and for cooperation on a worldwide level which would
also be viewed in the context of the regional and subregional
groupings. The conditions and procedures of such an institutionalization would have to be clearly defined.

Institutionalization should first be decided on a high
political level, with respect for the sovereignty of the member
states of the Group of 77 and of the nonaligned countries. In
view of the urgency which is largely acknowledged by the
parties concerned, the decision ought to be taken as soon as
possible. Institutionalization then ought to be effected so as
to complete and strengthen the activity of international
organizations or agencies, such as UNCTAD or UNDP, without
competing with them.

The details of the institutions may vary greatly. They
may range from the establishment of a technical supporting unit
to that of a secretariat to deal only with problems of the
Third World. In this matter, however, a few precautions are
necessary. Such a secretariat should rather be set up <u>outside</u>
UNCTAD in order to preserve the latter's universal character
and to avoid burdening the system's finances which are known to
be in difficulty. UNCTAD could, of course, like UNDP, contribute technical assistance and institutional support to such
an undertaking, but the ideal would be its establishment in the
developing countries, as autonomously as possible.

The UNCTAD Secretariat has always been in favor of the
setting up of an appropriate secretariat for the Third World
which it considers to be related to the strengthening of its

own work. In any case, the way in which this would be done
would have to be examined very carefully by all the interested
parties.

Institutional Machinery for Regional Integration
and Cooperation

Collective self-reliance must be based on a common political
will expressed in cooperation or integration agreements and
carried out by institutional mechanisms adapted to the objectives fixed in the agreements. The Programme of Action on
the Establishment of a New International Economic Order devotes
an entire section (Section VII) to the promotion of cooperation
among developing countries and to the establishment and
strengthening of regional and subregional integration.

But merely proclaiming such a series of provisions is not
sufficient for their implementation. Different kinds of
support services to developing countries, which are sometimes
inexperienced in cooperation and integration practices, are
necessary. As regards information, UNCTAD has already provided
considerable support to the Third World countries by publishing
a series of studies on the present problems of economic
integration.

Apart from information and from models of institutional
machinery and agreements, treaties, and conventions, practical
assistance for the development of regional cooperation and
integration may be given by international organizations such as
UNCTAD and UNDP.

Measures to be Taken to Support Present and
Subsequent Programs

UNCTAD's medium-term plan, 1980 to 1983, depends on a strategy
for consolidating the regional groupings by means of aid
granted to their secretariats.(1)

To conduct and extend this policy would favor regional
administrative agencies that are still in the early stages of
organization and operation, since they would gain the experience acquired by agencies that are older or more advanced.

The technical assistance projects prepared by UNCTAD and
financed by UNDP should be renewed and/or extended in cooperation with the regional commissions.

It should be stressed that the international organizations
of the United Nations system would be unable to bring about the
establishment or extension of institutional machinery without
the political will of the states concerned. As the activity of
international institutions is limited by the principle of non-
interference, such procedures may only be started through the

free consent of the member states. Technical assistance may be called upon later with a view to their application. Participation in cooperation schemes is a right and not an obligation. But once participation has been agreed to, a duty is attached to it, which is to take care that the policies of the subregional or regional administrative authorities are consonant with the Charter of the Economic Rights and Duties of States.

The Arusha Programme for Collective Self-Reliance adopted by the developing countries recommends that UNCTAD should help to prepare specific proposals for measures to support the regional, subregional, and interregional economic groupings, at the request of the developing countries concerned and when the need for the measures is felt. Such assistance should receive a favorable response from the developed countries and be provided in addition to the assistance granted individually to the developing countries.

But the main thing is the first step in the process. This can only be taken by the developing countries themselves. They are unable, however, to strengthen their cooperation and integration systems without a ratification of the positions formally adopted by the Group of 77. For that purpose, each developing country concerned could draw up a complete list of its national needs and resources in order to obtain the appropriate measures of support, and to enable those needs and resources to be combined with those of the other countries in the region or subregion considered.

Responsibility for development first requires the mobilization of the parties concerned. Development will not be granted but will be gained by the pooling of the rationally organized economic forces, lined up on the international front by a strategy whose objective is to organize the dispersed abilities of the Third World on the regional, subregional, and interregional levels.

After World War II, Europe was ruined and struck by hunger, distress, and the destruction of its productive power. Its recovery was due to the coordination and integration of the economies of the member states quite as much as to external aid. One remedy would never have succeeded without the other, just as, today, aid to the Third World could not be effective without regional arrangements for its allocation.

The question arises concerning the models on which the new programs may be based. They are of two kinds: cooperation models and integration models. The corresponding structures are more or less elaborate and more or less cumbersome according to the objectives aimed at.

There are many models of regional economic cooperation among developing countries (a list of the existing arrangements is found in the Appendix). The most fundamental among them are the agreements, treaties, or conventions establishing regional groupings.

To work effectively toward the establishment of the NIEO, the regional or subregional arrangement should clearly define the corresponding objectives, methods of operation, and structure.

The objectives should be defined as precisely as possible either in the preambles to the treaties or, as is very often preferable, among the provisions of the agreement in the form of substantive rules. They should determine the sectors which allow the process of the economic development of the member states to be speeded up. Though limited to a particular sector of production, as in the case of agreements among producers of raw materials which are sectoral rather than regional, co-operation may also relate to exchanges among developing countries, investments, technology, and other matters. The objectives may be autocentered or may be directed toward an external common front of the countries of the region in their negotiations with the industrialized world.

Methods of operation may range from mere coordination of national policies to the establishment of common policies for the member countries. They may provide for the possibility of operational strategies, particularly by setting up multinational production or marketing enterprises, by developing means of transport and communication, by founding regional centers for acquiring technology, by establishing free trade areas or mechanisms for increasing intraregional exchanges, or by the regional financing of productive investments.

The structure of the regional mechanisms may vary on the institutional level, according to the type of objectives aimed at and the methods of action chosen. A few fundamental trends should, however, be recalled.

First, political difficulties often prevent the admission to the regional grouping of all the countries in the region. But the organization's success frequently depends on its membership. No union of producers or of commodity suppliers can, for instance, outside the future integrated program, work properly if one of the major producers remains outside the system or does not apply the principles of the consensus adopted by the others.

Second, the organs should have balanced complementary tasks. The conventional structure of a large number of institutions of this kind comprises a body of representatives of states or governments responsible for working out the system's general policies and having decision making or policymaking authority, an executive body, and a secretariat.

The models of regional economic integration among developing countries, which are more difficult to devise, often require the transfer of a part of the sovereignty of the member states to the supranational organization, and judicial control by the supranational legal system.

This kind of institutional machinery is introduced by stages, and generally begins with the establishment of a free trade area among members, coupled with a common external customs tariff. A common policy for agricultural and in- dustrial development may then be entered upon by the agencies of integration.

These agencies, which are basic elements of the integrated structure, inevitably comprise an intergovernmental organ but also a regional organ that is independent of the states and responsible for applying the constitutive treaties and pre- senting proposals for joint action. A regional tribunal supervises the compliance of the decisions of the regional bodies with the treaty that mandates them.

The aim of the legal structure of regional or subregional economic integration models should be to seek a constant balance between the characteristics of the member countries and the newly established economic entity. The institutions formulate rules of economic law in the form of decisions of general or particular application that are adopted unanimously and gradually by a majority of the contracting states, as and when integration takes place and the economies of the member countries merge and interpenetrate. The common authorities may, of course, formulate standards derived from the con- stitutive treaties in the form of resolutions, recommendations, or subsequent agreements.

It should be recalled, however, that legislation by itself is only effective in that it reflects a political will or an economic situation. It is also necessary for that will to be expressed and maintained once the institutions have been set up. While a state's withdrawal is, indeed, a display of sov- ereignty, it penalizes the entire region or subregion.

The constraints of an economic integration system are often difficult to accept, and doubtless explain why the devel- oping countries have not often favored mechanisms of this kind during the last few years. Many of the existing regional institutions are flexible cooperation mechanisms involving few constraints. Neither are they always as effective as their founders had hoped. In practice, these organizations do not always have the institutional, financial, and administrative means essential for satisfactory operation.

A Widening of the Geographical Areas and the Scope
of Regional and Subregional Authorities

Such a widening in scope should make it possible to increase the capacity of members for negotiation and development. Various measures intended to facilitate the participation in the cooperation and integration systems of countries which are now outside regional grouping may be requested by the countries concerned addressed to the agencies of the United Nations system, particularly UNCTAD. These will be adapted according to the type of grouping (cooperation or integration) and the type of applicant state (least developed, island, or land-locked). Consultations are essential between, on the one hand, the grouping concerned, and on the other, the regional commissions or any other appropriate agency and the interested state or states, in order to determine the conditions of the extension and technical assistance which the applicant state requires. Such consultations would also be useful to determine desirable fields of cooperation or integration not yet covered by the existing groupings.

Interregional Administrative Relations

Interregional administrative relations may be organized among the secretariats of the existing groupings. They may also assume very varied forms as regards their duration, since they may be permanent or periodical; their level, among high-ranking officials or representatives; and their nature which may, for instance, involve observer status, association, consultations, or visits, or be bilateral or multilateral.

THE ESTABLISHMENT OF MULTINATIONAL ADMINISTRATION

A "multinational authority" is an administrative authority with internal competence established as a result of the cooperation of two or more national authorities. Except in the event of political or economic integration, such an authority can only develop with limited objectives and under strict conditions.

Apart from the ever-present political conditions, two types of technical conditions should be fulfilled to ensure the effectiveness of such institutions. Some are connected with their organizational structure and others with their personnel.

Structural Conditions

Two kinds of structures may be contemplated for organizations of a multinational nature. In the first case, they would only be administrative structures common to various national agencies which would, in most respects, remain independent. In the second, actual joint enterprises would be established.

Common administrative structures might be set up, particularly to ensure cooperation among State Trade Organizations (STOs) in the three essential fields of activity: information, negotiation, and management.

As to information, there appear to be very few developing country STOs that have a real system for collecting commercial or financial data about the markets in which they handle business. Most Asian STOs depend on secondary sources of market intelligence to determine their trading strategy. With a few exceptions, the African STOs have to be satisfied with the information collected by their countries' commercial representatives abroad or with the data obtained by their own trading associates, particularly the transnational corporations. Likewise, in the Latin American countries, the need has been noted for trade enterprises to be better informed on topics such as surpluses and shortfalls, and prices of and marketing arrangements for the products in which they deal. All information of the kind now obtained from brokers, press agencies, or private companies is likely to be unreliable, out of date, incomplete, or biased.

To improve their trade and financial information, the STOs need to set up common information centers, at least in the principal markets so that, by pooling their resources, they may call in independent experts whose tasks would be to supply information and carry out surveys. On the one hand, they would collect the most recent data about commodities, consumption, world production and stocks, prices, suppliers, available quantities and qualities, arrangements for payment, periods and methods of delivery, shipping intelligence, etc. On the other, they would prepare surveys of the market in general.

With regard to negotiation, the very limited weight of the STOs, considered singly and facing the large trading conglomerates with which they have to negotiate, hardly needs to be pointed out. The formation of joint negotiating task forces comprising STO representatives might, in certain fields - fertilizers and pharmaceuticals have been suggested - facilitate the negotiation or long-term supplying contracts at preferential prices and terms, because of the existence of informal price agreements between important producers and manufacturers of the developed market-economy countries.

It is, above all, as regards management, owing to the more technical nature of the problems to be solved, that the formation of joint agencies may have the most immediate and effective results. This might involve, among other things: the installation of common storage and warehousing facilities that could be used to best advantage by the various STOs; the creation of a common inspection agency for verifying standard specifications and weights of products supplied to the developing countries, whereas the present inspection arrangements are made with private companies; and the establishment of a shipping coordination group, since freight constitutes a sizeable part of foreign exchange outlays, though, by pooling shipments of cargos, more reasonable freight rates could be obtained.

Joint enterprises are another possible form of multi-national administration. They are more elaborate and make possible a close association of the developing countries in defining and implementing a common economic and commercial policy. As an UNCTAD secretariat study has pointed out, the multinational enterprise solution implies the combination of three factors: the capital of the enterprise must entirely or at least in the majority belong to the developing countries; decision-making power must be effectively exercised by the nationals of those countries; and the objectives should be within a cooperation framework fixed by the member states. Multinational joint agencies of the kind might be set up or developed particularly in the fields of the marketing and production of the major commodities. The fact that several states control the domestic marketing of commodities which they consider important to their economies will facilitate matters. Another suitable field is that of transport, in which some progress has been made toward a multinational organization of the system of maritime transport of the developing countries.

Conditions as to Personnel

The establishment of the new common or joint structures implies efforts to train personnel in order to prepare them to perform their tasks. It is generally established that all the countries considered "face, in varying degrees, a scarcity of personnel skilled in purchasing techniques and procedures."(2) This statement concerning the countries in English-speaking Africa is similar, for instance, to that concerning the STOs in the Asian developing countries: "the need for continuous training and exposure of managerial personnel to difficult business situations is still pressing."(3) Some institutions are, however, offering training in this field. Some STOs have their own schools. Among them, the National Import and Export Corporation Ltd., Zambia, has, since 1976, in its school at Ndola, offered two-year courses in distribution and management techniques for its staff and that of its subsidiary companies. It would, however, be useful to place greater emphasis, in the long-established training institutions whose teaching is oriented toward management methods, on the importance of business management and the problems of international economic and trade relations.

It has even been suggested by the trade enterprises and organizations of the Latin American countries that an international trade school for public enterprises should be established to centralize international technical assistance and coordinate national teaching efforts in those fields.(4) It may, however, be asked whether strengthening the existing institutions and reorganizing their programs would not be preferable to founding new institutions.

The existence of permanent institutions does not, of course, preclude the organization of short – two to four weeks – seminars or sessions which should deal with very specialized subjects and be intended for limited audiences of senior executives from trade organizations and enterprises. Anything which can help toward the training of multinational administrative personnel in trade and production is an essential condition for the promotion of the regional administrative structures necessary for the implementation of the NIEO.

NOTES

1. PO/B/691, February 10, 1978.
2. TD/B/C.7/18 para. 97.
3. Ibid., 7/17, para. 60.
4. Ibid., 7/16, para. 41.

6 UN Decision-Making Structures and the Implementation of the NIEO
Robert Gregg

ESTABLISHING A NEW INTERNATIONAL ECONOMIC ORDER: THE INSTITUTIONAL CONTEXT

It is no secret that the campaign for a New International Economic Order is stalled. The Declaration and Programme of Action on the Establishment of a New International Economic Order were adopted at the Sixth Special Session of the United Nations General Assembly in 1974. Although no one anticipated instant and comprehensive implementation of this large and complex agenda, 1974 is no longer only yesterday; the hopes and expectations which were generated by the launching of NIEO have clearly met with disappointment. The sense of disappointment is unusually strong because the NIEO agenda is nothing less than the Third World's social and economic manifesto(1) and has been the subject of attention virtually without parallel in the UN's history. The high priority accorded to NIEO is succinctly summarized in a recent and authoritative volume:

> The NIEO is undoubtedly the most intensely debated item before the international community. Judging by the number of major international policy statements, declarations, resolutions, conferences, studies, reports, and the activities of various United Nations agencies, programs and organs, it is the number one issue for negotiation and resolution by the world's policymakers. It is outranked in urgency only by actual crisis situations, and it is only challenged for top position on the international agenda by disarmament. Yet even disarmament - as a host of other issues (most of which appear unrelated at first sight), such as transfer of technology, energy, food

103

production, ocean and space use, etc. - now come under the general umbrella of the NIEO in their actual treatment and negotiation.(2)

In spite of all this effort and attentive sense of urgency, the NIEO has lost its momentum. Dragoslav Avramovic, former Director of the Brandt Commission Secretariat, speaks for most informed and concerned observers when he states flatly that the "years of negotiations since the UN Special Session can be considered a failure. . . ."(3) The United Nations system is still seized with the issue, and in 1980 another special session of the UN General Assembly has been held primarily on NIEO. But, already, obituaries are being prepared in some quarters for NIEO and for the strategies which now characterize the Third World's approach to the North-South dialogue.

Explanations for the failure of NIEO are not hard to find. The one most frequently cited is the lack of political will, especially on the part of the developed countries, although this "explanation" is so superficial and simplistic as to be worthless for purposes of serious analysis.(4) Moreover, the economic malaise among the Western market-economy countries makes concessions of the magnitude envisaged by NIEO politically impossible. In any event, there is almost certainly blame enough to go around. One dimension of the problem, however, has received too little attention: the multilateral institutional framework within which NIEO is to be transformed, through a process of dialogue and negotiation, from a Third World manifesto into a working system of international economic relationships. It has been submitted that the United Nations, which has been cast in the role of midwife for the creation of the new order, is in fact one of the obstacles impeding the arrival of that new order.

It would be disingenuous to suggest that the UN is primarily to blame for the present impasse. No one who has been close to NIEO debate is arguing that the structures and processes of multilateral diplomacy are decisive for the creation of a new order. But the view is widely held that an efficacious United Nations system is a necessary, if clearly not a sufficient, condition for the realization of NIEO, and that the UN has been found wanting. The importance for NIEO of institutional factors is voiced repeatedly by UN officials and by diplomats accredited to UN organizations from both developing and developed countries.(5) The continuing quest for an appropriate forum (or forums) for the negotiation of NIEO is evidence of this widely held view that institutions do matter. Further evidence is to be found in the attention which has been devoted to restructuring of the economic and social sectors of the United Nations in order that the UN might better facilitate progress toward a new order.

This institutional dimension of the new order has two related but analytically separable aspects: 1) those elements which are explicit in the NIEO agenda or may readily be inferred from it, and which would presumably characterize the new order; and 2) those which are instrumental for establishing the new order. In the first category, the NIEO agenda, as elaborated in the Declaration and Programme of Action and certain other documents,(6) identifies several institutional objectives and implies several others. These objectives make the unmistakable point that the new order will require new or revised multilateral institutions, possessing in some cases new grants of authority, functioning in ways which afford a greater voice to developing countries, and operating to implement and to monitor the substantive economic reforms which constitute the new order. Sidney Weintraub has correctly observed that "the central issue in the NIEO relates to the processes of international decision making."(7)

The most frequently cited example of an institutional objective stated in the NIEO agenda is increased participation by developing countries in IMF and World Bank decision-making.(8) Other objectives may be inferred from the agenda. For example, a prominent NIEO objective has been an Integrated Program for Commodities, including a Common Fund for the Financing of commodity stocks and a variety of "other measures." The legislative history of efforts to negotiate a Common Fund reveals that this objective includes establishment of a new international council or board with responsibility for managing the commodity stocks.(9) Prospectively the first international financial institution of global proportions controlled by the developing countries, this controversial new body would be an important element of the multilateral machinery for implementing a new order. Similarly, the NIEO objective of providing equitable access to the resources of the seabed has come to include establishment of an International Seabed Authority to oversee deep seabed mining and an Enterprise to conduct the Authority's own mining operations.(10)

It is clear that the new order would have important new institutional features which would differentiate it from the existing order. These institutional objectives of NIEO are in themselves controversial to varying degrees. Because of the opposition they generate, especially within the governments of some of the more powerful developed countries, they may have contributed to the failure thus far of the NIEO program.

It is the second or instrumental aspect of NIEO's institutional dimension, however, that primarily concerns us here. Not only are institutional issues important in the new order; they are also important to the creation of that new order. The institutional context within which NIEO is planned and negotiated will presumably affect the content of a new order, the manner and speed of its coming into being, and the legitimacy it enjoys. Surely, a new international economic order devised essentially within the United Nations framework would be a rather different phenomenon than, let us say, one designed and implemented primarily within the IMF/World Bank context. The differences would be attributable in considerable part to dissimilar institutional histories, functions, and structures; to the fact that the memberships and predominant actors are not identical; to divergent decision-making procedures; and to dissimilar organizational ideologies. Each institution has its own essence; each vests and weights different interests and perspectives; each has different capabilities.(11)

Given the fact that NIEO is a Third World manifesto and that the United Nations, of all multilateral institutions, is most congenial to Third World purposes, it was logical and even inevitable that the UN would provide the institutional framework for efforts to bring about a new order. But the inevitability of a paramount role for the United Nations does not mean that a new order will be the outcome. A very important question remains: How are the negotiation and implementation of NIEO affected by the institutional framework provided by the UN? Phrased another way, what are the demands which NIEO makes upon the UN and, given the particular attributes of that organization, what is its capacity to accommodate those demands?

NIEO: Challenge to UN Capabilities

The nature of NIEO virtually guarantees tension between the task which the United Nations has undertaken and its capacity to perform that task. It constitutes a formidable challenge to the United Nations which is no less real because the UN appears to be the inevitable setting for efforts to create NIEO (and also the preferred setting for doing so as far as the overwhelming majority of governments is concerned).

Those characteristics of NIEO which pose a challenge to the United Nations and its capabilities are neither subtle nor latent. They are very obvious, even to the casual observer. To begin with, the Declaration and Programme of Action for Establishment of a New International Economic Order are not everyday, garden-variety UN resolutions. They are considerably more ambitious even than such landmark resolutions as the Declaration on the Granting of Independence to Colonial Countries and Peoples and the resolution which launched the first United Nations Development Decade.(12) To build a New International Economic Order is, indeed, a dramatic undertaking, requiring a forum which is capable of generating and sustaining a sense of the dramatic.(13)

Moreover, NIEO is sweeping in its scope, embracing objectives in the fields of trade, finance, industrialization, development assistance and debt, technology transfer, sovereignty over resources, and many more. There is nothing sectoral or selective about the NIEO; it is broadly comprehensive. It requires a forum comparably broad in its mandate.

NIEO is, as the name implies and as any short list of its major objectives makes abundantly clear, an economic agenda; it raises and proposes to deal with many complex issues which are essentially economic in nature and presumably require detailed and expert analysis and sophisticated bargaining. Therefore, NIEO requires a forum in which economic and technical competence are present in abundance among both secretariat personnel and government representatives.

Although the economic objectives of NIEO are many, they pertain primarily to the external environment or international economic framework within which development is to take place, rather than to support given by the international community to the social and sectoral aspects of national development efforts via technical and financial assistance. This distinction, to which UNCTAD Secretary General Gamani Corea has given the labels "hardware" and "software" respectively, directs the UN's attention to the systemic and, in the process, focuses responsibility for failures of development in the Third World squarely on the creators and principal beneficiaries of the existing order, the developed market-economy countries.(14) This emphasis reinforces the requirement for a forum with strong economic capabilities, but it also underscores the normative character of the North-South debate.

Whatever the economic objectives of NIEO, it is a conspicuously political program, which means that the forum needs to be a political forum where political influence can be brought to bear.

NIEO emphasizes the political concepts of rights and duties, spelled out most fully in the Charter of Economic Rights and Duties of States.(15) NIEO asserts the economic sovereignty of states; its thrust is insistently egalitarian. The rules governing important areas of international economic relations and resource transfers are at issue, as is control of the processes whereby those rules are made and implemented. As Sidney Weintraub observes, "The NIEO deals with the classic kind of conflict between those who seek more - more growth, more power - and those wishing to preserve their special interests."(16) There are, indeed, many who would argue that NIEO should more appropriately be termed the New International Political Order, or at least the New International Economic and Political Order.

Finally, NIEO is not self-actualizing; nor can it be brought into being simply by nation-states complying with UN resolutions. Most resolutions and declarations of the UN are,

in effect, appeals to governments to do something or not to do
something. The UN exhorts and then watches critically while
states do or do not respond.(17) In the case of NIEO, although
unilateral or bilateral actions by states would contribute to
its implementation in some areas, what is required is follow-up
action by international institutions in international institutions. NIEO is a call for continuous, wide-ranging, multilateral diplomacy and negotiation. What is required is a forum
which not only demands and monitors results, but is capable of
producing results through its capacity to function effectively
in the negotiating as well as the deliberative mode.

The UN's task is thus shaped by the sheer magnitude and
audacity of the NIEO concept, by the fact that NIEO embraces
such a wide range of substantive issues, by the economic
complexity of so many of those issues and their interrelationships, by the conscious emphasis upon the global framework
for development, by the political character of the agenda, and
by the necessity of delicate and extended negotiations. This
is the challenge which the United Nations has set for itself,
or, more precisely, the challenge which the member states have
set for the United Nations.

THE INEVITABILITY OF UN RESPONSIBILITY FOR NIEO

The responsibility of the United Nations for the implementation
of NIEO would seem to follow logically and inevitably from
certain historical and institutional facts of life. The UN
gave birth to NIEO; it seems natural that it should nurture its
growth as well.

Although NIEO had its origins outside of the United
Nations in the 1973 summit meeting of the Non-Aligned Countries
in Algiers, the brief history of the NIEO has unfolded largely
within the UN framework.(18) It was the UN General Assembly,
meeting in special session, which promulgated the Declaration
and Programme of Action. If the Sixth Special Session represented the challenge by the developing countries to the
existing order, the Seventh Special Session was the occasion
for the developed market-economy countries (and especially the
United States) to pick up that challenge and join the dialogue
in a seemingly constructive way.(19) Whatever the balance
sheet on UNCTAD IV in Nairobi in 1976, this pivotal UN body did
produce a consensus decision to initiate negotiations on what
many believed to be the most important single objective on the
NIEO agenda, the Integrated Programme for Commodities and
creation of a Common Fund. Within the framework of the United
Nations, the nearly unalloyed confrontation of 1974 was
replaced by limited and tentative steps toward accommodation.

It was in this spirit, part confrontational and part
accommodationist, that the locus of efforts to implement NIEO
shifted away from the UN to the 18-month long Conference on
International Economic Cooperation in Paris. Had CIEC succeeded in one or more critical areas, arguments that the UN
must have primary responsibility for bringing about a new order
would have been less insistent. But the failure of CIEC, which
has been attributed in part to the fact that it took place
outside of the UN framework, has only intensified the con-
viction that the UN must not be by-passed. There are, of
course, many reasons for the lack of success in Paris; institutional factors are only a part of the explanation.(20)
Nonetheless, the UN's central role has been asserted even more
vigorously in the post-CIEC period, and UN resolutions now
routinely reaffirm "that all negotiations of a global nature
relating to the establishment of the New International Economic
Order should take place within the framework of the United
Nations system."(21) The history of efforts to implement the
NIEO agenda seems to support the paramountcy of the United
Nations for negotiating the new order.

Institutional logic seems to point in the same direction.
The NIEO agenda is sweeping in its scope; the UN's mandate,
while diffuse and in some respects residual, is comparably
broad. While other multilateral institutions have mandates and
expertise which make them relevant for particular components of
the NIEO, none outside of the UN has been charged by constitution and by the cumulative demands of member governments with
responsibility for development generally and for what might be
termed the equity issue in international economic relations.

The breadth of the UN's mandate is reflected in the
organizational structures which have evolved to discharge that
mandate. The Economic and Social Council was to have been the
keystone of the UN system for international economic cooperation in its broadest terms, but ECOSOC gradually acquired a
reputation among developing countries as a rich man's club and,
eventually, lost so much prestige that Gunnar Myrdal could
observe that it had "sunk to a level of unimportance which must
appear almost scandalous in view of (the) declared purposes" of
the Charter.(22) The failure of ECOSOC probably has more of a
bearing on the capacity of the UN to play a major role in
establishing a new order than is presently acknowledged. But,
for most proponents of UN paramountcy, it is irrelevant. The
UN, under prodding by its developing country majority, has been
resourceful and resilient, filling the void created by ECOSOC's
default with the United Nations Conference on Trade and Development (and, to a lesser degree, the United Nations Industrial
Development Organization).

Moreover, the UN General Assembly itself has acted to
strengthen its already substantial role in economic matters
and, more particularly, in the implementation of NIEO, most

recently with the establishment of the Committee of the Whole to act as the focal point for a number of NIEO-related tasks and with the decision to launch global negotiations leading to a new order at the 1980 special session of the Assembly.(23) At the same time, UNCTAD has been actively seeking a broader role both within the UN itself and with respect to other institutions such as the IMF.(24)   While the issue of which UN body has responsibility for which aspects of NIEO may remain open and contentious, there is no question but that, in both Geneva and New York, UN institutions are trying to position themselves for the task of implementing the broad and ambitious NIEO agenda.

Almost invariably, the principal argument advanced in justification of the UN's central role in the implementation of NIEO is its universal membership plus its egalitarian decision-making procedures.(25)   It must be remembered that the developing countries have been participating in an international order which most of their number entered late, whose rules they had no part in drafting, and in which they find themselves at a decided disadvantage.   Not surprisingly, the overwhelming majority of governments want the active participation of all states in deliberations and negotiations about the next international economic order, which will profoundly affect all states.   They do not want NIEO to be created by only some states (including an emerging group of elite states within the developing world).

Full participation by all sovereign states in the establishment of NIEO is thus defended as both just and economically and politically necessary, and the UN is the logical forum for such participation.   The General Assembly and the UNCTAD Conference include all UN members, while the Committee of the Whole and the UNCTAD Trade and Development Board are open-ended in membership.(26)   In effect, the key UN bodies have global membership or the nearest approximation to it among multilateral institutions (contrast the IMF and World Bank, which are most representative of the old order, or CIEC, which had a much more limited membership of 27).(27)

Moreover, a form of direct democracy prevails within the New York and Geneva wings of the United Nations.   The full membership is continuously and directly engaged in the North-South dialogue, and the one-state, one-vote principle is employed in reaching decisions (at least formally; in practice, voting frequently yields to decision by consensus).   The leading role of the UN in efforts to establish a new order is obviously a function of its egalitarian/majoritarian voting system, which anticipates the new order and is believed to facilitate its implementation.(28)   The case for the United Nations is vigorously argued by Bedjaoui, who states that "The Third World possesses for the first time in these institutions [the United Nations, ILO, UNCTAD, and UNESCO] a 'right to the creation of law' thanks to the strength of its numbers."(29)

Three other attributes of the United Nations contribute to its status as the "inevitable" institutional framework for implementation of NIEO. In the first place, the UN, pre-eminently among multilateral institutions, is political. Of course, all intergovernmental organizations are political, no matter how technically or functionally specific their agenda, but some are more political than others. The UN has always been more political in the sense that several of the special-ized agencies, such as the World Health Organization (WHO), have long and disparagingly claimed it to be. Today, con-fronted by the need to convert economically and politically ambitious objectives into a New International Economic Order, the great majority of governments seem to welcome the political leverage which they see in the UN, and especially in the General Assembly. That leverage ostensibly results from the fact that issues of high politics are on the agenda, compelling high level attention by governments and making it more likely that officials close to the seats of power will be engaged in formulating national policies toward issues on the UN's agenda and representing their governments in UN forums.

Also working in favor of the United Nations, at least in the conventional wisdom, is the fact that the group system is most highly developed there. Although the group system functions somewhat differently in New York and in Geneva, its dominant feature in both places is the negotiation of a unified position on developing country demands within the Group of 77, followed by reaction to that position on the part of the Western industrialized states (Group B), by confrontation between groups, and finally by negotiation of a consensus by those groups.(30) Were there no group system, it would have to be invented in order to provide the North-South dialogue with elements of structure and discipline, facilitating both ag-gregation of interests and the negotiation of differences.

The group system is reinforced by the presence within the UN, in the UNCTAD secretariat, of a staff which gives the developing countries a technical capacity considerably greater than would otherwise be the case. This arrangement by no means gives the Group of 77 parity with the developed countries in the quality of its economic staff work, but it has become an accepted if still controversial corollary of the group system, and helps to make the UN the locus for efforts to establish NIEO.

The United Nations thus possesses the broad mandate necessitated by the scope of NIEO: intergovernmental bodies with comparably broad terms of reference, universal membership, and egalitarian/majoritarian decision-making modes which are consistent with the ethos of the new order; political as opposed to technical representation and orientation, and hence relatively greater political leverage for a politically freighted agenda; and a group system, together with a secre-

tariat for the developing countries, which presumably are more
conducive to progress in the realization of a new order than
less structured and less symmetrical bargaining. These
factors, taken together, argue for the paramount role which it
was widely assumed the UN would play, and which it is, in fact,
now playing, in the creation of a new order.

IMPROVING THE UN'S CAPACITY TO ESTABLISH THE NEW ORDER

Unfortunately, the United Nations is as much impediment to, as
facilitator of, the establishment of NIEO. Implementation is
lagging, if not moribund, and, while the problem is much
broader than the UN and its decision-making structures, processes, and capabilities, the UN is an important part of the
problem. To understand the problem, it is necessary to recall
the characteristics of NIEO and the demands which they place
upon the United Nations. The NIEO agenda was characterized as
dramatic in scale and comprehensive in scope; economically
complex, with emphasis on the external environment for development; and highly political. Perhaps most importantly,
extensive multilateral negotiations are required to translate
the NIEO objectives into a functioning new order. Some of
these characteristics are consistent with the UN's central role
in implementation. No other institutional framework in being
or realistically conceivable is better suited for the task of
dealing with an agenda which is so dramatic, comprehensive, and
political in nature.

On the other hand, the UN appears less well-suited for the
implementation of an agenda which is so economically complex
and which must be so painstakingly negotiated in an atmosphere
conducive to positive sum outcomes. Its traditional role has
been characterized as "resolution therapy," in which the
majority passes resolutions which the minority frequently
ignores.(31) The UN, and especially the General Assembly, is
accustomed to exhorting member governments to comply with its
resolutions; that is usually the extent of its role in implementation. But NIEO, as we have noted, contains numerous
interrelated economic objectives which cannot be realized by
mere exhortation, or for which UN responsibility stops with the
adoption, however overwhelmingly, of resolutions making demands
upon the developed countries. Those objectives almost invariably lack necessary specificity; the details which will
make them workable and bring them to life can only be filled in
through bargaining which, even in the right forum, would be
difficult and time-consuming. In the UN, it is probably
impossible.

Thus we have, in some respects, a good "fit" between the
NIEO and the United Nations, while in others the UN is mani-

festly poorly constituted to serve as institutional framework
for implementing the new order. Awareness of the UN's deficiencies as a vehicle for implementation of NIEO has led to
efforts to improve the UN's capacity for discharging this role.
Developing countries have, as might be expected, taken the lead
in mapping strategy for reforming or upgrading UN capabilities.
In some instances, the impetus for NIEO-related reforms of the
UN has also come from international officials. Not surprisingly, these efforts have been controversial; they do not
proceed from a broad consensus as to the nature of the institutional problem, but rather from an impulse, not shared by
all of the key actors in the system, to force the issue of UN
authority.

By common consent of virtually all interested parties, one
of the UN's most egregious deficiencies where NIEO is concerned
is lack of experience as a negotiating forum; UN authority for
negotiating about NIEO is suspect, and the structures and
processes which served so well to raise consciousness and
promulgate the Declaration and Programme of Action are poorly
adapted to the task of negotiating. The corrective efforts
which have been undertaken within the UN cannot, of course,
remedy the problem except incrementally. They could have
addressed the issue of structure and process, seeking ways to
adjust institutional forms and practices to the requirements of
negotiating a new order, but that has not been the primary
focus of reform. Instead, the Group of 77 and key officials in
the UN secretariat have stressed the issue of UN authority. As
a result, the debate over the appropriateness of the UN forum
for the next stage in the creation of a new order has not
addressed the question of whether the UN - be it the General
Assembly or UNCTAD - can negotiate a new order, but whether it
should.

Both the UN General Assembly and UNCTAD have sought to
bring (or keep) the NIEO agenda more fully under UN control,
although the two forums have been competitors more than they
have been collaborators. Inevitably, a thrust of this kind,
whether concentrated in Geneva or in New York or in both
places, has the effect of challenging other institutions and
potentially of reducing institutional options for debating and
negotiating issues raised on the NIEO agenda. The issue is the
degree to which further consideration of the new order should
be centralized. The United States, as well as other governments in the developed world, has preferred a decentralized,
nonhierarchical system of multilateral institutions, i.e., a
"soft center," and resisted efforts to concentrate deliberations and negotiations regarding the structure of the international economic order in the UN. The same governments
have also had reservations about the right or capacity of the
UN to oversee the work of other international organizations.
The developing countries generally wanted (and continue to

want) a "hard center," with negotiating authority vested
primarily in the UN and with the UN alone among multilateral
institutions in a position to legitimate measures pertaining to
a new order, wherever else they might be negotiated.(32)

The problem of negotiating capacity arises on two different levels: negotiation of specific objectives on the NIEO
agenda; and more general negotiations about implementation
strategy, priorities, trade-offs, institutional roles, and
monitoring of progress. It is the latter or more general
negotiations, ironically, which pose the most serious difficulties for the UN at this time. This is not to say that
negotiations regarding specific objectives will not be highly
divisive, the more so if the Group of 77 insists that they be
conducted within the UN, as has been the case with negotiations
regarding a Common Fund. Although strengthening of the UN's
negotiating capacity would presumably affect both levels of
negotiations, the most conspicuous reform efforts have attended
the creation of the Committee of the Whole, which has a general
rather than a specific mandate, and the convening of a special
session of the General Assembly to undertake global negotiations.

The Committee of the Whole was established by General
Assembly Resolution 32/174 in December 1977, another indication
of lack of confidence in ECOSOC and of a growing New York-based
challenge to UNCTAD's leading role regarding NIEO. Meeting
between regular sessions of the Assembly until 1980, the
Committee ultimately became merely a PrepCom for the upcoming
special session on economic issues. But a majority of UN
members wanted a stronger Committee, one which would, in
effect, have served as the successor organization to CIEC. The
rationale for the Committee of the Whole was expressed by the
Jamaican Minister of Foreign Affairs, who argues that there is
a clear need

> to have in the international institutional framework,
> a central body which would have the right to bring
> together the various elements involved, in order to
> move towards the creation of a just and equitable
> international system through the establishment of the
> New International Economic Order.(33)

The Committee's early existence was dominated by debate over
its mandate and especially over language which would give it
the capacity to negotiate action-oriented resolutions. The
very name, Committee of the Whole, is a telling commentary on
the disagreement over mandate and on the problems inherent in
efforts to strengthen the UN's negotiating authority. Ultimately the issue of the mandate of the Committee of the Whole
was mooted by the agreement to launch global negotiations
within the General Assembly itself. But the debate has not

ended; it continued throughout the preparations for the special session, during the special session, and beyond, as the parties quarrel over the nature and scope of the UN's negotiating authority.

UNCTAD, which opposed the Committee of the Whole and is the natural rival of the General Assembly for the central role in negotiation of NIEO, has sought to improve its own negotiating credentials. In part, this effort has been similar to that of the Assembly, an exercise in asserting its authority and making claims for an even larger role. But in the case of UNCTAD, greater attention has been given to the difficulties which attend the metamorphosis from an essentially deliberative forum to one with negotiating responsibilities. UNCTAD has tried to adjust its methods of work, and while the resulting changes have not been dramatic, progress has been achieved. Whereas the earlier Conferences were huge, protracted exercises in global stock-taking, UNCTAD has gradually achieved considerably greater selectivity in its agenda and has modified its "conference machinery" so that it can look at texts rather than merely hear speakers.

Nairobi (UNCTAD IV) brought a noticeable shift from the deliberating to the negotiating mode. Typically, three or four signs were up, rather than 150, in this "negotiating" conference, reflecting the discipline of the group system. Subsequent negotiations on a Common Fund have witnessed refinement of negotiating techniques. But sober analysis of UNCTAD IV and V and of the Common Fund negotiations reveals just how difficult the transistion has been, and how much remains to be done, before UNCTAD can sustain serious bargaining in an atmosphere of mutual confidence.(34)

One important "reform" in United Nations decision making has been the increasing substitution of consensus for the imposition of the majority's views in forums where the developing countries have the votes but the developed countries have the resources, and neither has an inclination nor an obligation to accede to the wishes of the majority. This practice, now well established in both Geneva and New York, has unquestionably eased some of the confrontational aspects of the North-South dialogue; consensus is clearly an improvement over the majority steamroller. It also makes negotiation essential, if only over language which will sustain the dialogue. Unfortunately, it also invites blandness and artificiality, and contributes to avoidance of some of the hard issues. Moreover, as Bedjaoui has reminded us, the technique of consensus is easily corrupted, and now seems to be losing its value in a tidal wave of reservations, both openly stated and tacit.(35)

One explanation for the difficulty which has been experienced in strengthening the UN's negotiating capacity is that, simultaneously, there has been a tenacious insistence upon the egalitarian and majoritarian attributes of the organization and a vigorous resistance to proposals which would dilute or compromise those qualities. Decision by consensus may be the prevailing practice, and small and informal groups of influential and interested delagates may do a lot of the hard negotiating in UN forums; but all efforts to formalize the use of limited member negotiating groups or to require suspension of voting while conciliation procedures are invoked have met with strong and successful opposition.(36)   Only recently, the UN sharply rejected a recommendation by a prestigious Group of Experts that consultative procedures employing small negotiating groups be established.(37)

Whatever the effectiveness of the measures taken (or, in some cases, of the postures assumed), there has been considerable attention devoted to the troublesome issue of the UN's negotiating authority and capacity. Somewhat less attention has been focused on the problem of the UN's economic and technical competence, which is marginal in Geneva and manifestly inadequate in New York. The UNCTAD Secretariat is generally regarded as superior to New York's, but its capacity for the quality of economic research and analysis necessary to give NIEO credibility is strained by the necessity for providing support services for the negotiations taking place under UNCTAD's aegis. The rationale for the General Assembly's involvement in the implementation of NIEO has never included the argument that either missions or secretariat officials in New York possess special competence in economic matters.

Against this unpromising background, the UN has been engaged in an effort to restructure its economic and social sectors. Restructuring, of course, is one of the objectives of NIEO, but prospectively more important is its instrumental value for the NIEO agenda. More of a concrete nature has been accomplished here than in any other area of UN reform, but the results are still limited and inconclusive. Most of the changes have occurred within the secretariat in New York. The potentially very important post of Director General for Development has been created, and the Department of International Economic and Social Affairs has been pruned and reshaped in ways which have encouraged UN observers from developed and developing countries alike.(38)

However, little has happened at the intergovernmental level within the UN or at the interagency level within the system. The proposed restructuring of ECOSOC has lagged,(39) and the conflict between the New York and Geneva arms of the UN has, if anything, been exacerbated rather than ameliorated by the campaign to strengthen the capacity of the UN in New York.(40) Moreover, restructuring has been regarded by many developed countries, including the United States, as a campaign to improve the effectiveness and efficiency of the UN for the conduct of its more limited role in the existing international order, rather than as part of a larger strategy for realizing a

new order. In spite of the limited results to date, however,
restructuring is at least an attempt to narrow the gap between
what the UN is undertaking to do in the economic sector and its
capacity to do it.

For the most part, however, the efforts which have been
made to turn the United Nations into a more effective vehicle
for implementation of NIEO have stressed those attributes of
the organization which anticipate the new order, rather than
those which would instill confidence among governments which
remain skeptical about the new order.

THE UN AS AN OBSTACLE TO NIEO

The United Nations is ideally suited, but virtue of membership,
voting sytem, scope of mandate, and tradition, to serve as the
forum within which the aspirant nation-states press their
demands. It is tailor-made for confrontation; and insofar as
confrontation is necessary to command attention and to demonstrate the breadth and depth of dissatisfaction with the
existing order, the UN is a vitally important institution or
set of institutions. But if NIEO is to be more than a manifesto, the dialogue must move beyond confrontation. If this is
not possible within the UN framework, the responsibility for
implementing NIEO must be transferred to institutions where the
modus operandi is more conducive to bargaining that will
produce a synthesis of position and, hence, movement toward a
new order.

Confrontation in its starkest form has, of course, eased
since the Sixth Special Session (although there have been
echoes of it on occasion, such as the early debates over the
mandate of the Committee of the Whole). While the atmosphere
may be less acrimonious, however, the dialogue and what passes
for negotiation is still, in the main, confrontational, at
least in the sense that the parties still tend to be locked
into positions and expect that others will make all the concessions. The bargaining that does take place is likely to
concern the language of texts, while joint analysis of difficult substantive issues is deferred. Confrontation in this
sense is inevitable and even a necessary element in negotiation. But it is not sufficient for the creation of the new
order, and it is especially regrettable when it results not
only from deep-seated differences among states and groups, but
from institutional characteristics of the UN itself.

This situation invites the question of whether the task of
implementing NIEO is divisible – whether the United Nations can
provide the requisite framework for some purposes, while other
multilateral institutions now in existence (adapted from
existing institutions, or newly created) can perform tasks

essential to the implementation of NIEO which are beyond the
capacity of the UN. However, the relationship of the UN to
NIEO has acquired a symbolic importance which makes it difficult to ask this question, much less to answer it affir-
matively. The dominating fact of UN-NIEO symbiosis has tended
to divert attention from, and even to obscure, important
aspects of the implementation problem. As the protracted
conflict over the mandate of the Committee of the Whole and the
launching of global negotiations reveals, the central institutional issue has been the UN and its role in establishing
NIEO, rather than the need to find or create multilateral
mechanisms and procedures which will facilitate tangible
progress toward a new order. The difference is an important
one, with important consequences for NIEO.

It is essential that the problematic character of the UN
as a vehicle for implementing NIEO be faced. If NIEO is to be
more than the manifesto, many things must happen; at the level
of multilateral institutions, one of three things must happen.
In ascending order of probability, they are as follows.

1.   The developed countries must acquiesce in the conversion of the UN into a world development authority, making
concessions demanded of them by the developing states majority.
In this scenario, international decision making would be rev-
olutionized and the resulting international order would indeed
be dramatically new. But there is no evidence whatsoever that
the developed states are going to follow this course and
abandon their vested interests and transfer control over
resource distribution to the aspirant nations in any such
sweeping manner.

2.   Confrontation in the UN must give way to negotiation,
i.e., to bargaining which demonstrates a willingness on all
sides to exchange rights and obligations, to give as well as
take. This means that the UN must be converted from a forum
which is dominated by aspirants and designed to amplify their
demands into one which facilitates synthesis of the opposing
positions of developed and developing countries. As we have
noted, some modest and rather superficial efforts have been
made to transform the UN into a negotiating forum, but those
efforts run against the grain of UN experience and capabilities. The well-established division of labor among multilateral institutions casts the UN in another role, and while it
is barely possible that the system may undergo a transformation
which enables it to serve as a forum for serious North-South
bargaining, that scenario is implausible.

3.   Confrontation in the UN must be accompanied by negotiation between developed and developing countries on various
NIEO issues, if and when they are ripe for negotiation and
developed countries can be persuaded to make concessions, but
primarily in other forums, not the United Nations, and least of
all in New York. The assumption here is that a synthesis may

be possible, at least in some areas of the NIEO, but only if
the negotiations which are required to achieve it go forward in
institutions in which the vested-interest states have greater
leverage than they do in the UN and in which the capacity to
deal with an economically complex and demanding agenda is
substantially greater. In this scenario, the UN's unsuit-
ability as a negotiating forum is acknowledged, and the task of
converting NIEO from manifesto to functioning reality is, in
large measure, reassigned elsewhere.

In practice, the processes of change in the international
economic system go forward in just such a decentralized
fashion, with the UN playing a marginal or indirect role in
many cases. The governments of developing countries support
this process, of course, and their representatives in such
institutions as the GATT, the IMF, and the World Bank participate actively in it.(41) Thus, governments which are
adamant about UN paramountcy in negotiating a new order are
simultaneously engaged in trying to extract concessions from
the developed countries elsewhere (and frequently succeeding),
as might be expected in a pluralistic system. This pragmatic
approach to international economic problem-solving will
certainly continue; but, just as certainly, the Group of 77
will continue to insist that the UN not be by-passed. They
will be particularly insistent that the main, overview negotiations on the NIEO be concentrated in the UN.

Because the first scenario outlined above is patently
unrealistic, and because the third risks emasculating NIEO by
shifting the dialogue to alternative forums which afford the
developed countries more scope for control of the negotiating
process, the Group of 77 promotes the second scenario. This
UN-centered strategy hopefully minimizes deviations from the
NIEO blueprint by confining negotiations to the UN where
aspirant states have the upper hand, and where the negotiating
process can be seasoned from time to time, as necessary, with a
little confrontation. The problem with this approach is that
the UN has to become an institution that it is not today.

We are confronted with a circular problem. NIEO creates
problems for the UN, making demands on it for which it is not
prepared. As a result, the UN poses problems for NIEO. If
NIEO must be established through the UN (the second of our
three scenarios), the UN's limitations and defects are imposed
upon NIEO, impeding progress toward its realization. Efforts
to remedy those defects and adapt the UN to the task of negotiating a new order (as opposed to demanding one) have not yet
produced the hoped for results and probably will not. The
problem is more fundamental.

Although the central issue appears to be the negotiating
role of the United Nations, there is a great deal of confusion
about just what "negotiation on the establishment of the New
International Economic Order" means. The term "negotiate" is

used losely by both those who want to strengthen the UN's hand
and those who reject such a strategy. One can regularly attend
public meetings of various UN bodies and conscientiously study
the documentary record of debates in those bodies without
acquiring a very precise notion of what "negotiation" really
entails. There can be no doubt, of course, that the United
Nations Conference on the Law of the Sea has been a negotiating
conference, and that UNCTAD is trying, albeit with mixed
success, to negotiate the establishment of a Common Fund.
Negotiation with respect to specific issues also goes forward
in numerous forums outside of the UN. But what is it that the
Committee of the Whole meant to do with a mandate to negotiate?
What do global negotiations, to be launched during the 1980
special session, entail? What is it that UNCTAD proposes that
it, rather than the Committee of the Whole or the General
Assembly, do?

Difficult as the negotiation of specific issues on the
NIEO agenda may be - and many are simply not amenable to
negotiated agreements now or in the near future - the more
immediately troublesome issue is negotiation in general, or
what might be termed catalytic negotiation. This is what CIEC
was trying to do, what its sponsors wanted the Committee of the
Whole to do, and what Secretary-General Corea has repeatedly
advocated that UNCTAD do. It involves negotiations about the
entire NIEO package. The scope of such negotiations was
suggested by the Jamaican spokesman for the Group of 77,
addressing the Committee fo the Whole in September of 1978,
when he argued that the Committee should have the responsibility "to negotiate in order to adopt the necessary political
decisions and conclude agreements on outstanding issues which
stand in the way of progress towards the establishment of the
New International Economic Order."(42)

Negotiation at this level is at once easier and more
difficult than the negotiation of specific issues, once they
have been factored out of the NIEO agenda and the parties have
agreed to negotiate. It is easier because such general
negotiations are still a stage removed from the detailed
bargaining which is required to create specific rules or
regimes for particular areas of international economic activity, such as a Common Fund for buffer stocks of commodities
or an effective code of conduct for transnational corporations.
But negotiation of this general or catalytic nature is also
more difficult than the negotiation of specific issues; the
latter presumes substantial agreement (in most cases) on the
need to act on at least some of the major guidelines for
action. Where the agenda is very broad and the commitment to
action vague and uneven, as has been the case with CIEC, the
Committee of the Whole and the global negotiations under
General Assembly auspices, the negotiating process is inevitably a very difficult one, with much of the participants'
energy invested in argument over what is to be negotiated.

In part, the problem lies in the package, in the need to negotiate about everything. NIEO is less an integrated program than a shopping list which lumps together demands of many different developing states. The result is a package which tends to be resistant to negotiation because the costs of compromise and concession are unevenly distributed and because the detailed discussions which serious bargaining entails risk exposing conflicts of interest within the Group of 77.(43) Everyone realizes that such conflicts of interest exist, but they have been muted and deferred by building an agenda which contains something for everyone and by maintaining group solidarity on behalf of that agenda as a whole. In these circumstances, even a decision to be selective, giving priority to some NIEO objectives while putting others on the shelf, is bound to be controversial within the ranks of the developing countries. The problems of obtaining agreement on trade-offs within the Group of 77 make intergroup bargaining very difficult. The negotiations on a Common Fund within UNCTAD are a good illustration of this problem, even though they fall within a relatively well-defined area of the NIEO agenda and follow an agreement in principle to establish such a Fund. The problem is also illustrated by the agenda of the global negotiations, which ostensibly involves some prioritizing. But the negotiations include major issues in the fields of raw materials, energy, trade, development, money and finance, i.e., virtually the entire NIEO agenda.

If negotiations at the general or catalytic level are to be meaningful and not merely variations on earlier statements of goals and calls for the exercise of political will, they must focus on such things as trade-offs, priorities, and issue linkage. What is required is negotiation about the parameters, content, and costs of further negotiations about NIEO.

In a recent essay, Robert Jordan and Thomas Wilson address themselves to this important "missing link" in the negotiating process. They advance the thesis that "the process of re-ordering the world economic system is proceeding along two related but nonetheless distinctive tracks, each with its own set of purposes, postures, and procedures."(44) They identify these tracks as the track of dialogue and the track of negotiation, and suggest that the failure of efforts to reorder the world economic system results in part from the fact that parties to the North-South dialogue frequently confuse the two tracks. Jordan and Wilson might have added that the confusion of the two tracks (functions) contributes to a confusion of institutional roles. Only if functions are well matched with institutions capable of supporting them will progress on the new order be achieved.

These two tracks or functions are really two elements of the negotiating process, as it is commonly understood. Negotiation, as used by Jordan and Wilson, is inherently confrontational, an exchange of claims and counterclaims; it is the "political process of trading concessions until a compromise is reached that can be accepted by all sides."(45) Dialogue is a necessary complement.

> Its agreed purpose, from the beginning, would be to search out shared or convergent interests and to find the way to consensus - about how to describe or define a problem in a way that is acceptable to all; about the identity of some major elements of a proposed solution; about next steps that need to be taken in the operational realm; about what needs technical examination by experts or what is ready for consideration at the political level by governmental authorities. This is the track of dialogue - or consultation, deliberation or joint analysis.(46)

This element has been conspicuously missing in so much of the North-South dialogue. It is what the global negotiations will have to supply if NIEO is to move forward. Bargaining is just as necessary to this "dialoguing" stage of the process as it is in the negotiation stage. Concessions must be traded and compromises reached as much in dialoguing as in negotiating. It may be that dialogue is more cooperative and less con-frontational than negotiation, but this is not always the case. In the UN, there is clearly a confusion of these tracks, much confrontation in both, and, as of the spring of 1979, five years after adoption of the Declaration and Programme of Action, very little substantive bargaining has taken place.

The problems of bargaining about the NIEO package in an egalitarian forum with some 150 member states are virtually insurmountable. At a minimum, the dialogue track requires a different kind of institutional setting, one freed from the constraints of high visibility, universal participation, group system rigidities, a UN-style voting system, and unrealistic timetables which force artificial consensus. Dialogue requires a setting in which the parties can dispense with stale rhetoric and proceed, through the kinds of exchange which are possible only in small, informal groups, to engage in serious joint analysis of issues. Virtually every international official and diplomat with whom the author has spoken has acknowledged the need to move important elements of the NIEO dialogue away from the universal, confrontational forums and into bodies more conducive to bargaining (although, not surprisingly, most of these same people also argue for UN paramountcy). The UN can surmount the problem of numbers if there is a will to move forward; but in the absence of such will, the size and nature of the UN constitute a massive impediment to true dialogue and to serious bargaining, and that will cannot be created in such a setting.

There is obviously no one institution for the role envisaged here, and it would be a mistake to try to create one. The task of implementing NIEO cannot be institutionally neat and tidy. But it is essential that the fixation with the United Nations and with negotiation en masse be overcome.

A useful place to begin the process of reevaluating the institutional framework for negotiating a new order is the late and largely unlamented CIEC. The Paris Conference needs to be reexamined, not with a view to reviving it but in order to determine whether there are lessons to be learned which might have applicability elsewhere in dialogue about the new order. As Jahangir Amuzegar has observed, CIEC's failure may be attributed to many factors: Widely different and quite excessive expectations, miscalculations of bargaining power, errors of strategy, inadequate staff support, poor timing, and even bad luck.(47) None of these explanations, nor any combination of them, constitutes a conclusive or even a persuasive case that a CIEC-like effort in the future is doomed to failure, especially in view of the deflation of expectations which has occurred regarding NIEO.

Amuzegar, in describing one of the reasons for CIEC's failure, makes a strong case for exactly the kind of serious joint analysis which Jordan and Wilson refer to as dialoguing.

> Not only did they [the CIEC negotiators] suspect each other's motives - which is normal in any bilateral negotiations - they lacked proper information about the limits of the other side's capability for making concessions, or altering demands. In direct labour management negotiations, the size of corporate profits, the strength and elasticity of consumer demand, the union's strike fund and other such pertinent information is usually known to both sides. The "overlapping zone" is thus extensive enough for bargaining maneuvers. In CIEC, the negotiators were largely in the dark regarding each other's possibilities and tolerances.(48)

A body such as the Committee of the Whole is almost certainly incapable of bridging this information gap. While CIEC did not bridge it in Paris, an institution more nearly like CIEC than the Committee of the Whole might do so, provided that the more debilitating defects of the CIEC were remedied. This would entail the improvement of secretariat support services, the modification of least common denominator decision making by consensus, and more attention to the legitimating linkages to the General Assembly.

CIEC is not the only model. Although the IMF/IBRD Development Committee is now in a state of decline and never did develop into a successor forum to CIEC, as some observers thought (and a few hoped) that it might, this interesting and little-noted 20-member institution was designed to play a catalytic role in the negotiating process which may be instructive for statesmen concerned with the future of NIEO. The Development Committee was intended to help focus the attention of finance ministers on development issues; its terms of reference call for it to maintain an overview of the development process, and to advise the Bank and the Fund on all aspects of the transfer of real resources to developing countries. It was intended to be an energizing institution, a vehicle for giving development issues more visibility within the Bank/Fund complex and for developing initiatives with respect to these issues by narrowing the differences among states to the point where agreed action is possible.

The Development Committee solved the representation problem more effectively than did CIEC. The Big Five have been directly represented, and other states have enjoyed representation in the same sense that they do through the Executive Directors of the Bank and Fund; thus the Committee members have had a legitimacy as elected representatives of constituencies which was only crudely and ineffectively approximated in the case of CIEC. The Committee has done its work in an atmosphere which is difficult but not threatening, which is devoid of incentives for political posturing, which scales down expectations to modest and realistic levels, which employs small working groups as a principal method of clarifying issues and readying them for action, and which favors direct, personal dialogue.(49) Unfortunately, the Development Committee has had a rather tenuous hold on life, even within the Bank and Fund, and it is doubtful if it could have played a major role in the North-South dialogue. Both its jurisdiction and the outlook of its participants would have kept it on the outer fringe of many North-South issues. However, it is an institution whose composition, terms of reference, and modus operandi, not to mention its successes and failures, should be of interest at a time when NIEO is much in need of forums capable of sustaining catalytic negotiations.

Both CIEC and the Development Committee functioned outside of the United Nations, and it may be that the dialogue function so necessary to progress toward a new order will take place primarily outside of the UN, if it is to take place at all. On the other hand, it is at least conceivable that an institution capable of undertaking elements of this task can emerge within the UN framework. UNESCO's experience is suggestive. An institution which is highly politicized and which might be presumed to share the UN's aversion to limitation upon the right of all to participate fully in the negotiating process, UNESCO, has, nonetheless, established a Drafting and Negotiating Group at each of its last two General Conferences. This so-called DNG, consisting of 25 members and working out of

the public eye, has been charged with facilitating negotiations, finalizing texts, and otherwise helping the General
Conference to come to closure on important issues on its
agenda.(50)

The DNG is even less balanced in membership between North
and South than CIEC and the Development Committee (only 5 of
the 25 have been from OECD countries), and its task is closely
tied to the calendar of the General Conference and to the need
to produce texts.(51) But this experiment is nonetheless
further evidence of recognition of the need for institutional
alternatives to universal participation.

The value of the United Nations in the implementation of
NIEO lies in its role as a confrontational forum where large
numbers of developing countries exercise their collective
bargaining power, mobilize countervailing pressure against the
vested-interest states, and apply leverage on behalf of
NIEO.(52) The developed Western states may not like this, but
for the most part they accept it, recognizing the division of
labor among international institutions which it implies.
Efforts to enlarge that role, giving the Committee of the Whole
(or, for that matter, the General Assembly itself) primary
responsibility for negotiating the new order, will not be
fruitful unless substantial modifications in UN practices are
introduced or a dialogue track is opened outside of the UN
which will enable the developed states to play a much larger
role in shaping and channeling NIEO measures. Substantial
modifications in UN practices are not likely, as we have noted
earlier, and in any event would not be desirable if they
weakened the utility of the United Nations as a confrontational
forum in which developing countries can press their case.

Insistence upon the UN's negotiating role, without
concurrent UN support for extramural dialogue in appropriate
forums which could make the negotiating process meaningful,
will simply render the organization increasingly irrelevant,
thereby depreciating its value for the developing countries.
The importance of what Ambassador Johan Kaufmann of the
Netherlands calls the "confidence factor" cannot be stressed
too much at this stage in the North-South dialogue.(53)
Concrete steps have to be taken to restore condifence in the
UN, especially among developed countries and notably in the
United States; concurrently, concrete steps have to be taken to
rescue the process of NIEO implementation from the UN.

Several developments need to be encouraged, all of them
with the objective of enhancing United Nations credibility and
promoting progress toward a New International Economic Order.
All will face resistance from one quarter or another, and none
can be achieved at one stroke. They are institutional goals
worth pursuing, however.

1. As Jahangir Amuzegar has observed, "the present
extensive configuration of the UN agencies, satellites, and
affiliates still lacks an effective mechanism for a 'planetary
bargain' at a high political level."(54) He recommends a
"relatively small but sufficiently representative standing
'council' of top officials from both the developed and developing countries who could engage in a truly global, politico-
economic dialogue."(55) That recommendation is warmly endorsed
here. If the proposed institution sounds like a variant of
CIEC or perhaps of the Development Committee, so it is. This
council - or whatever it is called - need not be the only locus
of dialogue or catalytic negotiation regarding NIEO, but that
would be its raison d'etre and it would be the focal point of
efforts to achieve the political compromises which are necessary for the realization of a new order. Presumably, the
General Assembly would be instrumental in the creation of this
council, and probably should be for the sake of its legitimacy.
But the council must not be bound too closely to the UN, or the
rationale for this kind of body will be compromised and its
advantages lost.

2. The UN, of course, will continue to be deeply involved
in the creation of a new order, even if a council for dialogue
is created. Confrontation over the NIEO agenda will persist,
and the UN will provide a forum for universal participation in
the exchange of claims and counterclaims which is a necessary
counterpoint to the small group dialogue. It is regrettable
that the UN forum for this purpose has shifted from UNCTAD to
the General Assembly and the Committee of the Whole. The New
York UN is a latecomer to this role; its ascendancy is not
attributable to any inherent advantages in the General Assembly, but rather is an inevitable consequence of the increasing
domination of the Assembly's agenda by economic issues (and the
restatement of the colonialism/imperialism issue in economic
terms).

The role of UNCTAD within the system is becoming increasingly problematic. The ascendancy of the General Assembly
is unlikely to be reversed, leaving UNCTAD with a substantially
reduced role unless it is merged with the GATT into a single
international organization for trade (not a near-term pro-
spect), or reshaped to assume the dialogue role which Jordan
and Wilson have described.(56) In spite of a tendency on the
part of Secretary-General Corea and his staff to overreach in
their desire to play the leading role in reordering the international economic system, UNCTAD possesses capabilities
which simply are not present in New York. It has been charged
that UNCTAD is too much dominated by technicians for the
political tasks associated with negotiating NIEO; that charge
will not hold water. It would be more accurate to say that the
UN in New York is insufficiently sophisticated in economic
matters to play the pivotal role to which it aspires. It is

true that the UNCTAD secretariat has been too closely iden-
tified with the Group of 77 for it to serve as broker between
North and South and for it to command the confidence of developed countries which is required if UNCTAD is to enjoy a new
lease on life in the UN context and perform effectively on
NIEO-related issues. But steps can and should be taken to
establish a secretariat for the developing states independent
of UNCTAD, as suggested by Miguel Wioncsek elsewhere in the
NIEO Library.(57)   Such a development could benefit the Group
of 77, encourage developed state confidence in UNCTAD, and
facilitate its transition into a forum which provides a
framework for catalytic negotiations and dialogue regarding a
number of NIEO issues. Whether UNCTAD can be reconstituted
along these lines is doubtful, but frustration about its
performance (among both developed and developing countries) and
uncertainty about its future suggest that the time may be right
to take a new look.

3. Further reforms are also needed at UN headquarters:
a) because they are intrinsically desirable and overdue,
b) because they may arrest the hemorrhaging of confidence in
the UN as a whole and thus indirectly benefit NIEO, and
c) because the UN will continue to be the setting for efforts
to implement NIEO if other institutions do not evolve as
suggested here. At a minimum, the General Assembly will be
expected to give its seal of approval to decisions and arrangements reached elsewhere in negotiations on the establishment of NIEO. It is the ultimate legitimating forum.

At the present time, however, the United Nations is in the
midst of a crisis which undermines its credibility as a
legitimating forum for the new order. It is a paradox that the
UN is being used to promote an unprecedented restructuring of
the international economic order while it is itself becoming
increasingly disordered, inefficient, and ineffectual. An air
of unreality pervades the "UN community" in New York; its
preoccupation with textual nuance repeatedly crowds out the
more important quest for tangible accomplishments. The work
habits of the UN and the performance of its bureaucrats simply
do not inspire confidence.(58) At a minimum, the lethargic
pace of restructuring must be accelerated and the problems of
unproductive and self-indulgent procedures and personnel should
be treated as if they were a real liability for NIEO, not
merely a minor and inevitable concomitant of multilateral
diplomacy. The General Assembly and the Economic and Social
Council are as much in need of reform as the Department of
International Economic and Social Affairs. While the occupant
of the new post of Director General for Development, Kenneth
Dadzie, commands respect in virtually all quarters, he has a
very general mandate and almost no staff, and must overcome the
suspicion that the high-water mark of restructuring may be the
creation of this top-level position for a Third World national.

If confidience in the UN is to be reestablished and if the organization is to play a significant role with respect to NIEO, the logic of restructuring must be pushed much harder and further.

There is an even larger restructuring agenda which has not been addressed by either the Group of Experts or the Ad Hoc Committee on Restructuring: the UN system as a whole. The phrase "UN system" connotes a coherent and cooperatively functioning set of institutions; the reality is a jumble of institutions and programs, created with little attention to their interrelationships, frequently feuding over jurisdiction and resources, each supported by constituent interests in capitals. The fact that the UN system is poorly integrated constitutes an obstacle to NIEO because it reduces the capacity of the system to make NIEO work and because it generates negative feedback in Western capitals, where support for NIEO is so essential if its objectives are to be realized.

Whether there is further progress toward a new order will depend on many factors, most of them beyond the reach of UN influence. But the UN has itself become an obstacle to realization of NIEO, and its role in that process must be reevaluated and a number of reforms instituted. Although many current elements of NIEO will surely be modified, postponed, or even abandoned, a new order may yet emerge with the help of a multilateral institutional framework which can sustain the dialectical process necessary for progress in this critical area.

NOTES

1. Remarks by Mr. Iqbal Akhund, Permanent Representative of Pakistan in the United Nations and former Chairman, Group of 77, in North-South Negotiations: Review and Prospects, Report and Proceedings of a Meeting organized by the Centre for Research on the New International Economic Order, Oxford, at Marlborough House, London, April 1, 1978.

2. Ervin Laszlo, Robert Baker, Elliot Eisenberg, Venkata Raman The Objectives of the New International Economic Order (New York Pergamon Press, 1978), pp. xv-xvi.

3. North-South Negotiations: Review and Prospects,   p. 16.

4. The author has not undertaken a content analysis of remarks made by delegates at various meetings of UNCTAD or other UN bodies, but can report from attendance at many such meetings that "political will" is invoked repeatedly, by one speaker after another, in many debates.

5. Research for a forthcoming volume by the author has included interviews with many secretariat officials at the UN,

UNCTAD, UNIDO, and several of the specialized agencies, as well
as with many persons accredited by their governments to those
organizations.

6. In addition to the Declaration and Programme of
Action on the Establishment of a New International Economic
Order, 3201 (S-VI) and 3202 (S-VI), May 1, 1974, the most
commonly cited sources of the NIEO agenda are the Charter of
Economic Rights and Duties of States, 3281 (XXIX), December 12,
1974; Development and International Economic Cooperation, 3362
(S-VII), September 16, 1975; International Development Strategy
for the Second United Nations Development Decade, 2626 (XXV),
October 24, 1970; and the Lima Declaration and Plan of Action
on Industrial Development and Cooperation, United Nations,
1975: PI/38, March 26, 1975.

7. Sidney Weintraub, "The Role of the United Nations in
Economic Negotiations," in The Changing United Nations, edited
by David A. Kay (New York: The Academy of Political Science,
1977), p. 96.

8. This objective appears in several of the basic NIEO
documents; a summary of its formulation and subsequent development through 1978 may be found in Laszlo, et al., The
Objectives of the New International Economic Order, pp. 110-12.

9. Ibid., pp. 45-65.

10. The literature on this subject is voluminous. See,
for example, the special issue of International Organization,
31 (Spring 1977); Richard G. Darman, "The Law of the Sea:
Rethinking U.S. Interests," Foreign Affairs 56 (January 1978):
373-95; and a host of other recent articles, most of which
focus on the seabed issue.

11. For development of this theme, see Robert W. Cox and
Harold K. Jacobson, The Anatomy of Influence (New Haven: Yale
University Press, 1973). The concept of organizational essence
is developed in Graham Allison and Peter Szanton, Remaking
Foreign Policy (New York: Basic Books, 1976), p. 21.

12. Declaration on the Granting of Independence to
Colonial Countries and Peoples, 1514 (XV), December 14, 1960;
United Nations Development Decade, 1710 (XVI), December 19,
1961.

13. There are, of course, critics who do not regard NIEO
as especially new or dramatic, but rather as a limited reform
which simply redistributes the benefits of the existing system
somewhat. A concise statement of this thesis is to be found in
Karl P. Sauvant, "The New International Economic Order: Toward
Structural Changes or a More Tolerable Status Quo?" in U.S.
Policy in International Institutions, edited by Seymour Maxwell
Finger and Joseph R. Harbert. (Boulder, Col.: Westview Press,
1978), pp. 125-46.

14. Secretary General Corea's views are most fully
outlined in The Role of UNCTAD in a New United Nations Structure for Global Economic Cooperation (Report by the Secretary

General of UNCTAD to the Trade and Development Board), UNCTAD
Doc. TD/B/573, July 30, 1975.
    15. See General Assembly Resolution 3281 (XXIX), December
12, 1974.
    16. Weintraub, "The Role of the United Nations in Eco-
nomic Negotiations," p. 96.
    17. Andrew Boyd terms this process, which has produced
over 3,500 resolutions in the General Assembly in 30-odd years,
"resolution therapy." Cited in ibid., p. 97.
    18. For a thorough treatment of the role of the Non-
Aligned Countries in the launching of NIEO, see Odette
Jankowitsch and Karl P. Sauvant, "The Origins of the New
International Economic Order: The Role of the Non-Aligned
Countries," in The New International Economic Order: Changing
Priorities on the International Agenda, edited by Karl P.
Sauvant (Oxford: Pergamon Press, forthcoming).
    19. For a detailed analysis of the Seventh Special
Session, see Branislav Gosovic and John Gerard Ruggie, "On the
Creation of a New International Economic Order: Issue Linkage
and the Seventh Special Session of the UN General Assembly,"
International Organization 30 (Spring 1976): 309-45.
    20. For an analysis of CIEC's failure, see Jahangir
Amuzegar, "Requiem for the North-South Conference," Foreign
Affairs 56 (October 1977): 136-59.
    21. Report of the Committee Established Under General As-
sembly Resolution 32/174, Volume I. General Assembly, Official
Records (33rd Session), Supplement No. 34 (A/33/34), October 4,
1978, p. 2.
    22. Quoted in Walter R. Sharp, The United Nations Eco-
nomic and Social Council (New York: Columbia University Press,
1979), p. 1.
    23. General Assembly Resolution 32/174, December 19,
1977, and General Assembly Resolution 34/138, December 14,
1979, respectively.
    24. See UNCTAD Doc. TD/B/AC.30/2, October 26, 1979, as
well as the reports of the Secretary General of UNCTAD to
UNCTAD IV and UNCTAD V (TD/194 and TD/245, respectively).
    25. This argument is presented most effectively by
Mohammed Bedjaoui, Algerian Ambassador to the United Nations,
in his recent book, Towards a New International Economic Order
(Paris: UNESCO, 1979), esp. Part two.
    26. A common explanation for the decline of ECOSOC is
that its limited membership made it increasingly unrepresen-
tative as the UN rapidly expanded in size; when the Charter was
amended to increase ECOSOC's membership to 27 in 1965 and to 54
in 1978, it was already too late.
    27. The principal difference in membership between the UN
on the one hand and the IMF and IBRD on the other hand is that
most of the states with communist governments are not members
of the international financial organizations. Although it is

not explored in this chapter, the absence of the communist states from the CIEC and their passivity and near nonparticipation in dialogue and negotiation of NIEO issues has troubled many observers. See essay by Miguel Wionczek elsewhere in this series of volumes.

28. The representative old order institutions either have weighted voting (IMF and World Bank) or reach decisions which do not require a collective vote (GATT, where reciprocal tariff reductions are, in effect, self-implementing).

29. Bedjaoui, Towards a New International Economic Order, p. 142.

30. There are actually four groups: Group of 77, Group B, Group D (the socialist states), and China, which has been a "group" by itself. But confrontation and negotiation is essentially between the Group of 77 and Group B. In New York, Goup B functions in a much less coherent fashion as a matter of choice on the part of the Western governments; as a result, the dynamics of the group system are somewhat different in New York than in UNCTAD, the "home" of the group system.

31. See note 17.

32. This campaign for a "hard center" is best revealed in the record of the Committee of the Whole.

33. U.N. Press Release GA/EC/21, September 8, 1978, p. 3.

34. The definitive study of UNCTAD as a forum for North-South negotiations is Robert L. Rothstein, Global Bargaining (Princeton, N.J.: Princeton University Press, 1979).

35. Bedjaoui, Towards a New International Economic Order, pp. 170-71.

36. It is interesting to note that UNCTAD has had such conciliation procedures (see General Assembly Resolution 1995 (XIX), December 30, 1964), but that they have never been invoked.

37. The recommendation is contained in A New United Nations Structure for Global Economic Cooperation, Report of the Group of Experts on the Structure of the United Nations System, UN Doc. E/AC.62/9, May 28, 1975, pp. 30-32. Contrast the position finally taken by the General Assembly in the restructuring resolution: General Assembly Resolution 32/197, January 9, 1978.

38. These reforms were reported by Secretary-General Waldheim in his first progress report on restructuring, UN Doc. E/1978/28, April 21, 1978.

39. Interest in amending the UN Charter to give all member states representation on the Economic and Social Council is once again rising. See draft resolution submitted during the 34th General Asembly, A/C.2/34/L.103, December 3, 1979.

40. For an analysis of UN action under General Assembly Resolution 32/197, see The Restructuring of the United Nations System: Implications for the Creation of a New International Economic Order, Draft Report of a UNITAR Seminar, Schloss Hernstein, Austria, July 12-15, 1978.

41. The use of other forums to achieve reforms of the existing order favorable to the developing countries is discussed in Weintraub, "The Role of the United Nations in Economic Negotiations."

42. UN Press Release GA/EC/21, Setpember 8, 1978, p. 3.

43. See Rothstein, Global Bargaining, for a detailed discussion of this problem.

44. Robert S. Jordan and Thomas W. Wilson, Jr., "North-South Relations and Conference Diplomacy: A Confusion of Postures," unpublished paper, p. 2.

45. Ibid., p. 3.

46. Ibid., p. 2.

47. Amuzegar, "Requiem for the North-South Conference," p. 142.

48. Ibid., pp. 152-53.

49. Robert W. Gregg, "The IMF/IBRD Development Commitee" unpublished paper, passim.

50. For a description of the mandate, composition, and working methods of the Drafting and Negotiating Group, see UNESCO Doc. 20 C/2, July 28, 1978.

51. Ibid., pp. 10-12.

52. Secretary General Corea of UNCTAD develops this thesis in a recent article. Gamani Corea, "UNCTAD and the New International Order," International Affairs 53 (April 1977): 184.

53. Johan Kaufmann, "Decision-Making for the New International Economic Order," in Partners in Tomorrow: Strategies for a New International Order, edited by Anthony J. Dolman and Jan Van Ettinger (New York: Sunrise Books, E.P. Dutton, 1978), p. 178.

54. Amuzegar, "Requiem for the North-South Conference," p. 158.

55. Ibid.

56. Secretary General Corea speaks eloquently of the need for continuous diplomacy and the staff to conduct it; but, for the most part, negotiations within UNCTAD have been tied to conferences or other meetings arranged long in advance and for predetermined periods of time. However, this problem is not unique to UNCTAD; in fact, it tends to characterize most multilateral institutions for quite obvious reasons.

57. Miguel Wionczek, "The NIEO: A Diagnosis of Failure and Prospects," in Structure of the World Economy and the New International Economic Order, edited by Ervin Laszlo and Joel Kurtzman (New York: Pergamon Press, 1980).

58. See comments on these internal problems of the UN in ibid.

7 The Impact of Research on Policymaking
Carlos Moneta

Future studies are designs of desirable or probable actions and events worked out by scientists in order to predict how mankind will most likely develop. World Order Studies focus their efforts on the formulation of future societies and on the speculation about how the world will evolve in accordance with man's present and future actions.

In spite of the fact that most current thinking on this subject openly acknowledges that the creation of a new world order will require at least a large scale restructuring of the present international system (which means a major political operation), relatively little attention has been given to several aspects of the political dimension of NIEO in the specialized literature. For example, there are few works analyzing the links between the theoretical schemes of NIEO (e.g., world models), the world's perceptions of the actors taking decisions about it, and the harsh and restraining conditions presented by the present international system.

The set of values, roles, and perceptions held by those who must rationally organize the societal and personal images of the world (the intellectuals and, in particular, the social scientists) and those who must make decisions about NIEO (the political decision makers) are very important, because they heavily contribute to the selection of courses of actions at the different levels of world politics. As an example, Sprout and other scholars have stated that "what matters in the process of policymaking is not the conditions and events as these actually are, but what the policymakers imagine them to be."[1]

The theorists carrying out these studies, the people whose actions and expectations they should take into account, and the decision makers that may adopt some of the proposals will be affected in their choices by a complex set of interrelated factors at the individual and societal levels. It is well known (but often ignored) that the conclusions reached in any study are strongly affected by the nature of the adopted initial assumption. Thus, it must be recognized from the beginning that, whatever they are, assumptions about the future – such as those related to NIEO – are political; any consideration of the future is based upon the views that mankind and each individual has of man as a decision maker.(2)

The study of possible or desired world orders is deeply imbued with values. The result will be that one set of the available present values will be imposed upon the future.(3) This imposition will cover a wide spectrum coloring the evaluation of the current situation, the setting of new goals, and plans to carry them out, as well as the negotiations and struggles in which men will be united for this purpose. Therefore, as Richard Falk has observed, "a world order outlook is based on the understanding that a key element for the build-up of an agreed desirable future is to know the place of values in the political process."(4)

Thus, the purpose of this chapter is to explore, from a political point of view, the effects on the management of world politics of the images and interactions related to world orders of two relevant actors – the theorist and the decision maker – on the different levels where they are acting (subnational, national, transnational, and international). From this understanding, we hope that it will be possible to advance some propositions with creative potential, thereby helping to reduce some of the existing obstacles to NIEO.

With this objective in mind, the first section analyzes the main features of the social sciences as a transnational subsystem of the world regime. The second part focuses on the role played by world order studies in the shaping of the external policies of the actors. The third part explores the interactions between intellectuals and decision makers within this context.

THE SOCIAL SCIENCES IN THE WORLD POLITICAL SYSTEM

Some Trends in the World Political System

The activities of the social sciences related to NIEO are carried out in a world system that is affected by significant changes in its regime and in its actors. Some of the trends that characterize the present regime are:

°   The emergence of transnational actors and transnational relations as an important modification of the previous state-centered system. This adds new nongovernmental actors gradually capable of generating (and successfully pursuing) a growing range of self-defined goals.

- The continuation of the confrontation between the "universalistic-nationalisms" of the USSR and the United States in their struggle for world dominance in a setting characterized by the presence of other major powers (Western Europe, Japan, China). It means the persistence of patterns of "dominant-dominated" and conflict-cooperation relationships with the national actors of the system. However, this has been somewhat modified by the rise of a limited but dynamic pluralism in the distribution of power in recent years.

- A certain degree of pluralism, based on new forms of power distribution related to the access to different privileged political, economic, technological, and military resources, enabling a more effective participation (varying in accordance with the issues and the sectors) of developing countries, and transnational and international actors in world politics.

- The type of development of most of the national actors has been determined to a great extent by: a) the predominant values and factual conditions imposed by the activity of an oligopolic, transnational, and techno-industrial capitalism;(5) and b) a techno-industrial authoritarian state-capitalism. Both economic models have deeply influenced the sociocultural and political subsystems of national societies.

- A rapid growth, on a global scale, of the problems related to ecological deterioration, raw material scarcity of the energy crisis, the arms race, etc. is due to the adopted economic, political, technological, and security models.

- The emergence of crucial disagreements - in most cases leading to serious confrontations - between the developed and developing countries with regard to the values, goals, policies, strategies, and means to be applied in the restructuring of the present order, which is considered unjust and exploitative by the latter.

- An increase of interactions among the units of the system, on a global scale characterized by a highly asymmetrical capacity favorable to developed countries and the TNCs to affect the behavior of the other actors.

As a result of these factors, a complete and thorough reevaluation of the role of the state, of life-styles, values, and in general the whole structure of the world system is in process, articulating in its contents different propositions for world order. In the construction of these models and proposals, social scientists play a major role, just as politicians do with regard to the decision-making process related to NIEO. Therefore, it is necessary to consider the

factors and interactions that affect the relevant behavior of
social scientists.

The Social Sciences as a Transnational-
International Community

A relationship between the theorist and the policymaker can be
established on different grounds. As members of social classes
in professional and national communities, they interact among
themselves and with the outside world. They are influenced in
their professional work and general behavior by a particular
set of beliefs, values, and attitudes, shaped by economic,
political, and cultural factors which act on the individual and
society as a whole. Accordingly, their function in society
will be: a) to provide the rationale to establish or maintain
the social hegemony of the dominant groups and guide the
governmental apparatus;(6) b) to articulate the rationale and
provide theoretical guidance to oppose the dominant groups.
    In addition to their values, other factors should be taken
into consideration such as the norms for pursuing these values,
the institutions through which people become organized for
action (e.g., associations),(7) their social bases, and the
specific circumstances that influence their image of the world
(e.g., membership in a basic social group or belonging to a
central or a peripheral country). All these factors are
capable of factually facilitating or impeding the pursuit of
particular values. Furthermore, the different perceptions
social scientists have of their respective roles and the set of
stereotypes that they share or by which they diverge from other
group structures (e.g., the university, a bureaucracy) must
also be taken into account.
    Depending on the type of their activities, social scien-
tists and policymakers have a high degree of exposure and
contact with the rest of the world. Both depend greatly on
outside specialized networks for information. Their word is
tested as to its credibility and applicability not only in the
national context but also on international and transnational
levels. They are linked either with a web of well-structured
sets of organizations at these levels, or, more loosely, with
what we may call the transnational-international community of
scientists.
    From the point of view of its political effects, the
scientific community plays a significant role in the framework
of the present world system, and it may be even more important
in the future. For example, transnational associations of
social and economic sciences acting directly or through their
members at the national or international level offer to politicians rationalizations, diagnoses, and proposals in critical
areas of national and world problems. Let us consider as a

first step, therefore, the interactions between social scientists within their own countries and their national communities with the transnational-international subsystem of the social sciences. Particular attention is to be given to the predominant patterns of relationships as well as to the influence of the ideological drive of the scientists on the content and orientation of their research.

The Existence of a Center-Periphery Dependence Relationship

A careful analysis of social scientists in all parts of the world shows that: 1) the patterns of asymmetry and dependence that characterized the international system are repeated in the social sciences. Centers of social sciences with vast human and material resources have been created in the United States and Europe, either as a result of state conscious political and ideological action or as a relatively more independent response to social tensions. These have become the leading focus in their field at the world level.(8)

Dependence relations emerge from and are reinforced by: a) Dominant theories and methodologies formulated in the industrialized countries according to their experience which become reference points for research and teaching influencing also the selection of themes of research and teaching; b) adequate disposition of funds which enable these centers to select and gather the best scientists not only from the developed world but also from the developing countries; and c) abundant opportunities for publishing and distributing research.

As an example, if we consider the size, growth, and composition of social science literature, we will find that the United States, Great Britain, France, and the Federal Republic of Germany together account for 66.9 percent of all literature published in the field. Meanwhile, the developing countries oscillate between 0.4 and 0.6 percent.(9) In terms of social science monographs published in 1980, the USSR had 18.3 percent of the world output; the United States, 13.1 percent; France, 4.9 percent; the Federal Republic of Germany, 13.1 percent; Great Britain, 5.7 percent; Japan, 6.7 percent; and the Third World countries between 0.7 and 1.4 percent.(10)

Conditions of Unequal Exchange

Unequal conditions of exchange, access, and participation should also be pointed out.(11) There is an unbalanced relationship between the high number of social scientists from industrialized nations studying the conditions of the developing world, and a relatively small number of researchers from

Asia, Africa, and Latin America who are analyzing the evolution
of developed countries. The Third World provides the "raw
material" - the sources of information. After being processed
abroad, the information is "reimported" in the form of sophisticated hypotheses.

    This disproportionate degree of participation is also true
of studies of world order. The participation of scientists
from socialist countries and from the Third World is very low
in studies conducted in the Universities of the most important
industrialized countries (the United States and West Germany).
Two models developed in these countries (The Limits to Growth
and Mankind at the Turning Point) show that only 28.5 percent
of the members of the team were from developing countries in
the former, and only 0.6 percent in the latter. There was no
participation from the socialist countries in either study.(12)
(It should be pointed out, nevertheless, that at that time and
for the cases in which it was required, collaboration of scientists from Eastern Europe was not easy to obtain. Since then
the situation has changed positively.)

    Contrasting with these figures, studies of world order
carried out in developed countries of minor potential and more
open attitudes toward the Third World, such as Sweden (the Dag
Hammarskjöld Report) and Holland (the RIO Project) increased
the participation of scientists from Africa, Latin America, and
Asia to 50 percent for the Hammarskjöld Report and 35 percent
in the RIO project. Eastern Europe is represented by 6.25
percent and 35 percent respectively.(13)

              Unequal Opportunities; Dependence and Autonomous
                      Thinking at the National Level

At the national level, those Third World social scientists who
have been trained in industrialized countries are, in principle, more likely to establish ideological ties with those
countries' theoretical models, interests, and images, although
these are not well-suited to the needs and predominant values
of their own countries.(14) It is a recognized fact that those
who participate in transnational activities continuously increase their opportunities for doing so. Furthermore, on
occasion, they have better chances of joining the government or
providing assistance to it compared with the rest of the
national social science community. Nevertheless, it should be
remarked that there are also cases in which the situation is
just the reverse. Social scientists trained abroad may be
aware of their acquired ideological and methodological charge
and use their knowledge to attempt to explain to their fellow
Third World people - as well as to the rest of the scientific
community - the possibilities available for the construction of
a more autonomous and adequate approach to the problems of

development and dependency. An example of this positive reaction is the "Latin American World Model" constructed by the Bariloche Foundation (Argentina). This mathematical model was formulated with political goals of egalitarianism, autonomy, and participatory democracy. It rejects consumption as an end in itself and promotes the use of resources for the social satisfaction of basic human needs instead of profit, stating total opposition to the features of dependence and exploitation that, in the view of these scientists, characterize the present international system. The emergence of this model on the arena of world order studies was a clear and positive alternative to the explicitly stated or hidden political content of conservative models and studies prepared in the industrialized world, such as The Limits to Growth. The Bariloche model very soon became the source of inspiration for several attempts at integrated planning at a national and regional level in developing countries. Staff members from the Bariloche team had adapted it to Brazil and other adaptations were made for Chile, Argentina, Egypt, and Venezuela. In Venezuela, possible applications are being studied by the Ministry of International Economic Affairs(15) for simulating the functioning of the international economic system, in order to test policies about NIEO to be supported by developing countries.

Ideology in Knowledge and in Action

Besides the problems of definition, what generally matters about ideology(16) and politics (which are deeply interconnected) is their role and relevance in the realms of knowledge. What is still being discussed is the degree to which ideology influences the content and orientation of knowledge; not enough serious consideration has been given to the function of ideology in politics. As González Casanova(17) and other outstanding social scientists have stated, all theoretical development is tied up from the beginning with ideology, even if the social scientist is not conscious of it. The influence of ideology extends to the themes selected for research, the variables chosen, the data collected, and, of course, to the interpretation of the facts.(18)

Faced with these problems, two opposite orientations have been adopted by social scientists: to attempt to ignore, deny, or "neutralize" the impact of the ideology (the latter through sophisticated but usually useless rationalizations proclaiming a "value-free" social science),(19) or to accept that ideology is a crucial and ever-present component of the system of political beliefs, and thus that it would be more fruitful to relate ideology to theory-building and to the whole social science field than to deny its existence.(20)

It is very important to point out that, in their search for a "depolitization" of the issues of NIEO to provide an "objective" or "pragmatic" ground that would ease the negotiations, scientists and statesmen alike tend to underestimate or misunderstand a crucial fact. They are not really opposing an "ideologically loaded" versus a "nonideologically loaded" set of policy proposals or positions, but two different cultural patterns: those derived from rationalism and empiricism.(21)

At the theoretical level, the presence of ideology helps to explain why some paradigms, approaches, and methodologies are chosen and others rejected. Present well-rooted and expanding examples of this situation in the Third World can be found particularly, but not exclusively, in Latin America and Africa. In both cases, the currently accepted scientific paradigms of developed societies have been rejected by a significant number of social scientists from these regions.(22) Thereafter, new paradigms are developed to explain the events in terms of the region's unique historical experience.(23)

In the Eastern European countries, the theoretical and axiological framework of what we call "official Marxism" (interpretation of Marxism that constitutes the doctrine legitimated by the state) is also under thorough revision in a new development carried out by the Marxist intellectuals of these countries.(24) Social scientists in developing countries are also separated from their colleagues in the developed world by structural differences in the sociopolitical and economic conditions of their respective countries.

In a broad and somewhat risky generalization, we may support the view that, for theorists of Western Europe, Japan, and the United States, it is easier than for their colleagues in the socialist countries and the Third World to be engaged in "pure" research on the subjects of their preference, without paying too much attention to the factors affecting their ways of thought, the possible usefulness of the knowledge they produce, or, to a lesser extent, the political turmoil around them. In developing countries the political and material requirements of development are highly pressing and urgent. Social scientists must produce research that can be rapidly converted into solutions to relevant problems.(25) Facing this challenge, social scientists are divided on how to deal with it. Some follow the forumulas originated in the industrialized countries, others adopt a more independent orientation. But for all, research and politics are constantly overlapping. The scholar in the social sciences, whether he likes it or not, is also heavily involved in politics. Therefore, his type and "quality" of work (judged by industrialized world standards), his attitudes and evolving ideology tend to differentiate his paradigms from those of his colleagues in the industrialized countries.

Therefore, the need for a careful consideration of the influence of ideology in the social sciences derives from its manifest and latent functions(26) in the social sciences as well as in politics. As Stavenhagen pointed out, "theoretical ideas at every level become political instruments."(27) Dominant paradigms already legitimized by the above mentioned factors are circulated. They help to enhance or to change, according to political goals, a given set of values, images, and theories, and to fulfill a function that is extremely useful for the decision makers in terms of either societal mobilization or control. Political consciousness may emerge, or a "false consciousness" may be enhanced.

Therefore, at the state level, the works of social scientists provide a quota of rationality for implementing one or another model of development, as well as help the political apparatus to obtain a certain "legitimacy." But they also may try, mostly unsuccessfully, to produce changes "from within."

An example that shows the importance of the paradigms is their use with regard to the problems of socioeconomic development. Most of the discussions about NIEO that relate to this theme have as their context an industrialist macro-economic conceptualization of "growth." The dominant paradigm presupposes "the validity of universally applicable and timeless standards of societal goal-achievement."(28) It does not take seriously into account the heterogeneity of religious, cultural, political, and philosophical values, reducing the whole world to the value system of one segment: the highly developed countries. A direct example of this thinking is the assumption that countries are required to reach certain levels of GNP in order to assure an adequate "quality of life."

The importance of paradigms lies in the fact that they pose the problem to be solved. The current one, which emphasizes "casuality, hierarchy, quantification, competitiveness and homogenization,"(29) stresses "economic rationality" and "empirical objectivity." It is inadequate to deal with present and future world problems. Chistakis summarized some of the limits of this paradigm as follows: a) lack of sensitivity to the emerging multifold cultural shift; b) emphasis on empirical level data in analysis, with not enough regard for the role of values and attitudes in decision making on people's behavior; c) overwhelming dominance of computers in macro-economic modeling, disregarding the ethical components of the data; d) nonplanetary, nonholistic analysis; and e) the tendency to apply technological solutions (due to the privileged value given to technology) to problems that require solutions which must be often fundamentally nontechnological. One more essential factor should be added to the above: the paradigm's high degree of compatibility with present structural patterns, favorable to the dominant actors in the world system.

What has been stated above does not mean that all social scientists act as conscious political activists or that politicians always take advantage of this situation. On many occasions scientists in developed and developing countries are not aware of the role they are playing in creating dependence relations, because "they lack self-consciousness about the social structure in their own scientific activities."(30) However, the manipulation of the results of research by social scientists for political purposes is a common occurrence. In view of these facts, within the scholastic circles of developing countries, contending ideologies create serious divisions, contributing to the fragmentation and polarization of the scientific community. This erodes the possibility of working toward a development based upon a sufficiently agreed paradigm which could represent the interests of developing societies as a whole.

To summarize, in the real world of politics, world order studies continue to reflect contesting sets of values and goals, hidden by paradigms that seem to offer the guarantees of scientific method. Therefore, it must be recognized that ideology exists, and affects the development of the social sciences and their output. The existing relativism in the social sciences, by which no one can claim to be in possession of the full "scientific truth," must be seriously taken into account and incorporated into the discussion of NIEO, as an element that supplies what is lacking in the current consideration of the issues.

It would be appropriate to have an "ideological confrontation and critique"(31) to understand the ideological elements of the theory related to NIEO, to see how and to what extent they affect the perceptions and proposals of social scientists and the inherent possibilities of the political use and misuse arising from them.

NATIONALISM, TRANSNATIONALISM, INTERNATIONALISM, AND THE SOCIAL SCIENCES

The prevalent trend is for social scientists to keep a national orientation. There are different reasons for this, but we would like to point out among them the commitment for social change and national development that permeates developing societies and the demands imposed by the state. Even where the development of social sciences is more regional in character, such as in Latin America, the national orientation maintains most of its force. Another example is Eastern Europe. In socialist countries, nationalism is a basic characteristic of the development of social science, given what are viewed as external menaces and the government's demand that social scientists support the task of national development.(32)

Nationalism can play an important role as either an obstacle or a creative force toward the establishment of NIEO. It is the growing perception of a sense of national self-identity and its link with nation-building that allows the social scientists of developing countries to find their own explanations for the sociopolitical and economic events of the world. They create their own centers of research, providing the politicians and themselves with a new rationale and a different set of demands, proposals, and strategies for action.

But nationalism is also the doctrinarian recipient of the so-called "national interest" - capable of sheltering a varied spectrum of misconceptions, narrow views, and the universal-ization of the interest of a dominant group as the expression of the whole societal unit. It is an agent for conflict or, at the least, a serious obstacle for the achievement of better and deeper cooperative action between the countries of the Third World. Definitions of national interest depend on the con-ception of the dominant groups that directly or indirectly control the state apparatus, and on what policies better serve goals that they consider vital for the survival, well-being, and power position of the nation-state.

For example, several governments of Western industrialized countries, as well as some influential intellectual associ-ations that express the interests of dominant groups, object to proposals of the Group of 77 about the management of an inter-nationally planned economy.(33) Underlying these objections is their apprehension that, if the proposals are carried out, it would mean the end of the free market system.(34) From an ideological point of view, the underground "scientific" sup-porting assumption is that the interplay of a free economic market (which in practice is, nevertheless, heavily controlled by private groups and a few states) is a pillar of economic and political development, promoting and sustaining the "democracy-freedom" package.(35) Reality seems to indicate otherwise: what is at stake is who will control what, and to what extent.

However, there is a third phenomenon that is relevant: the rapid growth and importance of transnational actors. Through them, a deep shift is taking place from national to trans-national identifications. Some social scientists in national organizations, as well as at the transnational and interna-tional levels, are gradually developing values and goals that differ from those formulated at the national level. The focus of identification, the style, and the spatial dimension of their work are progressively based on a global image and a world scale, linked in most cases with a vision that reflects the "modernization" of the values of the more developed seg-ments of their societies.

The transnational community includes not only the knowl-edge elites, especially in technology, but fundamentally the strata composed of the major owners of means of production, and the managers and professionals of the upper echelons of Third World governments and civil societies.(36) It includes, on more marginal and dependent positions, parts of the more developed segments of developing societies. This is the context in which the members of the transnational associations of social sciences interact with other privileged actors: the transnational corporations (usually through their research foundations), governments (serving in their bureaucracies and institutions of research), and international organizations (as advisers, technicians, etc.). The varied and often contradictory orientations that emerge from this complex - cooperative as well as conflicting - flow of interactions reaches the middle and lower levels of national societies through a web of various channels. Some of them are created by social scientists themselves.

What is relevant to emphasize is the fact that the growth of these nonterritorial actors implies that there is potential for the development of a different realm for the interplay of interests between the privileged and underprivileged segments of the world society. The transnational actors have their own articulation, sources of power, and rationale.(37) Some of them tend to reproduce patterns of domination in the international system; while others could offer new opportunities for the build-up of transnational intellectual networks in favor of the underdeveloped segments of national societies. National and regional chapters in the developing countries could be bases for this network. What is suggested here is the organization of a Third World Association of Scientists. This idea has been raised and discussed by members of other associations of Third World professionals, such as Ngo Manh Lan, a distinguished member of the Association of Third World Economists. The association would provide an adequate environment for the urgently needed articulation of efforts of research within the developing world with horizontal bases. It would increase the capacity of intellectuals in the pursuit of a just NIEO to deal more successfully with both their own national governments and other scientific associations linked with the developed countries as well with international agencies and institutions. In a system which grows and becomes more complex every day, a useful strategy is to develop mechanisms of cooperation adapted to the needs and possibilities of developing countries, capable of acting efficiently in the new transnational context. An association of developing world scientists is likely to be one of the tools to deal with new situations in the political context in which the social sciences are immersed.

With regard to the international scene, there are three basic models currently used to analyze the role of international organizations in world affairs: the "Imperialist" "Syndicalist" and "Corporate" models. In accordance with

Rittberger,(38) the first perceives international organizations as tools for the maintenance of dominant-dominated relationships between the central and peripheral countries. The
second presents the international units as a forum for the
syndicalist-type of representation of the interests of national
ruling elites. The corporate model points out that international organizations offer possibilities for concerted action
at different levels, with the object of pursuing collective
state interventions in international social processes.

     None of these models represents reality accurately, and
all deserve serious criticism. It seems that main elements of
all three are present in the everyday life of international
organizations, depending on the particular issue, institution,
or sector of activity in question. There are evidences of the
applicability of the imperialist and syndicalist models in the
treatment of, for example, nuclear policies and NIEO negotiations. However, the imperialist model assumes a direct,
dominant-dominated relationship between the national elites in
the developing countries and the ruling strata of the industrialized countries, without taking into account the basic
ambiguities (conflict-cooperation relationships) that exist
among them.(39)

     Assuming that there is an equal capacity for representing
the interests of developing countries in international organizations vis-à-vis the developed countries is a serious
weakness of the syndicalist model (except for a few cases, such
as OPEC). Precisely one of the major problems today is the
asymmetry in the distribution of power among these groups of
countries. Even at the negotiating table, huge differences
exist in capacities to carry out tasks with efficiency.
Developing countries lack qualified human resources and have
problems of logistics and infrastructure. The result is often
an insufficient and unqualified team in crucial negotiations.
This situation arises frequently when the negotiations are in
the main capitals of the developed countries. The representatives of developing countries are practically isolated from
their base of intellectual support, while the delegations of the
developed countries have a powerful network of universities,
centers of research, libraries, and scientific institutions at
their disposal.

     The developing countries themselves must be criticized for
this for several reasons, among them, the lack of political
will and the solvable problem of economic resources. These
states have not been able to organize pools of specialists
capable of providing advice and other services to the negotiating teams on the fields under discussion. Here is a
concrete area where Third World scientists could render a
service to their nations. Their colleagues, working under the
umbrella of international institutions, obviously have serious
limits on the degree to which they can commit themselves to

this task. 'But there is no intelligent use so far of the services of thousands of social scientists from Third World countries working in developed world universities and research centers, although in many cases they would be more than willing to cooperate informally.

The corporate model stresses the orientation of international organizations, such as the United Nations, to work toward compromise bargaining and problem-solving in conflictive issues at global or sectorial levels.(40) Nevertheless, international organizations suffer from serious limitations in their capacity to achieve these ends, given the "power politics" that constantly underlie the treatment of all significant issues. Scientists working in these organizations act within technocratic-bureaucratic structures, a context that is likely to influence their original views and positions, and make them search for the more homogeneous set of values of the "international civil servant."(41) A view of the world that shares an important part of the values of the transnational community still maintains national loyalties, however modified they are in their perception of what is in the "real interest" of their countries, adding merely elements of self-asserting, self-perpetuating, and expanding roles typical of techno-bureaucratic bodies. Taking into account their basic concern for the mediation of conflicting interests and their linkage with the other actors of the world system, international organizations can play a useful role in these matters, provided that there exists a clear understanding of their structural limits.

Therefore, nationalism, internationalism, and transnationalism are forces that cannot be denied, but must be consciously included in the scientific treatment of world affairs. These factors affect the perceptions, goals, and strategies of the social scientists and the decision makers. An important part of the task for social scientists and decision makers is to increase their understanding of these phenomena, and bring research and action to bear on them.

WORLD ORDER STUDIES AND THE EXTERNAL POLICIES
OF THE MAJOR ACTORS: AN APPRAISAL

To begin with, while limiting ourselves to a few selected elements in a complex process, there are some assumptions about decision making in foreign policy that must be pointed out. Policymaking is a deliberative and organizational process toward the achievement of specific desirable ends. It includes intellectual steps by which the decisions are reached based on obtainable information, perceptions of the situation, and formulas of "national interest." Conceptions of national

interests as well as psychological factors affect the behavior
of those who act as representatives of the state.

As has been previously stated, what matters most in the
process of policymaking is not the condition in which it
actually is, but how the decision makers imagine it to be.
Since it is difficult to assume without accurate confirmation
that top policymakers are adequately informed and advised about
the issues that they are working with, the characteristics of
the information inputs, situation appraisals, and policy
proposals that they receive are relevant, since they will
affect the resulting outcome. Examples of gross deliberate and
non-deliberate mistakes in the information policymaking process
are offered by the studies of international relations. Furthermore, this is often a case of incomplete information, which
by axiom is a given factor in decision-making theory. The
value system, as a factor that influences the type of information received, the perceptions of the situation held, and its
subsequent elaboration are elements to be taken into account
(e.g., geographic location, tradition factors of national
power) in the adoption of decisions related to foreign policy.
The same factors act upon the decision maker of other types of
units, such as international organizations, or transnational
actors (e.g., TNCs), the other elements being replaced by an
equivalent set of factors (è.g., purpose, privileged values,
functions, degree of autonomy of the organization vis-a-vis
other actors, sources of power).

Ideology and Planning in External Relations

It is necessary to comment at least briefly on the role played
by ideology in several dimensions: its effects on the mental
process of the decision maker and the objective use of ideological propaganda in external policies.

Within the value system of the decisionmaker,(42) his
philosophical stance becomes extremely important not only in
shaping his perceptions about what reality is but also in the
links between these perceptions, the desired state of affairs,
and the means to be applied toward this purpose. On this
issue, it has been stated that "ideology has unleashed human
drives far more powerful in their impact on societies . . .
than the force of nuclear energy."(43)

Thus, the analysis of the ideological dimension of international and transnational relations should be related to
the goals, strategies, and effects of the ideological interaction between the units of the system and the dynamics of its
interactions. One of the main focuses in the political arena
will be the role played by ideological confrontation in the
external policies of the units. For example, nation-states,
especially the central powers through the East-West issues,
have achieved a clear awareness of the importance of politics.

Foreign policymakers in the West have stated that "Today the diplomacy of public opinion is the emerging factor . . . ; its prime objective is to win mens' minds and loyalties."(44) Foreign policies include as a major element the psychological efforts directed at influencing the people of the world in accordance with the desired goals to be achieved. This is also true for international and transnational actors as well.

The Eastern socialist countries, especially the USSR, have consciously incorporated these elements into their theory of international relations, as well as into the operation of their foreign policies. For these countries, "at the center of international relations today are modern society's fundamental ideological problems. . . . Within the world's division into two systems not only every individual society and state but international relations became the arena of the clash between the two opposing class ideologies."(45)   In accordance with this view, the ideological struggle is an inevitable and necessary part of peaceful coexistence.(46)

Research about the future is widely accepted in the USSR as part of Soviet planning. The methods employed are quite similar to those used in the West, but they strongly stress that the use of sophisticated techniques cannot be a substitute for a deep and substantive understanding of the problems.(47) Soviet forecasting techniques - given its commitment to Marxist theory as an instrument for explanation and prediction - emphasize that, in the last analysis, the political goals of the system under consideration are what really count.(48) The development of social sciences (as well as other sciences) is under direct government control. It is concentrated in large research centers and academic establishments which must provide for the needs of the decision makers under the rule of administrative bodies.(49)

In the United States, the appraisals vary greatly with regard to the role played by ideology. The opinions split between those policy-oriented social scientists and policy-makers who stress the need to take into account all the dimensions of the ideological factor in the foreign policy of the United States(50) and those, such as Brzezinski, who still defend the "realistic view" in international relations.(51) Based on an image that is ideologically loaded, Brzezinski rejects the "ideologization" of foreign policy: "The USA has traditionally been the pragmatic society, free of ideological shackles and it will be unfortunate to succumb to it."(52) However, Brzezinski also has his own views on planning. It requires a staff deeply linked with the inner power circles yet simultaneously capable of drawing a coherent picture of the complex historical patterns that are observable, thereby providing meaning for the ongoing processes in the global system to obtain relevant goals based on a "non-dogmatic ideology."(53)

These comments have focused attention upon two sets of issues: the role of the ideological elements in the activity of planning, and the problems that arise from the attempt to plan in world politics. What has been emerging through the different and contradictory approaches to NIEO is the agreed upon need to establish certain planning capabilities for future global development. That means accepting the unavoidable task of including political planning as a central factor in the external policies of the actors involved, where this is not an already accepted and substantially developed practice. Huge differences exist in the attitudes toward planning among transnational companies and national and international actors. At the nation-state level, there are gross inequalities between resources, skills, and uses, as well as significant differences in the purposes of planning and the means to be applied. Distinct, specific goals are pursued by all the participants.

Planning is, in the end, a rational choice among different alternatives in order to get the best available solution for the fulfillment of an already agreed upon goal. The value elements include the criteria to select the "best" alternative as well as the fundamental perceptions of reality, goals, and permissible means. Values link the planning process to the belief system of scholars and decision makers. As we can see in tables 7.1 and 7.2, the theories of the scholars and the doctrines of the decision makers about NIEO present important similarities in terms of their basic perceptions of the world and their own political attitudes. Their final products (theories and policies) will be colored by the influence exerted by social settings, group membership, personal interests, and goals of satisfied or deprived human beings within the present state of affairs.

Differences arise between practitioners and scholars about the importance of theory and practice in the making of foreign policy. Practitioners are generally committed to handling it in a "pragmatic" way, preserving inherent policies, looking for similarities with the past, and avoiding the adoption of courses of action that have not already been proved.(54) In short, the Western political system basically encourages a short-term, problem-oriented approach to planning.(55)

The regimes of the Third World which are inserted in the center-periphery dependent relationships have been affected in their value assumptions and conceptualizations of foreign policies by the already commented upon liberal realistic tradition. Meanwhile, those who have adopted some sort of socialist models are somehow closer to the Eastern school of theory and practice. No clear solutions are available, however, and overlapping and mixed products are common, since cultural traditions are an important factor in modifying the basic patterns.

Table 7.1. Images of the World

	STATUS-QUO OR CONSERVATIVE	REFORM	TRANSFORMATIONIST
PRIVILEGED VALUES AND GOALS	1) Maintenance of "Cold War" era 2) Predominance of national interest and military security 3) Balance of power based on military predominance of bipolar competition able to accommodate and handle conflict and/or cooperation arising from limited multipolar interdependence. 4) Maintaining a "Power Politics" international system 5) Problems handled by statesmen and technocrats (decision making limited to a government machine with supporting elites) 6) National consciousness 7) Emphasis on "order" and "stability" 8) Maintenance of a "Laissez faire" economic system	1) Depending on the position taken by a particular study, basic liberal/radical values, or a combination of both. 2) "Pluralist" nonhegemonic distributive type of society. For some, a welfare-consumer model. In other studies, a satisfaction of "basic needs" scheme. Different degrees of state control of international markets. 3) Interdependence as a source of cooperation. 4) Progressive, gradual, orderly incorporation of people's visions, goals, and proposals to face shared world problems.	Mankind is able to shape the future in accordance with human preferences. Individual and world human consciousness will prevail with self-reliance and the creation of new models for society. Interdependence: a) a source of cooperation b) a source of dependence (on a North-South basis) 1) To reach a new system beyond "power politics" 2) Egalitarian, just, classless society 3) Planetary humanism 4) Self-development 5) Problems being solved by widespread active political participation of people at all levels 6) Replacing apathy with creative involvement
PARTICIPANT (PRIVILEGED) ACTORS	Nation-state; international organizations; transnational corporations. International system of the nation-state is the basic unit. Central states are the core of it. Presently, most territorial actors play marginal roles.	The Nation-state; international, transnational, and subnational actors maintain the nation-state as the core, incorporating other types of actors into the system with different degrees of participation.	Nation-state, international transnational, and subnational actors. Rapid weakening and transfer of national loyalties to transnational units.
SOURCES, SITUATIONS, DISTRIBUTION OF POWER	Persistence of the superpowers' hegemony. Military force is fundamental source of power. Entente or detente (according to particular study) is menaced by USSR attempts to undermine Western "unity and strength" to obtain strategic gains over the USA. Pluralism as a menace to USA security. Permanence of "Power Politics."	There is diminishing superpower hegemony (given the existing restraints on the use of military force). Actors within the system rely on various power sources (economic, etc.), in accordance with the issues, resulting in the diffusion of power. Detente is seen as basis for eliminating the use of military force, thereby aiding the formation of a pluralist, more diffuse distribution of power in a model that includes qualitative change in the sources and uses of power. (Shift to economic power.) Shift from "power politics" to "bureau-techno-economic politics."	According to the studies selected, there is multipolar or bipolar distribution of military force. Superpowers, the USA, or both (depending on the particular study) hegemony is eroded by a) the militant action of liberation movements; b) the common effort of developing nations through organizing joint activities as well as adopted policies in various fields. However, the present situation is one of 1) dependency or 2) imperialist exploitation (depending on the particular study) polarizing nations on a "North-South" confrontation basis. Shift from "power politics" to a "world order" politics.

(continued)

Table 7.1. Continued

	STATUS-QUO OR CONSERVATIVE	REFORM	TRANSFORMATIONIST
APPLIED STRATEGY	Persistence of East-West confrontation and maintenance of the predominance of military power, thus establishing limitations on the ability of the system to incorporate change or transformation. Therefore, it should be applied policy based on "bipolarity" and "limited interdependency" (O'Leary). Manipulation and controlled adjustments toward gradual evolution managed by the DCs. A strategy of "delinking" with the South, on "N-N" bases could be applied if a high degree of Third World unrest emerges.	Reduce the use of military power. Increase the level and scope of world interdependency through economic and technological net works. Growth and gradual strengthening of economic interdependence as alternative sources of power and easing of conflict. Redistribution of economic gains. Agreed regulation of world markets; diverse negotiated preferences and advantages for the LDCs in the commercial, financial, and technological fields.	Generation of political consciousness and self-awareness. To strengthen the world's institutional framework. Sociological evolution of mankind. Gradual or radical (depending on the particular study) reduction of the domination of central and superpowers. Functionalism, cooperation, development of new social units of transnational or subnational character, strategy to be applied: different versions of "N-S delinking" and collective S-S self-reliance. Abolition of high-control of the market system.
METHODS OF IMPLEMENTATION	Political; military; economic and technological power.	Economic exchanges and technology based on a more egalitarian system, including redistribution of wealth within and among developed and underdeveloped nations welfare policies.	Volunteerism, increased political activity. Self-development. Use of force (according to some studies).
ROLE STATE	Central, based on revitalization of the state as a military, technological, economic power.	Acceptance of certain decline. New actors of subnational, transnational, and international levels, limiting and gradually eroding the power of the state, this shifting the functions from the state to other actors. However, the state will adapt to the new environment.	Major erosion of the state by subnational and transnational actors. State adapting to individual requirements with the gradual emergence of a "global order."

Source: The organization of this table is based on multiple sources.   Major articles and books include: James C. O'Leary, "Envisioning Interdependence: Perspective on Future World Orders," ORBIS (Fall, 1978); Richard Falk, "Contending Approaches to World Order," Journal of International Affairs (Fall/Winter, 1977); Robert Keohane and Joseph Nye, Power and Interdependence, World Politics in Transition (Boston: Little, Brown, 1977); Silviu Brucan, "The Nation-State: Will It Keep Order or Wither Away?," International Social Science Journal (UNESCO), 30 (1) (1978). The models used as raw data are included in Table 7.2, based on C. Moneta, "Los modelos de simulación."

Table 7.2. Global Models and Studies Political Orientations

Project		Research: Actors localization and links				Composition of the research group			Focus of the study			Positions facing the system		
Model	Study	Sub-nat.	Na-tional	Trans-national	Inter-national	In-divid-ual	homo-gene-ous (a)	hete-roge-neous (b)	World Syst.	Sub-Syst.	Sec-tors	Main-tain-ing	Reform	Change
1. The Limits to Growth (Meadows and Associates)				X			X		X		X	X		
2. "Mankind at the Turning Point" (Mesarovic-Pestal and associates)				X			X		X	X	X	X		
3. "World Dynamics" (Forrester and Associates)				X			X		X		X	X		
4.	"Restructuration of the international order" (RIO) (Tinbergen and Associates)			X				X	X	X	X			X Moderate and middle reforms
5.	Dag Hammarskjöld Report about development and international cooperation	X (origin)	X		X		X	X	X	X	X			X Advanced Reforms
6. "Latin American World Model" (Herrera and Associates)		X (origin)		X (links)			X		X	X	X			X
7. "A new vision of development in function of the global restrictions" (Kaya and Associates)		X	X	X			X		X	X	X	X		
8. "The future of the World Economy" (Leontief and Associates)					X (origin)		X		X	X	X	X		
9.	The future of society: A critique of Modern bourgeois Philosophical and sociopolitical conceptions (Modrzhlaskaya)	X					X		X	X				X
10.	"Mankind and the year 2000" (Koso apov)	X				X			X		X			X

(continued)

Table 7.2. Continued

	Positions Facing the Structures		Does it include the treatment of the political problems?	POLITICAL OBJECTIVES	
	With change	Without change		1st	2nd
1		Changes which do not vitally affect the present distribution of the values (power, wealth, etc.)	No	Stability (Stationary equilibrium)	Development (certain development thanks to the technological change)
2	Institutional, Economic and Social Reforms (to diminish the developed-subdeveloped gap)		No (it recognizes that they exist; states changes in the role of the nation-state)	Balanced development (organic growth)	Stability
3		Maintenance of the present structure. Diminishing the growth of the developed fixing of actual patterns for the Third World.	Criticizes the inefficiency of the political decisions in the system	Stability	Limits to growth
4	Proposals with different degrees of change in all the power structures (wealth, etc.) of the world system.		it recognizes its existence but provides a very limited consideration to them. It does not explore the essentials (e.g. disarmament)	Equitable development	Stability
5	Proposals with different degrees of change, but rather advanced, to modify the power structures (wealth, etc.) of the world system.		yes	Self-sufficient development for the Third World "Own development" Styles.	Autonomy and equality for the Third World (Global system of selective relations)
6	Transformation of the world society: Shift from the consumption society toward a society where the production is done in accordance with the social needs.		yes (it considers the socio-political problems as a core)	Socialism (end of the historic exploitation of the underdeveloped countries)	Development starting from the satisfaction of the basic needs
7	Change in the patterns of industrialization trend and tending to improve the Third World situation maintaining the present system.		No (it recognizes that they exist)	Development (Diminishing the unequalities)	Stability
8	Proposals of change in the sociopolitical, economic, and institutional structures of the Third World.		No (but recognizes them as a core)	Development (accelerated growth)	Stability
9			yes (they are the core)	Socialist revolution (Transnational period between capitalism and socialism at world level)	Development
10			yes (they are the core)	Socialist Revolution (peaceful transformation toward socialism)	Development

(continued)

Table 7.2. Continued

Means and Factors	Appraisal of the Political position			Privileged values
	Conservative	Reformist	Radical	
1 Psychological Genetical (Control of Population) Economic (Control of industrial growth) Technological Ecological (Conservation of natural resources; decontamination)	X			Conflict: socioeconomic system-ecological system Equilibrium of the global system authoritarianism in the imposition of limits to the use and distribution of resources and the human freedom. Intellectual technology.
2 Economic and technical development based on regional goals. Regional interdependency. World industrial redistribution. Genetics Ecological Psychological		X (Moderate Reform)		Globalism; controled pluralism; evolution; global planning; organic growth. Harmonic relations man-nature.
3 Genetic Ecological Economic (Diminishing of growth oriented toward the achievement of better life standards). Technological Psychological	X			Intellectual technology as a new political power. Stability of the system. Authoritarian location of scarce values. Socioeconomic and political stratification. Elitism.
4 Ecological Economic Technological Psychological (Changes in behavior patterns and expectations) Political Genetical		X (Moderate Reform)		Negotiated reform of the system. Equitable development; orderly change; correction of inequalities; pluralism; world planning; democratization.
5 Economic Technological Political Psychological (Change in behavior patterns and expectations)		(Moderate Reform)		Self-support; satisfaction of the basic needs; abolition of unequal relations develop-subdevelopment; world economic planning; reject economies of trade; collective autonomy for the Third World.
6 Psychological Political and economic (drastic changes in the world society) Abolition of the consumption society Technological Ecological			X	Socialism; international society; solidarity and equality; satisfaction of basic needs; regional autarchy. National independence.
7 Economic and Technological (Important changes in the inter-national distribution of labor. Reforms in the global division of industrial production) Ecological		X (Moderate Reform)		National interest (of the developed actor). Diminishing of the socioeconomic inequalities. Interdependency.
8 Political (Changes in the political social and institutional structures of the developing countries) Economic (Important changes in the international economic order) Technological		X (Moderate Reform)		Growth; Diminishing of the inequalities between the developed and underdeveloped countries.
9 Political (Abolition of capitalism; socialist stage) Economic-Technological (Socialist economic system and technological revolution) Ecological Psychological			X	Socialist economic system and Technological and Scientific Revolution period of transition toward socialism. Fall of capitalism; world progress (Maximum happiness for the maximum number of people).
10 Political Economic and Technological Ecological Psychological			X	Technological and Scientific Revolution; Freedom.

Most of the developing countries lack enough human and economic resources and scientific and political traditions of autonomous thinking as well as institutional structures to be able to deal seriously with studies of the future in their foreign policies. This is not a minor obstacle, but a real pressure exacerbated by everyday problems, which inexorably postpone any attempt to think ahead.

This gap has far-reaching consequences for policymaking related to NIEO. At the national or regional level, the governmental apparatus hopefully would be able to rely for advice on their own experts. A "critical mass" of scholars may be obtained. The picture is different, however, when the delegates from Third World countries have to negotiate in the international organizations and forums. In many cases, they lack urgent and badly needed advice from experts who are located in remote places. On many occasions, their delegations are not adequately prepared to face the scientifically and technologically well provided teams of experts from the developed countries.(56)

Nations with sufficient resources and well-trained social scientists (e.g., India, Mexico, Brazil, Argentina) or those gifted with economic wealth, capable of creating a pool of resources and staff of trained personnel (such as the OPEC countries) are able to take part admirably on national, international, and intraregional levels. Yet, there still remains a very difficult barrier: those obstacles linked to the kind of goals pursued by the different political regimes in power and with the lack of understanding of and correspondence between the scientific and the governmental apparatus.

Scholars and Decision Makers Interactions

Since the nation-state still maintains itself as the primary focus of interaction among the different actors of the world system, scholars emphasize the relationships between decision makers on the national level.

To obtain their goals, nation-states have at their disposal a wide spectrum of instruments of statecraft. Among them are governmental and nongovernmental agencies which can provide assistance to the decision maker in terms of information and advice, as well as perform important tasks in the international system for the fulfillment of the state's goals.(57)

Foreign services usually have units for planning and research. Furthermore, the state apparatus is supported in its tasks by the services of specialized nongovernmental research institutions. As a result, direct and indirect links are established between decision makers and scholars. Each group has biases about the other that mutually reinforces their respective stereotypes. The scholars have, in general, em-

phasized the unreliability of the knowledge used by the decision makers, while the decision makers have proclaimed the
failure of theoretical constructs as guides for action.(58)
Many scholars, especially in the industrialized countries, tend
to assume that isolation in the ivory tower of the university
is more conducive to creativity than the "practical world" of
the decision makers.   However, this assumption has been se-
verely qestioned by the results of research on the subject.(59)

Decision makers argue that useful theories are those that
provide practical solutions.(60)   Meanwhile, this kind of
theory is not being provided by the scholars.   They have to
rely on doctrines, tradition, experience, and intuition.   The
practitioner believes that he is an experienced pragmatist and
a gifted generalist.(61)   However, most of the countries still
follow patterns of recruitment, training, and doctrine deeply
rooted in the experience obtained from the outdated models and
patterns of behavior of the international system.   Therefore,
usually the policymaker can choose between only a very limited
set of options which he is able to perceive, derived from his
everyday experience.   Since novelties are unpredictable (and,
therefore, potentially dangerous), the answer to the call for
fundamental change in the system tends to become incremental.

Unfortunately for the decision makers, change, complexity,
and novelty are the subject-matters of the present world
political system.   However, the information gathering and
policy-analysis apparatus of their institutions will not be of
great help.   As K. Boulding pointed out, they always tend to
"conform" to the existing image of the top decision maker, no
matter what it is.(62)   Furthermore, with regard to planning,
in general it is narrowly conceived, since it is organized
under the assumption that present trends will probably continue
into the future.

The importance of these patterns of behavior as an obstacle for NIEO should be emphasized, since a successful
achievement of NIEO that would be able to fulfill the present
and future needs of mankind depends considerably on the
capacity to provide new and creative political and technical
solutions.

This criticism of the decision makers should be matched
with a new look at the world of the scholar, how he perceives
his professional role, and what uses the theories that he
produces may have.

As has been commented at length, the social sciences in
the Western developed world have been dominated during the last
years by a paradigm that puts the emphasis on quantification
and behavioralism.   Through the mechanisms of transfer of
knowledge, it has also affected a great many of the developing
countries.   Emphasis on quantification and behaviorism has
helped to lead many scholars away from the world of the decision maker, since the concrete, urgent problems with which

the latter has to deal are not easily quantified in the way the theorist requires.(63)   In addition, the time framework in which both sectors work adds new difficulties. Furthermore, the obtrusive language of the "scientific subculture developed by social scientists to communicate their findings raises great barriers for the non-specialized public."(64)

It should be added that the practitioner's complaint about the quality and lack of usefulness of explanations and predictions produced during the last years in the area of socio-economic and political development has a considerable degree of justification. Furthermore, in the case of demands shared by governmental officials and non-governmental associations, requests from the scientific sector to provide specially trained experts in international relations and "forms of knowledge that can serve as guides to action,"(65) have not been generally fulfilled by the academic institutions.

Social Science Research and National Policy; Its Use and Misuses

The use to which governmental apparatus can put information provided by social scientists is a very important factor which is difficult to determine, given the limited verified data available on the subject. However, studies carried out in the United States may offer some preliminary insight, at least at the level of a great power.(66)

It seems that policymakers in the United States prefer to use information produced by their own agencies (51 percent of the total) and they almost ignore the research done in other nations. On the contrary, contacts with researchers of other nations point out that research produced in the United States is heavily used in policy-related decisions made by other governments.(67)

With regard to the information sources, the decision makers are eclectic. The purpose of this information is multiple: to keep the policymaker up to date with knowledge available and to get scientific support for the adoption of a decision.(68)   In terms of information needs, the data requested by the decision maker himself obtain the highest percentage of use (80 percent),(69) especially at the highest levels of the hierarchy and when the importance of the issue is great.

Rochester and Segalla questioned what it is that the foreign policy makers want from the scholars and found some differences from conventional wisdom.(70) They concluded that decision makers are interested in the treatment of specific problems, geographically confined, immediate or short-term in time span, and topically focused. In general terms, policymakers' interests seem to be centered at the country level, secondly regionally-focused, and, to a minor extent, determined by global or functional interest. The government is more interested in applied (policy guidance; problem opportunity analysis) than in basic research for most of its agencies. However, except for AID and a few other agencies, the majority seem to operate from a very specific geographical scope, while several others, such as the State Department, tend to operate at a macrolevel of analysis.(71)

In the realm of international affairs research, a high level of functional specification is founded. In 1975, in thirteen U.S. governmental agencies, less than 1 percent of the funds were spent on general studies, while sociopolitical issues accounted for 50 percent, economic issues 35 percent, and military issues accounted for 12 percent of expenditures.(72) (Expenditures in military themes are not totally reliable, since these figures only represent a small percentage of the total amount spent by the U.S. government.) In conclusion, it seems that conventional wisdom is only partially confirmed and that governmental agencies dealing with foreign policy issues support a significant amount of basic research, global in its scope, international in its orientation, and open-ended in terms of time span.(73)

Therefore, these preliminary and rather limited data provide some support for our previous comments about the heavy influence exerted by the intellectual production of the United States in the developing countries and the aggravation of its effects, given the dominant paradigms and, on a more general basis, the role played by research units linked to the decision-making apparatus in the shaping of decisions related to important sociopolitical and economic issues on the national, regional, and global levels.

Emphasis on the utilization of social science research by the nation-state doesn't mean that the rest of the actors in the world system are not increasingly applying the same research in the pursuit of their goals. A subnational actor might use these studies to influence public opinion, the policies of the state, or the policies of actors. The national actor might do the same, having in mind its own internal political needs and goals on the international level. International organizations, such as the United Nations, may also use these studies, for example, to legitimize their role and increase their bargaining and mediation positions vis-à-vis the state in the area of socioeconomic development. Transnational corporations might find it useful to promote sectorial studies related to their specific subjects of interest or, as with the nation-state, to support research of a global nature that would offer future scenarios harmoniously matched to their own desired models.

Of course, reality is often complex, with contradictory and simultaneous goals to be pursued. For example, the studies

of the future done by the RAND Corporation at one time had a
significant impact. They influenced "the way in which policymakers approach their task, define alternatives and assess
criteria for choice."(74) Herman Khan noted the influence of
the Hudson Institute: "The vision of the future of the Institute has influenced the policies of the government and
private corporations of the United States, and probably it will
continue to do so in the future."(75) Wienner, coauthor of
"The Year 2000," accepted that this work "approximately represents the ideology of Western capitalism."(76) Meanwhile,
soviet scientists have considered it a conscious attempt to
influence world opinion, more than a serious effort at prediction.

Several books, including those by social scientists from
developing countries along with issues of specialized magazines
have focused on the analysis and critique of the technical and
ideological content of studies such as the "Limits to growth"
model(77) and "Mankind at the Turning Point"(78) presented by
the Club of Rome.(79) According to Alker and Tickner "The Club
of Rome is itself a transnational actor, visibly affecting some
policy pronouncements, tending toward a Brzezinski direction"(80) - in this sense, something between a "global humanist" and a nationally oriented "power realist."

These studies of the future have had a serious impact on
the governments of the Western industrialized countries and, to
a varied degree, upon developing countries. The fact that the
theses presented were damaging for the development possibilities of the Third World aroused some opposition in the developing countries. However, relatively few systematic efforts
were made to thoroughly criticize its paradigms and conceptual
limitations and, in many academic circles, its basic assumptions were accepted. A gradual shift in the direction and
content of later studies promoted by the Club of Rome have
helped to change the level and character of criticism.

A serious problem may arise as a result of such studies
with the powerholders' positions that support the maintenance
of their own privilege and, if it is the case, the dependent
type of insertion of their country in the international system.
One of the more complete efforts in terms of modeling undertaken by Third World countries as an answer to the Limits to
Growth and Mankind at the Turning Point was the Bariloche
Model. Yet, the model found its principal enemies and de-
tractors on the internal level, among the members of the
dominant elite and the regimes in power in the countries from
where the scientists were nationals. For these policymakers,
the model was perceived as an ideological menace to the national values and life-style that they wanted to impose.

Nevertheless, it should be noted that, in many cases, the
studies about the NIEO prepared in the developing countries are
quite compatible, or at least not seriously antagonistic, with

the prevalent values and views of the governments of the developed countries and their dominant elites. Richard Falk examined the relationships between the most powerful intellectual groups linked to the subnational-transnational actors (e.g.; TNCs) and the governments of the developed countries, the "Trilateral Society" and the government of the United States (where many of these intellectuals now reside) and found that "there is an easy flow between playing official roles in policy formation within the existing system and the kind of image of global reform associated with Trilateral type of thinking."(81)

However, not all the studies undertaken in the Western developed countries about future world orders fully support the positions adopted by the state apparatus, the dominant groups, or the transnational corporations. Differences with the "official" value system and the various formulas of national and sectorial interests vary widely.(82) Many of these studies (see table 7.2), except those pursuing a complete change of structures (e.g., abolition of the state or the market sytem) usually considered radical, do not menace the essence of the present system and, instead, try to obtain different degrees of reform. In general terms, some of these proposals and models rest on a foundation that is close to the goals pursued by the Third World, or they have even tried to incorporate the Third World perspective into their studies from the beginning (e.g., the Dag Hammarskjöld Project and the RIO Project).

Some studies with Third World foundations are being undertaken. The "Second Round" of the RIO Project, the continuation of the activities of the "1975 Dag Hammarskjöld Project," and the participation of the "Third System" in the United Nations Development Strategy for the 80's Project of the International Foundation for Development Alternatives are only a few examples of the existing opportunities in which the developing nations may fruitfully participate.

Third World countries and their academic communities can expand their level of participation in this dimension of political confrontation with the more conservative, status quo segments of the developed world. It might also increase their chances of including their views in all the forums that they consider relevant.

Studies on the North-South Issue in World Politics

The purpose of this following section is to show which are the predominant perceptions and images of the present system as they are perceived and rationalized by scholars and decision makers from developing and developed countries. Since these perspectives are briefly presented in this section, they may suffer great variations, ranging from conservative and status quo conceptualizations of international relations to advanced, pluralist, transformative and egalitarian schemes of world politics. The power distribution, type of relevant participant actors, strategies, and means to be applied are some of the elements that are introduced by table 7.1. Several of the main studies and proposals prepared by scholars about the NIEO are presented in table 7.2, which emphasizes the political orientations, the values, privileges and positions adopted in the studies with regard to the world's present sociopolitical and economic structures.

Clearly, these are only crude and tentative elaborations that require a good deal of refinement; but, even at this stage, they may shed light on certain correspondences and similarities between the type of perceptions and models presented in the tables. What seems to be relevant for the purpose of this chapter is that there is a basic correspondence between the models and studies about the NIEO and the images of the world held by scholars and decision makers. Table 7.2 indicates the following categories:

1. Those models and studies labeled as "Conservative" don't coincide, in most cases, with the predominance given in the "images" to "power politics" (in the sense of the classical conception of privileged military power). However, the basic correspondence at the value and operational capacity levels remains. What they seem to offer is the equivalent of the dimension of economic power politics. A shift in the means and strategies to be applied, from military to economic power, cannot be seen as a great step forward.

2. In the "Reformist" colums we perceive the efforts of the more open-minded segments of the developed countries and developing countries to get rid of the military-power structure, emphasizing the potential for a more just redistribution of benefits. Nevertheless, in many of the proposals and views presented, the basic patterns of the present system still prevail.

3. The "transformative" proposals presented by the Third World national and subnational subactors (as well as by some advanced groups of the developed countries) reveal a high degree of idealism and, therefore, can easily be charged with lacking practicality. However, there are some serious and realistic elements in their conceptions. Those who don't appeal to violence offer two relevant possibilities: 1) a quota of enthusiasm and political will and a necessary bit of idealism (in terms of goals) that must exist if a commitment toward real and effective changes in the present regime is pursued; and 2) some "practical" strategies that would be combined, on a selective basis, with those of some of the proposals of the "Reformist" grouping. If we return to the field of "power-politics" realities, several factors must be emphasized: 1) following the rules of the "power game" the LDCs must

substantially increase their bargaining power in order to achieve a minimum satisfactory level of benefits from the negotiations with the DCs; 2) it doesn't seem that this level could be obtained without a real commitment to some degree of collective self-reliance between the developing countries; 3) unfortunately, it doesn't seem that there are great chances of success, given the search for better positions in the present international stratification to which several important countries of the Third World (many of those considered "Middle Income" Countries) are really committed under formal banners of cooperation.

A significant level of correspondence exists between the world images and studies within the operational field of the North-South negotiations such as the North-South delinking on North-North basis, and some Reformist approaches corresponding with the positions adopted by the developed countries. Also, Reformist and Transformative views within the Third World, include a wide range of positions, such as the search for a better place in the present stratification for those who include the search for a North-South delinking on a South-South basis.

If we now consider the North-South negotiations we will find that the differences between the two groups of countries are multifold with respect to: a) the order of priorities; b) the type of action proposed to solve the problems; and c) the approach adopted for the resolution of the problem.

Industrialized countries use a pragmatic, cause and effect approach, hoping to isolate the problems. As S. Arnau has correctly stated, the problems are perceived by this group only as "distortions" or temporary deviations in relation to a world that is basically correct in its order. Instead, the developing countries tend to consider it as an expression of macro-problems deeply linked with structures that function to their disadvantage. With regard to the measures to be adopted, the North proposes specific, ad hoc corrective actions, while the South aims for introducing the corrections that it perceives are at the root of the situation. Thus, the South demands structural changes.

Furthermore, the approaches to the problems also differ. The developed countries propose approaches that are integrated but acumulative; while the developing countries tend to adopt holistic approaches, looking for the patterns that govern the functioning of the entire structure. The result is an analysis that deeply affects the focus and the perspective of the debate and deeply affects the political and technical options available.

These differences have a relevant impact on practical matters. What problem must be given priority? Pollution for the First World and underdevelopment for the Third World. What

type of action should apply? A massive dose of technology or a
different pattern of consumption? Polarization on these issues
is not a monopoly of the interaction between the industrialized
world and the developing countries. For example, the concept
of the "postindustrialized society" has originated different
models that have managed to split the scientific communities of
the First World: a technological, urban, affluent service
society or a decentralized agrarian economy.(83) Again, all
these divisions appear often in world negotiations, such as
habitat, impact of technology, industrial development, food,
etc.

In short, a dynamic flow of ideological interactions will
mutually affect, to a varied degree, the work of scholars and
decision makers about NIEO. These interactions generate a
certain interdependency between them, affecting all levels and
contributing to the processing and creations, as well as
affecting the making of decisions that will put NIEO into
practice. The value systems affect the world vision of scholars as well as their proposals for which values and structures
NIEO should comprise. It also affects the rationalizations
made by the decision makers about the "situation" (the complex
set of interrelated forces and factors at national and international levels that impose restraint on demands for future
action), the alternatives available, the strategies to be
followed, and the probable outcomes.

Requirements for Intellectual and Political Studies

It is evident that we are facing serious shortcomings with
regard to studies of NIEO. Often, these constraints are
dangerous, and vary in what is presented to world public
opinion. As a general critique of these studies, there is a
need to seek the dynamics of change and take into account the
very real contradictions of this historical period.(84) The
bipolar elements of the present are dialectically related
rather than opposed. Dichotomous schemes emphasize the static
and mutually exclusive elements, which become easily divorced
from empirical reality.(85) Therefore, the dynamics of conflict are obscured by the fact that all changes are perceived
and understood from one or the other apparent irreconcilable
polar extreme.

Furthermore, political issues have been treated and
defined through nonpolitical variables (e.g., economic variables). That means a distorted reduction that attempts to
place politics in a disadvantaged situation vis-à-vis the
technoeconomic phenomena, modifying the real relationships
between the factors.

Taking into account the contents of tables 7.1 and 7.2 in
this context, we realize that the technocratic studies and

models can be adopted to the pursuit of quite different
societal goals.   This feature opens the way for different
political uses. Among them: a) to legitimize the socioeconomic
model pursued by the existent leadership (including the re-
assurances given to the people about the capacity of the
government to deal with the new challenges); or b) to oppose
this leadership, pointing out its weakness and ideological
assumptions.(86)

What is at stake is the dimension and nature of the
political participation of the people as a whole in the essential decisions related to the NIEO. Have the national and
the international systems the capacity to respond to the
demands imposed on them by NIEO? In what kind of political
participation are the intellectuals and the people allowed to
participate as a whole? Is it strictly a supportive role
organized by the national, international, and transnational
elite? Or, is it evident that these restrictions should
disappear if what is desired is a real global and just order
for mankind.

Many studies about political conflict tend to support the
fact that the ideologically committed political elite propor-
tionally increase their willingness and disposition to negotiate with the antagonist in accordance with two factors:
a) their feeling of self-assertion (degree of societal political support), and b) the relevancy and importance given to
the issue. If this is the case, an important element to be
added to strengthen the possibilities of success in NIEO's
international negotiations is the increase of the people's
level of awareness and exposure about the ideological and
political content of matters to be discussed. This reassurance
to the decision makers could be achieved by an honest process
of information to the public about the importance of the issues
at stake, a fair discussion of the alternatives that are
available, and the effective participation of the public in the
decisions. It would, indeed, be a better contribution than a
twenty-first century version of "cabinet diplomacy" to reach
the minimum requirements for a peaceful and just world order.

CONCLUSIONS

Taking into account what has been stated, we reach the following conclusions:

*   Studies of a global nature related to NIEO are functional
       as well as sociopolitical and technical tools for the
       pursuit of the external policies of the different actors
       in the world political system.

- Until the present, there are patterns of asymmetry and dependence. The use of world order studies is highly concentrated in the industrialized countries of the East and West, which provide most of the dominant paradigms and values to the rest of the world. Transnational associations compounded by private citizens and nongovernmental organizations that develop these studies have a highly predominant participation from the developed countries. The level of participation of the governments, private citizens, and academic communities of the developing world in these types of projects – as well as the generation and undertaking of projects of their own – is low.

- The Third World has concentrated its efforts on technical negotiations of a practical nature, limiting its activity in the field of world order studies to a weakly organized criticism. However, it seems there is a growth in participation on this subject, with more social scientists and private citizens from the developing countries taking part in the activities of transnational associations and centers of research. As yet, a majority of the developing countries and their subnational and transnational actors have not taken full advantage of the existing opportunity to increase their limited capacities to present their views to the world, and to pursue their goals in a way that can increase understanding and, hopefully, also increase the potential support of important segments of the public and the decision makers in the industrialized countries.

- Among other factors, cooperative interaction between scholars and decision makers is very often impeded by the existence of strong biases. Given structural restraints, the decision makers are seriously limited in the search for creative solutions to the problems raised by NIEO. Scholars, on many occasions, have not provided satisfactory forms of knowledge that can be used as guidelines for action. When they were able to do so, the initiatives have not been carried out due to the conflicting political-economic interests involved.

- The relatively low level of understanding between scholars and decision makers becomes aggravated in many developing countries by the existing structures of internal domination. Lack of adequate infrastructure and human resources creates further restraints.

- In spite of the existent misunderstandings, decision makers and scholars can perform quite complementary roles. Theoretical research and planning expand the world horizon of the practitioner. It helps to ask the right questions and to foresee the consequences of the political decisions in a holistic context. It gives the scholar the opportunity to test theoretical findings, closing the gap between theory and practice.

PROPOSALS

The main demand and proposal presented in this chapter is the
urgent and unavoidable need to improve, expand, and increase
the dialogue between the actors of the world system to be
politically relevant. It is the value system which, in the
final analysis, will determine the finalities and proposals of
the world system.(87)

Taking into account the different aspects of the problem
considered in this chapter, we suggest the following proposals:

A)   Asymmetries and dependency of the developing
     countries in the social science subsystem.
     -   To build up strong and self-assertive social
         science communities in the developing coun-
         tries.

It seems worthwhile to attempt to participate in the use of the
scientific apparatus of the central powers in a way that will
lead toward a positive confrontation of the rationales and
underlying systems of values of the South and North.   The
underlying assumption is that no realm should be ignored in the
confrontation of ideas and that the abandonment of this field
has a high political cost for the developing countries.

This participation is considered a complementary resource
to be added to an unavoidable self-reliant effort to build up
global studies and models that expose the developing countries'
own visions and goals of the world in the future. This should
be the core of the effort to be done in this area. A concrete
proposal is the organization of the "Developing Countries
Association of Social Scientists."

In terms of financing this effort, the role of the OPEC
countries could be highly relevant. A relatively low amount of
resources could be channeled by them, together with other
contributions, to allow for the organization and the scientific
human resources of the Third World under an agreed upon basis
for a joint program of research on NIEO. The adoption of such
a program would greatly contribute to the knowledge of the
problems and would also improve the negotiating power of the
developing countries.

At the operational level, work and discussions related to
NIEO usually take place in the capitals of the industrialized
countries where the headquarters of the major international
organizations are located. This fact creates a serious imbalance between the level of expertise and support that can be
provided to their representatives by the developing and developed countries.   Therefore, what associations and institutions (including those of the UN system) could be used to
gather, organize, and provide assistance to the developing

countries must be considered. In other words, the build-up of a "Developing Countries Research and Planning Staff" is required. President Julius Nyerere of Tanzania, addressing the Ministerial Conference of the Group of 77 in Arushe (February 1979) stated that: "I am sometimes apalled by the handicap under which Third World Countries' negotiations enter into important meetings. . . . Our delegates have very little help. I believe similar situations exist for most if not all Third World Delegations to UN or N-S negotiations . . . and with this kind of support they are to meet highly experienced people, armed with all the preparatory material done by sophisticated domestic and OECD staffs and their computers."

    B)   <u>Ideological issues and the conceptualization and neogitation of NIEO.</u>
        -   <u>To point out the ideological elements related to NIEO contained in the discussions between developed and underdeveloped countries.</u>

There should be a great effort made in terms of research by coordinated and integrated teams of social scientists from developed and underdeveloped countries that works on the themes of NIEO, to clarify and fully articulate the ideological elements contained in the studies, proposals, and negotiations. The goal will be to contribute toward a better understanding of the different value-bases of the main literature, policies, and decisions referred to in NIEO, with the purpose of facilitating the achievement of an agreed set of goals, policies, and strategies between the South and the North.

    C)   <u>The role of the actors of the world system in the pursuit of NIEO.</u>
        -   <u>To fully incorporate new relevant actors of the world political system in the achievement of NIEO.</u>

The growing forces of new actors (such as transnational, international, and subnational agents) searching for different sets of values and goals to be introduced in NIEO should be fully taken into account not only in the studies about this subject but also in the institutional build up required for it (e.g., the growing role being played by nongovernmental organizations in economic and social development; and the activities undertaken by nongovernmental associations in the development of studies of the future world order).

NOTES

1. H. Sprout, and M. Sprout, Toward a Politics of the Planet Earth (New York: Van Nostrand 1972), p. 100.

2. R. Jackson, "Politics and Futurology," Futures (October 1977).

3. Jib Fowles, "The Problem of Values in Future Research," Futures (August 1977), p. 303.

4. R. Falk, "Contending Approaches to World Order," Journal of International Affairs 31 (2), (1977).

5. S. Amin, Accumulation on a World Scale (New York: Monthly Review Press, 1972).

6. A. Gramsci, Selections from the Prison Notebooks (New York: International Publishers, 1976), pp. 12-14.

7. Neil J. Smelser, Theory of Collective Behavior (New York: 1963); and T.R. Gurr, "The Revolution - Social Change Nexus: Some Old Theories and New Hypothesis," Comparative Politics (April 1973), p. 362.

8. C.F. Alger and G. Lyons, "Social Science as a Transnational System" (Collective Report of the Seminar on this theme held at Bellagio, Italy, by the Study Conference of the Rockefeller Foundation, July 16-21, 1973), International Social Sciences Journal, UNESCO, Paris, 26 (1), (1974).

9. M. Line, and S. Roberts, "The Size, Growth and Composition of Social Science Literature," International Journal of Social Science, UNESCO, Paris, 28 (1), (1976): 133.

10. Ibid, p. 147.

11. Alger and Lyons, "Social Science as a Transnational System."

12. Carlos Moneta, "Los Modeleos de Simulacion Global en la arena Politica: algunas considerationes preliminares," paper presented to the Conference "Alternative Visions of Desireable Societies," World Futures Federation, WFSF-CESSTW, Mexico City, April 1978.

13. Ibid.

14. Alger and Lyons, "Social Science as a Transnational System."

15. S. Cole and H. Lucas, Models, Planning and Basic Needs (Proceedings of a UNESCO-sponsored conference held at the Institute of Development Studies, University of Sussex, Oct. 29 - Nov. 3, 1977), p. 17.

16. In this chapter, "Ideology" is understood as all action-related systems of ideas (C. Friedrich, Man and his Government, New York: Mc Graw-Hill, 1963).

17. Gonzáles P. Casanova, Las Categorias del desarrollo Economico y la investicacion en Ciencias sociales, Instituto de Investigaciones Sociales, UNAM, Mexico, 1970.

18. Alger and Lyon, "Social Science as a Transnational System," p. 143.

19. Verifiable examples of this type of thinking are the thesis of the "End of Ideology" stated by relevant scholars from the Western industrialized countries such as A. Crozier, R. Dahrendorf, E. Haas, S. Lipset, D. Bell, R. Bendix, and E. Shils, during the 1960s. With respect to the "value-free science" paradigm, the cases are countless. Most of the behaviorist school of thought in the U.S. is an outstanding example of the efforts to obtain a "value free" social science.

20. González Casanova, Las Categorias.

21. A "cultural pattern is characterized by the forms, or the matrixes, with and within our mind stores and order whatever it absorbs (See G. Sartori, "Politics, Ideology and Belief Systems," American Political Science Review 63 (June 1969): 402.

22. For Latin America see, among others, the important article of Jose Nun, "Los paradigmas de la Ciencia Política; un intento de cónceptualizacion," Revista Latinoamericana de Sociología 1 (1976). In Africa, the works in the economic field of Samir Amin and his followers as well as the revisionist thinking based on "African Socialism" seems to be developed in accordance with their own African experience.

23. G. Lagos, in Alger and Lyons, "Social Science as a Transnational System.", p. 142.

24. See, for example, A. Sivinski, "Is and How a Vision of Desirable Society Possible Today?," and M. Marcovich, "Humanist Socialist Vision of the Future," papers presented to the Conference "Alternative Visions of Desirable Societies," WFST-CESSTW, Mexico, April 1978.

25. Alger and Lyons, "Social Science as a Transnational System."

26. "Latent functions are those objective consequences contributing to the adjustment or adaptation of the system which are neither intended nor recognized." R. Merton, Social Theory and Social Structure (Glencoe, Ill.: Free Press, 1957).

27. G. Stavenhagen, in Alger and Lyons, "Social Science as a Transnational System."

28. Christakis, "A New Policy Science Paradigm," Futures (December 1973), p. 543.

29. Ibid., p. 545.

30. Alger and Lyons, "Social Science as a Transnational System," p. 147.

31. Brucan, ibid., p. 143.

32. Ibid., p. 141.

33. See B. Persuad, "The Commodity Problem and Negotiations to Establish a Common Fund: A View from the Third World," Symposium on the Common Fund, London School of Economics, February 1979.

34. C. Ries, "The New International Economic Order: The Sceptics' Views," in The NIEO: Confrontation or Cooperation between North and South?, edited by H. Hasenpflug, and K. Sauvant, (Boulder, Colo.: Westview Press, 1977).

35. See Toward a Renovated International System, A Report of the Trilateral Commission, New York, 1977; and "La Comisión Trilateral y la coordinación de políticas del mundo capitalista," CIDE, Cuadernos Semestrales, no. 2-3, México, 1978.

36. E. Fuenzalida, and O. Sunkel, "Capitalismo Transnational y Desarrollo Nacional," Revista Estudios Internacionales, Centro de Estudios Internationales, U. Nacional de Chile, Santiago, 1978.

37. On this subject, the article of Galtung is very interesting: "Non territorial actors" in On the Creation of a First World Order, edited by Mendlovitz, (New York: Free Press, 1975); also see K. Skjelback, "The Growth of International Nongovernmental Organizations in the Twentieth Century," in Transnational Relations and World Politics, edited by R. Keohane, and J. Nye, (Cambridge, Mass.: Harvard U. Press, 1971); Fuenzalida and Sunkel, "Capitalismo Transnational y Desarollo Nacional."

38. V. Rittberger, The New International Order and United Nations Conference Politics: Science and Technology as an Issue Area, Science and Technology Working Papers, No. 1, UNITAR, 1978, pp. 24-25.

39. Ibid., p. 25.

40. Ibid., p. 26.

41. See, for example, B. Urquhart, "The International Civil Servant," in The International Executive, World Order Studies Programme, Occasional Papers No. 6, Princeton University, March 1978, as well as the other papers included in this publication.

42. As it has been pointed out elsewhere, there is a great ambiguity in the sense assigned to the concept of "value." The concept has not yet achieved an agreed upon content. At least, it should be noted that there is a difference between an objective approach (values as things or property of things) and the subjective approach (values as a function of human perception). See A. Sicinski, "The Concepts of 'Need' and 'Value' in the Light of the Systems Approach," Social Science Information, (SAGE, London) 17, (1), (1978): 84-85.

43. P. Coombs, The Fourth Dimension of Foreign Policy: Educational and Cultural Affairs (New York: 1964), p. 13.

44. W. Benton, (former U.S. Assistant Secretary of State), The Department of State Bulletin, Feb. 6, 1961, pp. 185-86.

45. G. Arbatov, The War of Ideas in Contemporary International Relations (Moscow: Progress, 1973), pp. 36-37.

46. Ibid., p. 276.

47. R. Randolph, "Social and Technological Forecasting in the Soviet Union," Futures (December 1976).

48. V. Kulivov, Kommunist (Moscow: May 1976) and J. Erickson, "The Soviet Union, the Future and Future Research," Futures (August 1977), pp. 335-38.

49. M. Gapotchka, and S. Smirnov, "The Social Sciences in the USSR: Status Policy, Structures and Achievements," _International Social Science Journal_ (UNESCO, Paris) 28 (1) (1976): 69.

50. Robert A. Packenham, in his work _Liberal America and the Third World_ (Princeton, N.J.: Princeton Univ. Press, 1973), offers an interesting and useful analysis of the role played by ideological factors in theory and doctrine applied to foreign policy.

51. A lucid criticism and analysis of realism in contemporary international relations is offered by R. Rothstein, _Planning Prediction and Policymaking in Foreign Affairs_, (Boston: Little, Brown, 1972), pp. 67-81.

52. Z. Brzezinski, "The Implications of Change for the United States Foreign Policy," (Washington, D.C.: 1967) cited in Arbatov, _The War of Ideas_, p. 117.

53. Z. Brzezinski, "Purpose and Planning in Foreign Affairs," _The Public Interest_, (Winter 1969), pp. 56; see also Rothstein, _Planning, Prediction, and Policymaking in Foreign Affairs_ (Boston: Little, Brown, 1972), p. 86.

54. Rothstein, ibid., p. 47.

55. G. Lyons, "Science and Politics: Four Case Studies," _International Social Science Journal_ (UNESCO, Paris) 28 (1), (1976); 35.

56. For a useful example of the political and technical problems that have to be faced by the developing countries, see J. Manher, _A preliminary assessment of National Papers as a basis for UNCSTD Conference Programming_, UNITAR, Science and Technical Working Papers No. 3, 1979.

57. Sprout and Sprout, _Toward a Politics of the Planet Earth_, p. 143.

58. Rothstein, _Planning, Prediction, and Policymaking_, p. 118.

59. G. Gordon, and S. Marquis, "Freedom, Visibility of Consequences and Scientific Innovation," _American Journal of Sociology_, no. 72, (Sept. 1966).

60. Rothstein, _Planning, Prediction, and Policymaking_, p. 155.

61. Ibid., p. 157.

62. K. Boulding, "The Learning and Reality-Testing Process in the International System," _The Journal of International Affairs_, no. 21 (1967), p. 10; and Rothstein, ibid., p. 181.

63. Rothstein, ibid., p. 124.

64. J. Rosenau, _International Studies and the Social Sciences_ (London: Sage, 1973).

65. Ibid., p. 80.

66. N. Caplan, "Social Research and National Policy: What Gets Used by Whom, for What Purposes and With What Effects?" _Social Science Journal_ (UNESCO, Paris) 28 (1), (1976).

67. Ibid., p. 189.
68. Ibid., p. 190.
69. Ibid., p. 194.
70. M. Rochester, and M. Segalla, "What Foreign Policy-makers Want from Foreign Policy Researchers: A Data Based Assessment of FAR Research," International Studies Quarterly 22 (3), (September 1978).
71. Ibid., pp. 447-48.
72. Ibid., p. 445.
73. Ibid., p. 459.
74. Smith, The Rand Corporation, pp. 226-27; and in Rothstein Planning, Prediction, and Policymaking (Boston: Little Brown, 1972) p. 107.
75. Cole, op. cit.
76. Cited in ibid.
77. D. Meadows, and H. Meadows, The Limits to Growth (New York: Universe Books, 1972).
78. M. Mesarovic, and E. Pestel, Mankind at the Turning Point (New York: Dutton, 1977).
79. "The Limits to Growth Controversy," Futures (special issue), 5 (1) (February 1973); "The Ideological Background to the Limits of Growth Controversy," Futures, 5 (2), (April 1973); Varsasky Furtado, et al., El Club de Roma, anatomía de un grupo de presión, Edic. Síntesis, México, 1976; "The No Growth Society," Daedalus, (Fall 1973).
80. H. Alker, and A. Tickner, "Some Issues Raised by Previous World Models," in Problems of World Modeling: Political and Social Implications, Edited by K. Deutsch, B. Futsch, H. Jaguaribe, and A. Markovits (Boston, Mass.: Ballinger, 1977) p. 30.
81. Falk, "Contending Approaches to World Order," p. 183.
82. To have an accurate survey of the present world order studies, see, among others, the works of Freeman Jahoda, Ed. World Future: The Great Debate (Univ. of Sussex, 1977); and ibid. An analysis of the main trends of world order studies, perceived from a very conservative and status-quo position, is the work of James P. O'Leary "Einvisioning Interdependence: Perspective on Future World Order," Orbis 22 (3), (1978).
83. M. Marien, "The Two Visions of the Post-Industrial Society," Futures (October 1977), p. 16.
84. Rudolph, p. 10.
85. J. Bill, and R. Hardgrave, Comparative Politics: the Quest for Theory, (Ohio: C. Merrill, 1973).
86. Falk, "Contending Approaches to World Order," pp. 175-83.
87. Elmandjra Mahdi, "Power, Values and Political Reality," Development (Rome) 20 (2), (1978): 15.

Appendix

PROGRESS TOWARD A NEW INTERNATIONAL ECONOMIC ORDER:
THE BASIC POINTS PRESENTED BY THE MEXICAN DELEGATION TO THE
MEETING OF THE LATIN AMERICAN PARLIAMENT, JULY–AUGUST 1978

1. Bringing order to trade and prices for raw materials would be of only limited aid to developing countries, for although they supply 38 percent of the total value of all minerals produced in the non-socialist world; more than 50 percent of the world production of tin, copper, bauxite, manganese, sugar, and cotton; and 90 percent of all world exports of coffee, cacao, tea, hard fibers, and natural rubber, the marketing of those products is handled by transnational corporations. Even so, the Latin American countries will continue to make every effort to obtain agreements on the prices of those articles and on trade conditions that will tend to shift the scales to the side of all exporters of raw materials.

2. At the regional level, the creation of such specific mechanisms as the Latin American Economic System (SELA) proves the feasibility of integration projects sponsored by countries producing raw materials and fuels, as well as of the formation of multinational enterprises such as the Caribbean Shipping Corporation. The idea of bringing these producers' agreements and multinational enterprises up to the level of a general economic system for developing countries is already beginning to be put into effect.

3. The apparent confrontation between the highly industrialized countries (particularly the United States, Germany, England, and Japan) and the less-developed ones must be overcome and replaced by true cooperation, based on under-

standing of the overall problems of development and on acceptance by the world community of its joint responsibility for survival and of the consequent need to establish better living conditions for all the world's inhabitants, without detriment to the sovereignty and independence of any member state. It is important to face up to the fact that our only alternative lies in establishing purer and more democratic and peaceful forms of survival.

4. The problems presented by the inequitable distribution of world wealth are linked to the operation of an international economic system that spontaneously accentuates disparities instead of lessening them. The permanence and gravity of those disparities are not a result of technical problems, but rather of the lack of political and economic elements at the international level that might serve to enrich and complement the socioeconomic and political factors existing within the individual countries. The absence of such elements is what makes it so difficult to arrive at more equitable international agreements that would provide positive evidence of solidarity between industrialized and underdeveloped countries, and even between the different classes and groups in each nation. This must be achieved if there is to be any real hope of more just international relations.

5. There can be no question that the progress made in formulating the basic precepts of the NIEO is due to the initiative, determination, capacity for work, and solidarity of the developing countries. The effectiveness of such action in the future will depend not only on their maintaining the same spirit and level of effort, but also, and primarily, on their upholding the justice of their cause by the action each of them takes within its own borders to effect the necessary socioeconomic and political changes.

6. Therefore, the first important step to be taken is to find means of actively accelerating the process of integration of the economies of developing countries without reducing the freedom of the individual peoples to retain the type of valid sociopolitical organization they prefer. The term valid organization refers to the fact that international cooperation should be the rule among countries on condition that each of the states involved operates with fundamental respect for the sovereignty of the others and for the principles set forth in the Charter of Human Rights, since it would be incongruous to support countries with repressive regimes that violate the principles of human dignity in the manner of Nazism, Fascism, and the like.

7. The second step that governments of Third World countries
    should take is to negotiate as regional or producers'
    blocs with transnational corporations in order to demand
    that they pay a price for their access to natural re-
    sources whose sovereignty and control unquestionably
    belongs to the state, as well as for access to the
    existing and potential markets afforded by the growing
    populations of Third World countries. It must be stressed
    that there has already been too much talk about how to
    solve the structural problems of foreign financing that
    affect the Third World, and that such a solution can be
    achieved by aquiring the necessary capacity to influence
    real economic variables and even by increasing the ability
    of developing countries to defend themselves against
    fluctuations in the prices of raw materials; by seeking
    access for the manufactured products of those countries in
    the international market; and, above all, by negotiating
    on the basis of the import market and of self-sufficiency
    as regards such basic needs as foodstuffs, energy sources,
    steel production, and others.

8. Thirdly, it must be considered that the only way to
    achieve satisfactory results over a relatively brief
    period of time is to adopt a global approach that entails
    a single coherent strategy based upon greater Cooperation
    for Development. Thus, it would be illogical, for ex-
    ample, to advocate the production of sufficient food for
    their own needs by Third World countries without also
    promoting the production in those countries of fertilizers
    and other industrial inputs required for agricultural
    development.

9. The international economy is rapidly being transformed by
    the action of multinational and transnational enterprises
    into a world economy. World trade, production, income,
    and finance are not matters to be decided by private
    interests or by a small handful of nations, but rather
    among groups of nations that agree at the world level on
    orderly standards for the supply of basic raw materials,
    their markets, technology, finance, and the mobility of
    manpower. Those are the problems that must be dealt with
    by the NIEO.

10. As a counterpart to NIEO proposals, a real trend is
    underway toward concentration of economic activity at the
    center of the world system of market economies, at the
    expense of its periphery composed of the developing
    countries. The ongoing process of concentration may be
    noted in the deterioration of the terms of trade derived
    from the international division of labor that has taken
    shape since World War II which increasingly limits the
    less-developed countries to the role of suppliers of raw
    materials and products in which value added is minimal,

while assigning them a far more active role as importers
of manufactured goods, technology, and financing, as well
as of foodstuffs and strategic inputs.

11. Patterns of trade in marginalized areas depend more on the
supply of competitive industrial products in international
markets than on domestic economic and social requirements.
This creates inappropriate and inflexible production
standards that lead to inflationary pressures and monetary
instability and also has the even more serious effect of
contributing to unemployment, to a rising foreign debt,
and to the growth of political and social tensions in the
most impoverished sectors of the population.

12. In view of the fact that the present international economic order still has as its underlying strategy the
accumulation of capital, which in developing countries is
expressed by the economic stabilization policies outlined
at Bretton Woods and interpreted and applied by the IMF
and the World Bank, there is obvious need to review the
validity of that strategy. That need arises from the
political unrest the strategy has helped to cause by doing
away with democratic forms of organization and from the
fact that it has not, in the end, prevented economic
instability, while it has accentuated social inequity in
terms of unemployment, the unequal distribution of income
and wealth, and the social and cultural marginalization of
a growing strata of the Latin American population.

13. The relative loss of U.S. hegemonic power over the evolution of the system in this continent is reflected by the
deterioration of the international monetary system based
on the dollar. It opens new possibilities of reinserting
Latin American economies into the dynamic joint growth
process of all centrally planned market economies.

14. The polarization and disintegration of center and periphery countries tend to hinder overall development because of the eruptions of violence that come in their wake
- the exaggerated use of repressive measures in dealing
with the justified dissent of marginalized sectors of the
population and the narrowing of the margins of democratic
and independent coexistence.

The progress developing countries have made in their
utilization of the highest international forums shows that
a perfectly serious view can be taken of the real possibility of strengthening domestic development policies in
Latin American countries without falling back on such
schemes as the substitution of imports and other relative
advantages, which tend to diminish the number of options
for regional development open to the people of those
countries without providing efficient means of economic
growth.

Similarly, the presence and experience of countries that have undergone a "disintegrating" process of the integration of nationalist alternatives for regional and subregional growth can be of great aid in designing the specific measures to be taken by economic and social authorities in the effort to develop a real political identity, shared by all Latin American countries, that will lead to the effective integration of the region.

15. In the absence of a Latin American political and economic front, the best that can be done is to suggest certain basic criteria that might form part of a regional stand on behalf of establishment of NIEO that would respect the sovereignty of the states least favored by the present international economic disorder.

For countries like ours, the value of NIEO depends on the tangible impact it makes on the attention of the less privileged sectors of the population in growing terms of:

- Employment, food supply, health, and education.
- Access to informed and democratic political participation that is respectful of human rights.
- National independence and sovereignty.

16. Basically, this implies a new national economic, political, and social order, since history has shown that independent development is unlikely to be attained as a result of efforts made by parties other than those most directly interested in achieving it.

A new international economic order can only emerge from the sum of analogous national efforts made in this respect, with the complementary support provided by the cooperation and action of international organizations. The Latin American position, therefore, calls for reinforcing those general components that receive support within the political and social organization at the national level, so as to create the political support that will make it possible to do the same at the regional level.

Where relations with other countries are concerned, the Latin American position is that the industrial nations should observe the formal context of the NIEO action program approved by the General Assembly of the United Nations by agreeing, within a given period of time, to refrain from any obstruction or alteration of specific measures taken at the international level to complement the efforts made by less-developed countries to accelerate democratic and independent national development.

17. Latin America particularly rejects the patterns of the international division of labor, which offers comparatively

limited opportunities for the diversification of the economies of the region. Its goal, moreover, is integral inclusion of the region by means of the elimination of the existing gap and imbalances between the center and periphery countries based on agreements permitting economic and political deconcentration and preventing any sub-imperialist exploitation of the most underdeveloped countries.

18. The Latin American position with respect to disarmament and security is that mere cancellation of the armaments race by the great powers will not suffice to meet the needs of developing countries, since it will not result in any redistribution of world wealth unless it is followed by satisfaction of the food, health, and educational needs that must be resolved at the international level.

19. A monetary and financial system in line with the needs of Latin American countries would imply the gradual elimination of the persistant implantation by international lending institutions of stabilizing policies which take a simplistic and money-minded view of the structural characteristics of these countries' economies and promote antiinflationary strategies that further lower the living standards of the masses, weaken democratic states, encourage monopolies and exacerbate class conflicts.

20. Latin American countries seek to establish a regional strategy for the exploitation of the natural resources they have in common, as well as for environmental protection centering on better use of efforts aimed at satisfying the food needs of the population.

As regards industrial and trade development in the region, national efforts focus on a general revision of the processes of accumulation and capital formation in order to overcome the crisis in that area by reassigning responsibility for guiding economic development to institutions that guarantee progress toward democratic, popular, and independent procedures in national and, consequently, in regional organizations.

21. Finally, it is the opinion of the countries of Latin America that NIEO implies redirecting and regulating the action of transnational capital so as to contain the spreading of relations of dependence and the flow of subcontinent assets to other nations.

This calls for a contributory effort to be made within their own spheres of action by the industrial nations, which should revise their laws on the matter to include complementary regulation of the proliferation of transnational activity, which undermines the sovereignty of the state in every country in which it occurs.

Index

About the Contributors

ARMANDO LABRA, Colegio Nacional de Economistas, Mexico City, Mexico

JAVIER CABALLEROS, Colegio Nacional de Economistas, Mexico City, Mexico

BYRON CARDOSO, Colegio Nacional de Economistas, Mexico City, Mexico

DAVID COLMENARES, Colegio Nacional de Economistas, Mexico City, Mexico

EDUARDO NOVOA, Universidad Central De Venezuela, Caracas, Venezuela

JORGE CASTANEDA, El Colegio de Mexico, Mexico City, Mexico

GERARD TIMSIT, Universite de Paris XI, Paris, France

MARIO BETTATI, International Institute of Administrative Sciences, Paris, France

ROBERT GREGG, Washington, D.C.

CARLOS MONETA, UNITAR, New York